The Black Hole

The Black Hole

Wendy Donnelly

Lulu Books

2009

Published by Lulu Enterprises, Inc

3101 Hillsborough Street
Raleigh, NC 27607

Cover painting by Laura Martin

ISBN: 978-1-4452-4111-1

Now, will God not judge in favour of his own people who cry to him day and night for help? Will he be slow to help them? I tell you, he will judge in their favour and do it quickly. But will the Son of Man find faith on earth when he comes?

Luke 18:7-9

THE BLACK HOLE

So there it was. The black hole. A mile wide and deep, deep, deep. Disappearing into nothingness.

I held on to my mother's hand. She took no notice. I looked up at my father; his face was grey and grim. Nothing there. I looked around; everything else seemed normal. The houses, neighbours, the road – all were there as usual. Only the house was missing.

And there was that great black hole…

No one spoke. There, next to our house was a field where my friend Horace, the magnificent Shire horse grazed and dozed; I had been persuaded to stand on steps and feed slices of apple to him and felt somewhat horrified when my four-year-old hand had totally disappeared into his capacious mouth, but Horace, a gentleman and true to his breed, had gently disentangled my hand, eaten the apple, and continued his ruminations on the stupidity of humans.

But Horace had gone. The cows were still there, placid and silent, lying on their sides. "What are my cows doing there?" I asked my father. "Why are they lying so still?"

He seemed disinclined to answer. "They are dead, I'm afraid," he said finally. "It was the bomb; it has taken our home."

This was not remotely important to a four-year-old. "But what has happened to Horace?" This was the most pressing consideration.

No answer.

A sudden, terrible thought seized me. "What has happened to my *doll*?"

"Gone, I'm afraid."

What has happened to *all* my toys?"

"All gone, I'm afraid. It was a direct hit…"

One

So this was Hong Kong. The business friend I had been introduced to before I left the UK was due to arrive shortly and would be in touch.

We had been in our allocated hotel for a fortnight, having been flown out on a cramped Forces flight and arrived in the August heat. We now had a week to settle in before being introduced to our new school. It was wonderful to venture out after the sticky day to wander the streets in the evening wearing no more than light dresses and cardigans, and to sip coffee in the pavement cafes and eat (with difficulty) rice with chopsticks.

"We can't use chopsticks," we complained, but soon found we could when we were hungry enough. But in the local Chinese restaurants (…and who wanted to eat the tourist way?) there were no knives and forks.

"Why is that circular hole in the middle of the table?"

We were given frightened looks. "We speak no English."

No? Well they had, a minute ago. We later discovered that the circular hole was where a central part of the table could be removed, if necessary, for discerning guests. A monkey would be placed discreetly beneath the table and a waiter would, with a flourish, slice off the top of its head so that the guests could pick at the expensive delicacy, monkey brain, while it was still warm and gently steaming. We became a little more particular in our choice of restaurant…

The school was new, and hard work. Air conditioning had not yet been installed and the temperature and humidity were well above eighty degrees. On arrival, I discovered that my new school was situated above Repulse Bay, then an empty palm-strewn bay with a golden, gently shelving beach sliding down towards warm, crystal waters. Because of the heat, teaching began at 8.00 am and finished, with only coffee breaks, at 1.00 pm. Then straight down to the beach and into the water. We ate our picnic lunches and then, refreshed, returned to the hotel.

However, after a fortnight, the novelty was beginning to pall. The hotel was not air conditioned – one could just about sleep if sufficiently exhausted and, of course, we could wander out and explore the exotic streets in the evening, but our salaries were certainly not compatible with top hotel entertainment and lifestyle. We all began to feel claustrophobic; it was pointed out that unless we had an escort who could afford Hong Kong prices, our lifestyles were going to be very limited indeed. I began to long for the promised phone call from the businessman who travelled extensively through the Far East and who had promised to 'show me Hong Kong'. Finally, at the end of the fortnight, he rang. Joyfully, I sailed off in full evening splendour for my first experience of true Hong Kong nightlife.

It was wonderful. Dinner at the Miramar with its glass pillars that were in fact, aquaria. As we dined, I watched the golden carp swimming up and down and around the huge pillars. The Hilton Grill Room had amazing food and deep, plush seats to recline in. Then there was the Repulse Bay Hotel, in all its Raffles colonial glory – sitting out on the huge balcony overlooking the balustrades with giant arms at intervals, we admired the trailing exotic blooms over the parapet, and the terraced formal gardens with fountains, leading down to the palm encircled beach.

Then on to the Mandarin Hotel. That evening there was a cabaret – Peter Maxwell from the Quaglino's Club in London. He played; he sang; he told jokes. He came from Southampton, he said.

"Southampton!"   exclaimed   my   escort   enthusiastically. "Southampton! He comes from Southampton!" He handed the waiter a note: *WE are from Southampton. Please invite Mr Maxwell over to have a drink with us.*

He came over. He was charming. Were we together? No, we explained, we had met at a party in Southampton and my escort had promised dutifully to look me up and show me Hong Kong. Which he was beginning to enjoy…

We had indeed got on very well over the past few days. Not more than holding hands and looking at the moonlight, but he had already made plans for future visits and felt it was time he 'settled down', having made a success of his small empire. I enjoyed his company and certainly the entertainment, but I had come a long way and was just tasting *freedom* and a fantastic lifestyle. Give it up and return to a very nice house in Southampton… when I had just left one?

Peter Maxwell joked and chatted. Finally, as we prepared to leave, he said to my escort, "You are due to leave in a couple of days. Now why don't I take Wendy and introduce her to the 'right people' in Hong Kong? After all, once you have gone she is going to be stuck alone again in her hotel."

He was an ex-RAF pilot, had been stationed in the Far East for many years, had kept in touch with the 'top' Hong Kong families through his night club trips, and would introduce me. When he had to leave they would, quite naturally, invite me out with them. My escort was less than pleased; but I was delighted, and I accepted.

I promised to keep in touch with my first escort, but after that, I was collected every evening from my hotel and dined at the Mandarin, after which Peter would take me to a nightclub to dance until the early hours. He was due to leave for London and the Quaglino Club at the end of the week. Would I help him with the publicity involved and go with him – in the stretch limo provided by the Mandarin to see him off in state – to the VIP Lounge at the airport?

With difficulty, I tore out of school with the children – no time to tidy up – whisked back to the hotel, changed, jumped in a taxi to the Mandarin and arrived (late) to a barrage of photographers.

"You're late!" Peter hissed. "Get in the car."

Flashlights erupted; I smiled dutifully, though no one noticed. It was merely Peter Maxwell driving off in state with, of course, a lady by his side.

Arriving at the airport, we were ushered straight through to the VIP Lounge where champagne was flowing freely and I was introduced to the farewell party. Eventually, after circulating, we sat down to await his flight home.

"Let me introduce you," he said, "to my special friends. We've been in touch since we were all serving as Wing Commanders in the RAF."

His two friends settled down to discuss old times in the Far East. However, I was not forgotten.

"Wendy is new to Hong Kong; I expect you to look after her while I'm gone – not *too* well," he laughed. "I'll be back for another engagement at the Mandarin, but unfortunately not until the Christmas season. So, until the end of November, I will leave her with you."

His friend, the Wing Commander still serving in Hong Kong, and I had got on very well. I had already been invited to the next RAF function – in fact there was a race meeting at Happy Valley the next day, followed by a beach barbecue and a midnight swim... would I come? I'd love to!

I checked with my escort. Without speaking, he got up and went to sit beside his RAF friend, and had 'a quiet word'. Returning, he said, "I've just had a word. Now, I'm leaving you in my very best friend's capable hands... perhaps a bit *too* capable, he's a bit of a ladies' man, I'm afraid. Married, but er... enjoying life. I've warned him off – I'm sorry, – although he's my best friend, *do not* accept any invitations from him." He smiled fleetingly. "I noticed you getting on very well; er... I have therefore asked my other friend to see you home. He is one of Hong Kong's most eligible bachelors and I can rely on him, as a *determined* bachelor, to wine, dine and look after you – without complications – until I return in November."

His friend turned round to survey me. "Oh fine," he said. "I'll see she gets home!"

I was furious. I had been looking forward to going to Happy Valley racecourse; a midnight swim sounded wonderful in exotic Hong Kong, romantic and exciting. But time to go... I waved Peter Maxwell off.

"I'll ring," he said. "Wait for me."

I turned to go. The RAF Officer designated to see me home said, "Got a car?"

"No."

"Oh hell," he said. "Better get a taxi."

"Thank you," I said civilly. "*That* I can manage myself!" I stamped out to the taxi line. There were none; everyone had gone. What in the world had I come here for? Stranded now at the airport – miles from the Island – and no taxi!

A figure loomed up. "Er... you're waiting in the wrong place. The taxi rank is over there. You're waiting in a disused car park, which is why there are no taxis..."

Still stamping, I followed him and got into the taxi.

"I promised Peter I would see you safely home," he remarked.

"Well thank you, but I am quite capable of seeing myself home."

He unbent sufficiently to say: "So how long have you been teaching?"

"Six years," I replied.

"And then what?"

"Then I applied to come to Hong Kong." Out of three thousand applicants, I had been offered the one plum job in Hong Kong. I tried not to sound too proud of my achievement.

He collapsed with a snort. "You're *not* telling me you're only twenty-six? Good God, you're more than that."

Something inside me exploded. "I had," I said with quiet ferocity, "a major car accident and spent the next three years in hospital recuperating. Now I am here minding my own business and getting used to the idea that there is a life here in Hong Kong for me... which I intend to enjoy."

He made a few desultory placating remarks, for which, fortunately, I had sufficient reserves of courtesy to resist comment. We completed the journey in silence.

"Where are we?" I asked as the taxi drew to a halt.

"At my flat."

And I had thought he was seeing *me* home. "Oh, fine," I said, and then to the taxi driver, "drive on to the Star Ferry."

"STAY WHERE YOU ARE!" he bellowed to the driver. "Now look," his voice was controlled as he spoke to me, "I promised Peter I would look after you and see you home."

"I told you – I am perfectly capable of seeing myself home."

"Really? How? The last Star Ferry left half an hour ago."

I was shattered. The Island was totally separated from the mainland and the last ferry went at 10.30; after that, one was marooned. I was tired and fed up and extremely hungry. My day had been exhausting – teaching non-stop from eight o'clock until one, then the dash home to change, before diving into the stretch limo, and now, after several glasses of champagne (which I was beginning to regret), I really wanted to go home. My back, after all the operations, was beginning to give way.

"Then I'll walk and find a sampan, or a hotel, or something," I snapped.

"Oh for God's sake," he said. "I'm not on my own; I don't bite and the amah will have a meal prepared. At least come in for a meal, and meet my flat mate... and we'll discuss how to get you home."

His flat mate rose to his feet as we entered. "Where the hell have you been?" he asked. "The meal's cold... oh, hello?"

"This is Wendy," said my reluctant escort. "We've been to see Peter off and he left me to see Wendy home. And she missed the last ferry!"

"Oh, trust Desmond to see you missed the last ferry," said the flat mate. "My name's Tony; now, let's eat."

Two

The meal was a success, but there had been an altercation before we arrived, between the amah and Tony. The meal was obviously burnt and the amah hotly defended herself, finally bursting into tears and disappearing into the kitchen, Tony apologized profusely, and most charmingly, for the mishap. Tall, dark, Italian and incredibly handsome, he exuded charm.

In contrast, my host for the evening pointed to me, infuriatingly. "Wendy was cut up; I had to see her home. We've seen Peter off, met up with Ian, and... Peter didn't trust Wendy to get back home safely."

"I am," I said indignantly, "perfectly capable of seeing myself home."

Tony, the ultimate lounge lizard, smoothed oil over troubled waters. "Not the most tactful of men, our Desmond," he said, "but honestly, had you thought how you were going to get home, I mean... rushing off like that, straight from school... to the reception at the Mandarin... to the reception at the airport? What time was the flight...? Seven o'clock... and Peter did say Desmond must see you home. Certainly he expected you to have dinner before going home – and the last ferry leaves at ten-thirty pm." He raised an eyebrow, questioningly.

Oh hell. Now I was stuck. Living on the island, my business friend had ensured I caught the last ferry home – or else wined and dined on the island. Now I was stranded on the mainland; 11.30 and no ferry...

"Spare room!" said Tony, as if reading my thoughts. "No problem, we have a spare room." He called the still snivelling amah. "Make up the spare room – now. Pronto!"

"No," I protested. That really was the last straw. My flat mates were waiting for me on the island, already highly suspicious of my being invited out by a newly acquired 'businessman friend' – a strictly platonic relationship that involved expensive dining out – then a cabaret artist doing ditto – and now staying overnight with 'a friend'. No. Absolutely not.

I had achieved great things; I had beaten a life sentence of being relegated to a wheelchair, endured excruciating surgery, tricked my way through an Army medical, and was now back into teaching... with the offer of a Deputy Headship. No way was I going to ruin everything by staying overnight with an overgrown bully – no matter how many spare rooms.

I thanked them for the meal and the offer of hospitality. "But I have to get back to the island tonight."

"The ferry's gone."

"There'll be a sampan." The only way to get back, (I'd been told) was to use the local sampans. This was the usual drug-runners' route – highly undesirable, and the Colonel had warned us all not to use it.

"We've no car and can't seem to get a taxi – you'll have to stay."

"I'll walk." I collected my coat, thanked them again for the meal and went to leave.

Desmond, apologizing profusely for having obviously offended me, couldn't have been more helpful. He 'found' a taxi, drove me down to the Star Ferry, organized a sampan and as we, with considerable trepidation, wove our erratic way across to the island, apologized for the meal, for being rude and for the inconvenience. He then found another taxi and finally delivered me back to my hotel.

Having arrived home before midnight, I was expected to relate all my experiences to the others. But never, *ever* again; even if it meant being incarcerated in this hot and smelly hotel forever – no, never! Still, it had been fun.

The next day a note was delivered under my hotel room door:

Will meet you on Stanley Beach at 5 pm – you did say you were teaching at Stanley Fort – so you should finish by 3.30 pm. You didn't leave a phone number so it's the only way I can get in touch. Desmond.

One of the staff had arranged to give us all a lift back that week, since we had no transport. But how could I say I had an appointment with someone I didn't know, on the beach at five o'clock? I rang her, saying I would find my own way home the following day.

She brushed that aside; as the outgoing Deputy Head it was her *duty* to see me, as her successor, comfortably back to my hotel, until I had my own transport. Was there, she enquired, any important reason for my staying on? She would wait…

"No." I said. "Not a problem. Thanks for the lift." I received at least three phone calls every evening for the rest of the week… *please ring… forgot to leave phone number… you weren't on the beach…*

School seemed to be going well, anyway. Everyone had settled in and all was fine. Eventually, I took a chance and rang back.

"A Mister Jon*elly*?" they said. "No one of that name here."

I discovered the number I had been given was that of the Correspondent's Club. (I should have been warned!)

The following day I had a call back to my other number. Eventually the hotel manager begged me to return the call: "Mees Leego… I have many calls… you ring back… yes?"

I rang back. This time I spoke to Tony. "Hold on," he said, "hold on, I have Desmond here – he's right here, coming now!"

When he did get to the phone, he was still apologetic. "Missed you on the beach… I left calls. I just wondered… now Peter's gone, would you care to have dinner at the Mandarin?"

I had been at the third-rate hotel for over a month now, without air conditioning; I had flat-hunted throughout Hong Kong after hot, hectic days of teaching, with staff meetings most days and yes, okay… brief relaxations on the fabulous beach, but no funds for anything else but to return to a stuffy hotel room – oh yes, *please*, I *would* like to go out for a luxury evening!

Desmond arrived, and wined and dined me at the Peninsular; he was cheerful, amusing and full of anecdotes about work. A barrister, he had worked in London, divorced, moved to Singapore and lived in the Far East ever since.

I was delivered back to my hotel at midnight. I had to deal with others at school, in their early twenties, reported for arriving back in the early hours of the morning, unfit for work, so it was important to me that whilst *I* went out, I got home in good condition and at a reasonable time. This was 1972; I had my position back and I was determined to keep it.

However, after that, Desmond rang every evening and I was wined and dined every other night.

We were then invited to an Army Ball – one of Hong Kong's festive occasions. I was invited by one of the Captains and went. I heard nothing from Desmond for a week. Finally I had a phone call.

He could hardly speak. "How could you?" he said. "We have been going out every night (we hadn't) and I now gather you are going out with someone else – it would have helped if you had told me yourself."

I had no idea what he was talking about and said so.

"Oh... *that*!" I said when enlightened. I explained that we were expected to take part in Hong Kong social life – as a school, we were invited and as a teacher at the school, I went; a duty dance.

After that, it was made clear that I was Desmond's partner and he was not prepared to tolerate any competition. I was now wined and dined two or three times a week at luxury restaurants, returning home (by the Star Ferry) meticulously before midnight and, obviously, with the utmost propriety. Any mention of male members of staff, contacts, etc were treated most suspiciously.

Finally, I accepted that everything had worked out in Hong Kong. The post was excellent, I adored Stanley Fort and I was committed to Desmond. Either I left, and joined in the general activities, or I accepted Desmond's tacit ultimatum... I was his private, platonic (enforced) partner, or else. It took a while, but eventually I decided that, yes, I wanted to be with Desmond more than anyone else, no matter what the inducements from elsewhere.

So we dined out most evenings: the Peninsular, Hilton, Repulse Bay and Mandarin. Finally – and realistically – Desmond said could we not have a quiet meal at home? Problem. I had never cooked in my life. Mary and Elizabeth jumped at the chance (I now had a flat and flat mates).

"*We'll* cook the meal. Love to. Invite Desmond back here. All we ever see of him is arriving in full evening gear, enthralling us with his scintillating conversation, and then you rush him off."

I put their suggestion to Desmond. No. He was not prepared to spend an evening with the three of us, however charming – he wanted a quiet evening, just us on our own. Fair enough. I went back to his flat. His flat mate, Tony, was totally charming. I gathered that the elevator kept breaking down (they were on the twenty-third floor). Desmond blamed Tony.

"If," he said, "…if there were not a permanent shuttle service of airline stewardesses using the said lift" (a different stewardess every night, I gathered), "then: a), Tony would be fit to work in the morning and b), the lift may have a chance, also, to recover."

Tony looked across at me, smiling sweetly and forebore to answer.

After that, I regularly ate out at hotels with Desmond or, more and more often, ate with them and managed with increasing difficulty to find a sampan to take me back to the Island and make it in time for work in the morning.

The crunch came after a couple of months when, one night, the sampan stopped halfway; another pulled alongside and a transaction took place.

"What's going on?" I wanted to know.

"Take no notice," advised Desmond.

Transaction completed, there was a distinctly nasty moment. A silence… then a conversation. Desmond joined in – he spoke some Cantonese. Then we proceeded to the Island. I was somewhat unnerved; I had not understood a single word, but it was obviously an unpleasant exchange.

We reached the other side. Desmond would not return to his flat that night. Taciturn, he said he would put up at Repulse Bay. We got in the taxi to drop me off at my flat.

"Last time I do that," he said.

Apparently, halfway across, our sampan had arranged to drop off a drugs haul. The sampan had pulled in and the drugs were handed over. He'd explained that Desmond had hired him to take us over and he could do that at the same time – to earn extra cash. However, the drugs dealer had explained that it would be far cheaper and safer to stick a knife in his passengers, to safeguard the haul. Desmond had then intervened, explaining that he was the QC who undertook all the Leaders' trials and murder convictions; he was on good terms with the Leaders and if anything happened to him, there would be repercussions. We had then been allowed to complete our journey, although Desmond had politely declined the return journey on the sampan.

Thoroughly chastened, I agreed with the difficulties of continuing our wining and dining as we had done and accepted that, if it were to continue, I would in future stay at Desmond's flat, on his terms.

I turned up the following evening and Desmond promptly explained to Tony that in future I would be staying over.

"Oh, thank God for that!" was Tony's response. "Couldn't stand the strain much longer of Desmond trying to be a gentleman."

After that, I had to admit, we could eat out as we chose, and return when we wanted; more and more frequently it was 'a quiet night in' – just a frantic rush for me to get the first Star Ferry back, taxi to my flat, pick up the car and zoom out to Stanley Fort on the other side of the Island, arriving blown and puffed out by 8.00 am.

Desmond, of course, took a leisurely air-conditioned taxi to Chambers at 10.30 am.

That was the end of any social life for me in Hong Kong. At school by 8.00 am, put in a hard day, having turned down the Deputy Headship of a new school – not being suited to all the paperwork. I was opted in to scale three posts, with responsibilities for Drama, English, Art and Divinity throughout the Primary School. This I accepted on condition that I would have full responsibility for the School Zoo – a collection of ill-assorted creatures: African talking parrots, parakeets, squirrel monkeys, guinea pigs, turtles, etc. They were all leftovers from various servicemen's families at the end of their terms. I was slightly fazed by the two white rats (a couple of skeletal, smelly, yellowy-grey creatures in a tiny bird cage), but was relieved to discover that when fed properly and sufficiently, they turned miraculously into two snow-white, plump charmers. Having been cruelly incarcerated in tiny cages and malnourished almost to the point of starvation, they became delightful and much loved pets.

I was beginning to enjoy Hong Kong. Exhausting, yes. Trying to live in both Desmond's flat on the mainland and my own on the Island, there wasn't a moment wasted. I was more than willing to accommodate Desmond's wish that we spent the evenings in his flat and the days working on the Island, with an occasional evening out.

Three

Things were going well. Liz and Mary, with all the other staff, had met up with their Army Officers – it was balls, functions, dinners and *work* (with a spell of lazing on Stanley Beach and a swim, to get our breath back).

Stanley Fort School had a breathtaking position – high up on a mountain, overlooking the Pacific Ocean and a few uninhabited islands and an incredible view of a Far Eastern sunset every evening. But the toll of settling in – the wining and dining, the workload and travelling and, ironically, supervising the children down the mountainous slope – all proved to be my undoing. I lost my footing, jerked my body backwards in an effort to regain my balance... and my troubled back gave out.

It would have been another slipped disc – except now I didn't have any; the whole fused four discs, now solid bone, went. I struggled back to my car and made it back to my flat, but I couldn't get up again. Three days off work. I managed to get to the Army doctor, but then had no alternative but to explain what I had done. He listened attentively and then simply said, "You appreciate this is a hospital job? I'll have to report you for treatment...?"

"Oh, *yes*," I said. "Not a problem."

I had enjoyed Hong Kong. I'd met Desmond and was totally entranced – the job was fantastic – the scenery straight out of a Bond movie – swimming in the Pacific Ocean – wining and dining in unbelievably stunning hotels – oh yes, I'd enjoyed it, and how – but all things must come to an end. Fair enough...

Mr Wilkinson had said he was sure I would be fine provided I had no X-rays and no one knew the extent of surgery that had been performed.

No alternative, then. Off to the hospital. X-rays. And then sent home in disgrace.

Off I went by ambulance to the Services Hospital. Everyone was charming and very helpful. X-rays; three days strict bed rest. No change. The surgeon would be round the following afternoon. I was ready for him.

A charming fellow in a white coat wandered in the next afternoon and promptly sat on my bed.

"Well, and how are you?" he asked.

It wasn't what I had been expecting; I was being treated as a friend. Determinedly I explained, with what dignity I could muster, that I had tricked my way – knowingly – through an Army medical.

There had been three thousand applicants for just two plum posts available in Hong Kong. A Deputy Head and one assistant. I had taken the Deputy Head's post and obviously was unfit, and now they would need to incur the expense of sending me home as well as re-advertising for my replacement. A waste of time, money and everyone's patience – a Court Martial, perhaps? Total at any rate. If I could have stood to attention for the firing squad, I would have done.

"Trouble is," my companion said cheerfully, "you've rather done your back in and there's no way of keeping it quiet now. I have contacted the Brigadier – who happens to be here at the moment – and explained the situation."

Do I get blindfolded, I wondered, or do they just aim and fire…?

With that, the door burst open and a flurry of nurses heralded the arrival of a new visitor.

"You can all go!" he said, and they fluttered off.

"Now, what's the problem?"

I explained it all again, this time with a stiff upper lip and a calm, determined demeanour.

"Hah! Well," he said, "I see the problem. Now, point is… can you do the job? Spoken to the school, oh yes; good job… done a good job. Heard about the play you put on… on our telly, eh? What next?" He turned to my friend. "Did you hear about it? Great stuff." He then began to talk about the play and what I had intended doing in the future. "But do you think you can?" he asked. "No point damaging your back; no good at all. But we want you to stay… don't we?" Again he turned to the consultant.

I said, carefully, "I know I can do the job and I love doing it. The problem is pretending there is nothing wrong with my back and not being able to rest it when I need to, so soon after the operation. If I'd had time to settle in, I would have been fine." (I thought it best not to mention the late evenings out, the mad dash to get back and drive out to school at the crack of dawn, travelling between the Island and the mainland.)

"That's settled then," said the Brigadier comfortably. "Keep it under our hats, eh?" he said to the consultant. "Nice to have met you – look after yourself." He leaned forward confidentially. "You take it easy," he said earnestly. "You're doing a good job and we want you to stay, but don't work too hard… it doesn't pay."   And he was gone.

So I could stay! I was over the moon. I was also speechless; this wasn't the Army as I had expected.

The consultant calmed me down. "You're not out of the wood yet. I'm not sure what you've done to your back – I think just a strain, but it means you'll be flat on your back for the duration."

"What about school?"

"I'll deal with the school," he assured me.

In fact it meant bed rest for half the term. The Headmaster fumed and spluttered, but the Brigadier was adamant. Not a word of explanation was given. I had been hospitalized and that was an end of the matter; I would be back when the Brigadier decreed. Until then, I must delegate.

I felt crushed… then elated; upside down and inside out and incidentally, heavily under drugs now. Dozing, at around 9.00 pm, the hospital being quiet and darkened, the door of my private room slowly opened and a bunch of red roses appeared round the door.

"Got past the door," a voice whispered.

"Only five minutes!" snapped Matron. "This is *not* visiting time."

It was, I assumed, a friend of Desmond's – another barrister from his Chambers that I had spoken to on the phone and met a few times in passing.

"Brought you these," he said, holding out a bouquet of gorgeous blood-red, long-stemmed roses. "And this," producing a bottle of champagne, "to cheer you up… and me as well, hopefully."

He sat down on the bedside chair. "Now," he began. "Now, at last I've got you all to myself. Look, since you arrived in Hong Kong, no one else has seen you or spoken to you – I know Desmond, and he has seen to it. You are kept in that flat of his and he makes a point of keeping you for himself." He sat forward, interlocking his fingers. "I've tried and tried – then I heard at Chambers that you'd been brought in… your friends rang, so I've come. I go back to the UK in the summer – only here for a year. I want you to come out with me, wherever… however… and I want you to come back with me. I know you don't know me, but I know *you*. I have a nice house in the UK, and a good job; we can have the summer together and then go home, get married and stay in the UK."

I stared at him, speechless.

"Don't answer now," (well, I wouldn't… couldn't…) "just think about it. I don't know what Desmond has said, but *he* will never *marry* you. Desmond is the original Irish charmer. He's Hong Kong's most eligible bachelor and intends to keep it that way."

I listened, unable – or unwilling – to stop this most informative outflow, which was becoming more interesting by the second.

"Before you came, both he *and* Tony had worn out the list with an endless supply of stewardesses – each trying to outdo the other, you see. He is a pillar of all the night clubs and hotspots and – the ultimate in heavy drinking clubs – the Correspondents Club. Oh, I know he's stopped now, but only to make sure you don't go out. Get out *now*, while you can. Granted he's clever – cleverer than me – he's witty, nice looking and charming, but how long do you think it will last? I have to leave in the summer, but think it over. Don't throw your life away on Desmond, he's not worth it. Come back with me in the summer. Leave him." He paused for a moment, looking at me. "Now, what chance do I have?"

I thought about it for a moment and then, to my surprise, I heard myself saying, "I'd rather have a fortnight with Desmond than a lifetime with anyone else."

"Ah…"

As his mouth opened, forming the word, the door opened again and another bouquet of blood-red roses appeared – accompanied by none other than Desmond.

"Brought you this," he said, putting a bottle of champagne down on the table with a box of marrons glace. Then he froze. Looking across the bed at Alan, he went white. He looked at me, at Alan, at the roses, and at the champagne. He said nothing, but simply sat in the chair at the other side of the bed, opposite Alan.

The nurse walked in. "I've brought you some glasses for the champagne…" and stopped dead. "I'll get another one," she mumbled, and disappeared.

I rubbed the drugs out of my eyes and said brightly, "Well, this is nice, *two* visitors on my first night!"

Neither of them answered. The next half hour was extremely difficult as I attempted to chat to both of them. Alan gave monosyllabic replies – obviously determined not to be made to leave; he would stick it out. Desmond merely sat and glared at him, leaving me – the invalid, suffering, and now drugged – to make polite conversation: the weather, school, life abroad, the rain forest…?!

Finally, to my relief, Matron decided that I had suffered enough. In she marched. "Ten o'clock!" she snapped. "*Out!*"

Forget two of the most important legal personages in Hong Kong, used to laying down the law to all and sundry – *out* they went. It had been a tough old day.

After that, Desmond visited every evening; but now at least I knew why. He barely spoke, brought the *Financial Times* with him to read and left when he was sure no one else had visited.

At half term I went back to school. My Headmaster was barely on speaking terms and I returned wiser, though saddened, and took the Brigadier's advice and eased up. That was the end of any social life for me in Hong Kong – I watched enviously as Mary and Liz went out to balls and dances. I looked at all my long dresses and sighed. Once in a while Desmond and I went out for a festive meal. It was now accepted that we were a couple and preferred to stay in. (Desmond certainly did.) No one dared question Desmond… if Desmond decreed that we stayed in, we stayed in.

Alan went back in the summer. He rang once to enquire politely how I was. I told him. I never heard from him again.

Tony obviously thought the whole thing a huge joke and, I gathered, mocked Desmond unmercifully when I wasn't there. Finally, he lost his sense of humour and, for once, spoke seriously. "What *are* you doing, Wendy?" he asked me. "Everyone has remarked on it; Desmond doesn't do the Town any more. You do know… he used to have a woman here every night?"

Yes. So I had gathered. I could only repeat that I would sooner have a fortnight with Desmond than a lifetime with anyone else. I'd given up dancing and watched everyone else going out for an evening's entertainment, dressed to kill. I stayed in with Desmond.

He looked at me rather sadly. "You do know he's not the marrying kind?"

Well, if I didn't, I did now.

So that was what I said I wanted and that was precisely what I got. And I had no one to blame but myself.

Four

"**S**usan and Peter are coming this weekend," said Desmond. "You'll meet them."

I hadn't met any of Desmond's friends – I didn't think he had any. He was very friendly with the solicitors who provided him with most of his work.

He had taken us out to the Golf Club; Desmond had no hobbies and didn't play golf, but insisted on inviting all the national heroes of golf back for dinner. I had been asked to meet him there and, having seen a small dog with its owner on the terrace, took mine.

Desmond dropped me off in the morning to amuse myself whilst he had some 'business' in the New Territories. He would pick me up for lunch at the club and then drive me home. At ten, I had strolled the grounds with Susie Chow... permit me now to digress from the Golf Club to explain how she came into my life...

Desmond had rung me one day to tell me that a group of Chinese were dicing outside his Chambers for a dog – a small black Chow (the best kind for eating in Hong Kong!). Not that he was prepared to do anything about it, but he abhorred violence. I rang the RSPCA and then later collected the dog from them and took it home – with some difficulty. The poor animal was thoroughly fed up; it had taken four officers armed with pole loops, dragging it in different directions so that its feet barely touched the ground – a picture of snarling teeth and claws. It was obviously one of the pack of wild Chows that roamed Hong Kong until February – Chinese New Year – when they were ceremoniously tortured (most people beat their beef on a board to tenderize it, but the Chinese prefer to do it on the wok). The dogs were put into a sack, hung and beaten before being cooked and eaten.

This one, naturally, had objected. The Officers looked at the dog and then at me; wouldn't I prefer to take one of their puppies, they pleaded?

...ɔ. The puppies would soon find a home; having rescued it, I would keep it.

"What do we do with it?" they asked.

I hadn't a clue. "You'd better put it in the back of the car."

As I drove up the eight-lane main Nathan Road I was conscious that the dog had uncurled from its foetal position, huddled in the back of the car, and was crawling on its belly, inch by inch, towards me.

I couldn't stop the car; I was surrounded by crazy taxis driving at break-neck speeds across Hong Kong's busiest road and intersections. Nothing I could do. I had been talking to it, hoping it would gradually relax. It seemed to have worked only too well; now I had a very cross feral Chow aiming for my jugular.

A black nose appeared between the bucket seats of the Toyota Celica which, fortunately, was automatic; I had too much paralysis to handle gears. A head appeared, and out of the corner of my eye I could see teeth flashing as it snarled up at me.

Then suddenly, it plunged its head – not at me, but into my long, wide kaftan sleeve. With its back legs still between the seats, its head stuffed firmly inside my sleeve and its rigid little body across mine, we reached my flat. I took hold of the string round its neck and it followed me in on its belly, head bowed and tail tucked out of sight... a gorgeous little dog without an evil bone in its body...

So, at the Golf Club, I strolled the grounds with Susie Chow. We went up to the terrace for coffee.

"Sorry, no dogs allowed," I was told.

I pointed to the terrier being walked nearby.

"Ah, that's the Chairman of the Club."

I explained my position, that I had been dropped off and wouldn't be picked up until the evening; I would like a coffee and the dog needed a drink – it was now well over 34°C and *humid*.

By seven o'clock I was, I must admit, somewhat hysterical. Susie Chow had survived in the open heat – all day without water and after a long walk – and so had I. Desmond alighted from his taxi at seven o'clock and greeted me absentmindedly. I moistened my parched lips and then told him exactly what he could do with his precious golf clubs; what he could do with his precious dog – in fact, come to think of it, what Desmond could do with himself – which, though physically impossible would give *me* a great deal of pleasure.

Officials came running. "Er, I am the Secretary. Is there a problem?"

Problem? I had been at their Club, which I had mistakenly assumed was run by gentlemen, not amoeba-like creatures with one function in life – to insert food in one end and expel it at the other, leaving a wide open gap where civilised creatures kept functional organs; having now discovered life below the level of the green slime at the bottom of most ponds, I did not intend to sully either my dog's superior intelligence or my own more limited reasoning powers by trespassing on their misbegotten property a moment longer.

I opened the door of Desmond's taxi. The driver was still staring, open-mouthed.

"I am now," I said grandly, "going back to my flat with *my* dog. I do not wish to see the Golf Club again. I do not wish to see *you* again. Unfortunately I have no alternative but to see Hong Kong again tomorrow – but be sure I will rid myself of *that* as soon as possible."

Desmond stood like a statue, also with his mouth open.

"No. No, wait," said the Secretary. A crowd had gathered on the terrace and several wives had come out to see the fun. Three or four of them came down the steps.

"Quite right, too," one said. The others joined in. One snatched a drink from a gaping waiter and thrust it into my hand. "You poor thing," she said. "I wondered why you didn't come up for a drink."

"And that poor dog," said another. A bowl of water appeared. Now there was no way I could leave.

Susie Chow, beautifully mannered until now, pulled free of her lead and slurped desperately at the bowl, skidding it round as she hoovered the water up before that, too, disappeared. All four feet planted firmly, she was not budging. She'd had a ghastly day – thought her end had come – she was staying put where the water was.

By now, apart from anything else, I had been standing with Susie Chow for nearly eight hours and I knew that if I didn't sit down – or more importantly, get home and lie flat on my back – my spine was going to collapse again, which would mean another hospital job. At which point, my knees gave way and I allowed myself to be sat down and made a fuss of, although the star of the day was Susie Chow.

Everyone wanted to hear the story of her rescue – her impeccable manners were admired. Then the women turned on the Secretary.

_m sorry, I... I'm sorry," he gabbled. "I... I didn't know!"

"I thought," I said coldly, "that I had explained my predicament fairly clearly and succinctly on my arrival. There was therefore no excuse for what was obviously an individual example of natural ill manners, and not that of the Golf Club management."

"Indeed..." he blustered, but was surrounded by a crowd of indignant and influential matrons exuding evil towards him.

He soft-pedalled. "It will be made up to you," he said. "What can I offer you? Free membership for a year? What is your present position at the Club?"

Desmond, quick to capitalize said, grandly, "We are not in fact members. We are visiting!"

"Free membership for a year," the Secretary gabbled on. "*Anything*!"

"*Nothing,* thank you," I said haughtily. "I would not care to join such a club if I were paid to."

"Since you insist," said Desmond, taking the Secretary's arm and walking away...

Eventually, I was shepherded into the taxi to be driven back to my own flat – to lie supine – it would be a miracle if I made it back to work on Monday. Desmond dutifully tipped me out of the taxi, and the incident was never mentioned again. I did in fact stagger back to work on Monday and when Desmond rang the following week he was in high good humour. In the ten years he had been in Hong Kong, he had never been invited to join the prestigious golf club – now he had at least a year's free membership and various other unspecified 'perks' he had managed to squeeze out of the Secretary.

Now Susan and Dennis were visiting and were to meet the famous Susie Chow and, of course, be taken to Desmond's new venture – the Hong Kong Golf Club.

I returned from work to be introduced to Susan. I was, however, totally unprepared for the vision of loveliness that descended the stairs to greet me. A figure Marilyn Monroe would have died for and a face that Elizabeth Taylor would have done likewise. I stood and gaped, my mouth open, as she teetered down on four-inch heels, carefully showing everything to advantage.

From then on disaster.

We were out wining and dining every evening in every nightspot in Hong Kong, arriving back around 4.00 am, when Desmond would happily sit us round the bar and dispense exotic drinks. I was expected to entertain them although, as I pointed out, I was the only one working, and I had to be up at 6.30 to get back to the Island, where I was then expected to put in a full day's work.

Still, finally they left, and I collapsed in a heap.

"Not to worry!" said Desmond. "They've invited us back to visit Taiwan and Manila next weekend – for a fortnight – you'll be on holiday then."

"Well, it has to be a restful fortnight," I told him.

"Of course," he replied absently.

School finished and I tore home; we were just in time to get the plane to Taiwan, where Susan and Dennis met us.

We all trailed round after Susan on her shopping spree as she twirled and preened before us. Then more wining and dining until the early hours. Then on to Manila.

"I *must* show you the fabulous shops here!"

She did. Non-stop.

"We *must* go out to the new Mercato Centre," said Dennis. "The showplace shopping centre, newly built – cut out from the jungle. It's supposed to be truly awe-inspiring… only we have to leave early in the morning because we have to drive through the jungle – under armed escort – bit of a bother to get there."

It certainly seemed so. It was a bit disconcerting to have a fellow carrying a sub-machine gun at the back of the traditional jeep.

It was a long drive through the jungle, but worth it. The Centre was a fantastic, fairy-tale place. Every five-star hotel was there, and the shops were out of this world – only Couturier standard shops allowed there, of course. All the Parisian labels… Susan was in her element.

We seemed to stop at each shop, gathering parcels at each one, until Dennis and Desmond, trailing behind Susan like adoring puppies, could carry no more. Suddenly, I felt it… my back… "I can't walk any more," I said. "I'll have to sit down."

"Me too," said Desmond. "But where?"

The Mercato Centre had certainly opened, but no one had got round to putting chairs or rest centres in place. We were practically the only ones there. There were fabulous restaurants everywhere, but none open yet. And then it was too late... I felt all four fused discs slip to one side.

So there it was. Done.

What to do now? I looked around.

The Sheraton Intercontinental was over the square, Dennis pointed out, helpfully. "Wendy wants to sit down; so do I," he said.

"It really doesn't matter now," I said, taking one look at Susan's face, which forecast a storm ahead. "Whatever I've done to my back is done now."

Dennis looked thoroughly uncomfortable. "Look," he said. "We left the hotel at nine, and it's now gone two. We've had a long drive out here and done nothing but shopping ever since. I'm exhausted, Wendy's had it... and if Susan buys one more thing, I'm suing for divorce."

Susan looked thunderous now and an explosion appeared to be imminent.

Desmond solved the problem. "I need a drink," he said. "We go to the Sheraton."

As we walked up to the entrance, two guards with machine guns took up positions at either side of the door.

"Oh," said Dennis. "Something's up. Hold on, I'll go and find out what's happening."

He came back shaking his head. "We're not going in there; Marcos and Imelda have arrived. The two kids are expected up in the Disco – and the police are moving in."

Dennis had spent some time in Taiwan and knew the situation in and around Manila. We had to have an armed escort to drive us out and the political situation was distinctly fraught.

Susan spotted the Marcos entourage and was on the shopping trail again. Off we traipsed again, behind them, while Imelda tried on scarves, jewellery, and shoes with gracious admiration, obviously enjoying herself.

So was Susan. As Imelda put down scarves, earrings and brooches, so Susan hastily picked them up. "I'm shopping with *Imelda*," she whispered to me, while Dennis panicked in the background.

"Get her away," he hissed at Desmond. "She'll buy the *shop!*"

They were both loaded to the gills with expensive parcels and packages and, as Desmond said – which was of paramount importance – he needed a drink.

The Sheraton was now out of bounds – a small army of machine guns defended the entrance. Dennis advised – and we all readily agreed – it was time to leave. The trouble was, all transport had disappeared and Dennis's armed escort, scheduled to take us back to our hotel, failed to materialize. As Dennis explained, once there was a *problem*, all sensible inhabitants simply vanished. We had been regarded as foolish to attempt to drive out to the complex, but Dennis and Desmond had totally overruled this – mainly thanks to Desmond demoralizing Dennis over a few drinks: *Huh, too scared, eh?* And Dennis's furious rebuttal… *very well, I'll take you there!*

Now Dennis had been proved right – it had been a foolhardy venture and everyone, even Susan, demanded to *go home*.

Dennis, walking behind the rest of us, suddenly exclaimed, "Wendy; she's tipped over!"

To everyone's consternation, so I had. I pointed out that I had been on my feet all day, walking for a further two hours with a slipped spinal fusion and – as I had already mentioned, it made no difference now what anyone said or did; it was an accomplished fact. All I needed now was to get back to the hotel, and for once we were in universal agreement.

By now, there were guards with machine guns everywhere; no one knew whose side they were on – I doubted if even Marcos knew. Since the situation was now life-threatening to Desmond, his *full* attention was concentrated on getting back to the hotel. So was mine.

Finally, very late in the afternoon (and we had been on our feet without a rest since nine o'clock that morning), we managed to get a taxi back. I do not remember quite how; I was by now tipped over sideways at an angle of 45° and even Desmond had noticed.

Eventually we arrived back at the hotel, where I was able to collapse in a heap. Well, thanks for the spinal fusion and thanks for the hospital picking me up and putting me back on my feet… but now I was surely for it. End of job; end of career; end of everything.

I tried lying flat. Totally impossible. My spine was twisted.

Desmond, once back in the safety of the hotel, was concerned and devoted. What could he *do*, he begged. "Anything?"

Fortunately, my innate good manners and total exhaustion came to my aid. I took a double dose of painkillers (morphine – to be taken for extreme pain only) and said politely that all I needed was to be left alone.

"Oh, fine," he said with relief.

"Ready for an evening out?" Desmond was on the phone to Dennis and Susan. "Good. Wendy's not up to it, but she insists that I *must* go out and not waste the holiday. What... going where? I'll be there."

"Sure you don't mind?" he looked at me through the mirror as he straightened his collar, then buttoned his jacket – ready for off.

"Oh no," I said, truthfully. "I don't mind at all; not at all."

After that, the fortnight's holiday went into a blur. Desmond left each morning on a trip, returning at mid-afternoon to change into tuxedo for a flash evening out. In the early hours of each morning he returned to tell me of the fabulous entertainment:

"Even the waiters wore white gloves..." "The chandeliers were bigger than Buck House..." "The dinner was twelve courses, with truffles, caviar knee deep and excellent champagne to wash it down..."

How lovely.

He came back high on alcohol and joined me – high on morphine.

My only route was to stay totally flat and hope to God (and pray) my spine went back into shape.

God – I will never do anything again to upset anyone. I will repent of any wrongdoing, I will do anything. God – get me back on my feet...

And he did. By day ten, in defiance of all my doctors' prognoses, I was attempting to walk round my bed. Hopefully, I rang the Airline; they could get me *out* of Manila and back to Hong Kong. It would take time and they would ring me back with flight details. I sank back on the bed, exhausted but triumphant.

At that moment, Desmond stormed in. "Just time to change before I go out," he said. "We're going to this fabulous place – Marcos and Imelda use it. So sorry you can't come." The phone rang as he opened the wardrobe door. I went to answer it but, slow and clumsy as I was, I was not in time.

Desmond picked up the phone and froze as he listened to the caller. "The flight is cancelled!" he snapped. There was a very brief consultation. "The flight is cancelled!" he repeated and slapped the phone down. "How could you do such a thing?" he asked me.

"Thinking of leaving without me, without a word..." Tears rolled down his face. "What have I done to deserve this?"

I lay on my bed, I have to say, somewhat bemused by the drugs. "I do not have a problem with you, Desmond," I replied. "I wanted to be with you – to the exclusion of all else, no problem – but you offer no security. I have worked hard; I have a good home bought and paid for (almost) by my own efforts. This has proved totally worthless as a relationship and now all I want is to get back to Hong Kong and my job. You can offer me nothing... I am leaving."

"I will not leave here," he said. "I will stay with you – I won't leave you."

Frankly, with the pain I was in, I didn't much care, but no way could I have him with me. I said fine, he could please himself; I would be happy just to stay there and relax – he had cancelled the flight (I'm not sure I could have made it, anyway). But tomorrow, if I could manage to walk round the bed... who knows?

The next day, finally, I *was* able to walk round the bed. Tentatively, I edged down, out of the door of the hotel and made my way to the coffee shop. Bliss! I was finally in the land of the living. I ordered coffee and a bacon sandwich and relished it. Somewhat exhausted by my exertions, I retired to my room and collapsed.

However, the next day, flushed by my success, I tottered out, not only to have a bacon sandwich, but on the way I had seen, through the patio doors, a lush swimming pool and complex. Of course! The one thing I needed. The original spinal fusion had been the first in the UK *not* using full plaster encasement of the spine, but hydrotherapy. Provided I stayed in water, I could get moving again. I enjoyed my bacon sandwich in the coffee shop and no longer thought enviously of the other three in full evening kit living it up happily at lush hotels – they could keep their king-sized chandeliers and their white-gloved waiters – I had beaten it a second time and was now *on my feet*. Now I knew my back would recover. No, let the other three enjoy their entertainment – I knew what I wanted.

I left the coffee shop and made my way very slowly, but far less crab-wise than before, to the pool. Very few people about, so no one to see my hesitant movements. Very carefully and very slowly, I stretched myself out on the nearest lounger. Oh, bliss!

I looked down at myself and discovered that I had turned a most delectable shade of yellow – my tan having somewhat dissipated after ten days in a hotel room without daylight. However, it would soon pick up now and I would go back to work with a healthy tan – at least I would *look* healthy…

Suddenly there was a shout from the shallow end of the pool. "Hi! Hi, Wendy! It *is* Wendy, isn't it?" One of the girls was climbing out of the pool. "We met you at one of the meetings – we're from Gun Club and the guys are from Kowloon," she said, pointing towards two men in the deep end. "What are you doing here?"

I explained that I was here at Dennis's invitation, had hurt my back and they hadn't seen me for the simple reason that I'd been incarcerated in my room. No point trying to hide it any more – at least I was mobile.

They were full of sympathy. All four left the pool and gathered round. The guys got drinks and we all chatted – shop talk, of course – but at least it was human contact. I lay back in the sunshine, cosseted by friends and colleagues, sipping my drink, listening to their news, and wallowing in their sympathy and understanding. Bliss.

Then the patio doors swung open and out strode Desmond – white to the gills and obviously in a fury, followed by Dennis and Susan who looked equally condemnatory.

"I looked for you in our room," said Dennis crossly. "We came back early, and this is the way I find you!"

"Yes," I said, happily. "I can walk now – not quite straight, but at least not listing at 45°. These are…"

"I *know* who they *are*," roared Desmond. Turning to Dennis and Susan, he said, "I knew there was a man; that's why she's been locked in her room all this time! *WHO IS IT?*" he was positively bellowing now… *which one… WHICH ONE?*"

I said, "Let me introduce the Deputy Head of Gun Club and three teachers…"

Dennis immediately backed out; Susan remained, totally disbelieving.

"We are going," said Desmond grandly, "to *our* room," holding out his hand to help me to my feet (which took some time).

The teachers immediately rose to their feet – at least *their* manners were impeccable. "We are staying at the hotel (three star) over the road," said one, "but we pay every day to use the pool." She smiled.

"The heat…you know…anyway, sorry if we disturbed you people; I think we'll go back now."

There was little I could do but go back to *our* room with Desmond. Once there, he attempted to break the silence with his idea of an apology. "I realized," he began, "you had been left on your own for over a week while we were out being wined and dined by Dennis's bosses. You were so… cross, I came back early; then I found you gone and came looking for you – only to find you at the pool side with those men – I didn't know what to think." He had the grace to look slightly sheepish.

"No problem," I said, "but no way were you going to embarrass my colleagues, or me, any further. Frankly, I just want to get back to my flat. I can get my job back, that's the main thing, and that's what I will concentrate on in future."

"Oh no," said Desmond. "No. We are not finished. Tomorrow night is our last night here. Now I know you are back on your feet and you say there is no one else, we can all go out for our last evening. Let's forget the last few days."

Forget the last ten days, (with Desmond arriving back in the early hours of the morning after a luxury night's entertainment, courtesy of Manila's richest entrepreneurs, suffering the after-effects of a surfeit of rich food and (mainly) alcohol, with me lying flat on my back suffering the after-effects of a surfeit of morphine) and go out *together* for our last evening in Manila.

Desmond's fearsome reputation as a protagonist prevailed. I agreed to one last effort.

He nodded, pleased. "I promise it will be a night to remember."

It was.

My one and only chance to sample the nightlife of Manila before I left for good, was irresistible. I spent the day selecting which evening dress to wear. It would, I decided, be a white cotton sheath dress; with long gloves and perhaps the long drop pearl earrings. Definitely *yes*. No, I promised Desmond, I would not go back to the pool again. Although I needed to swim to regain my strength, if Desmond even suspected I had been using the injury to meet someone else, then I'd rather not go again. (I doubted anyway, after that experience, whether the two young men from Gun Club/Kowloon would want to risk another fearsome encounter.)

I rested throughout the day. I was going out that evening, but it was most important (desperate, even) that a) I was on my feet to make the flight back to Hong Kong and b) able to teach, having arrived there. Desmond arrived back late in the afternoon after an extensive excursion involving yet more shopping for Susan. He bathed and changed into full Manila-type evening wear – no tuxedo; instead the fine look evening shirt of Manila. Both he and Dennis had bought several and this was their opportunity to wear them.

Whilst I climbed into my evening dress and began to select jewellery for *my one evening out*, the phone rang. Desmond answered it, listened, spoke a few words and hung up. "Dennis," he said. "Susan says this evening is casual; wear slacks and top."

"Slacks and top?" I repeated. "But every evening you have been going out to vastly expensive locations, dressed to kill and no expense spared in *seven star* hotels! No," I said decidedly, "that cannot be right." Dennis, being a man, of course, wouldn't understand. "His bosses have been entertaining us lavishly for the fortnight," I argued, "their last evening won't be casual. And in any case, I will be wearing a white cotton dress, albeit full length, which will go anywhere; I stay as I am!" With that, I continued dressing.

"This fortnight," said Desmond crossly, "is at the expense of Dennis's bosses, and if they say casual – it's casual."

I was unimpressed.

"Perhaps I'll ring Dennis," said Desmond, and did so.

"Afraid not," he informed me, after a brief exchange. "Dennis has checked with Susan and it's definitely *casual*. They are entertaining us, so it's up to us to do as they say."

I had to agree and reluctantly climbed back out of my regalia; the long sheath dress had to go. Instead I had to think *casual*. However, I had a pair of white slacks which normally travelled anywhere; plus, I had bought on my first day in Manila a gossamer fine blouse, simply held together by magnificent and colourful embroidery. A local beauty. It could disgrace no one. A pearl necklace and I was ready. Desmond in full evening dress – albeit Manila-style – and me in local folksy dress.

We went downstairs to the foyer. The chauffeur was waiting. He was concerned; it was late and he was without an armed guard. He could only proceed through the gates of the hotel, at which we were to be entertained, by a certain pass; time was of the essence.

Dennis rang through to his room. "Susan, it is imperative that you come down *now*, or else the evening is *out!*"

Five minutes later, the lift whined down from their floor.

"Thank *God*!" said Dennis with feeling.

The lift opened and out stepped Susan… in all her regal beauty. In a satin, sequinned sheath, décolletage near her navel, cut at the back to allow her to walk (and then with difficulty). Her hair was piled in profusion on top of her head and sprinkled with diamonds, and the long drop diamond earrings and white satin shoes with four-inch heels completed the effect. She looked a million dollars. All eyes swivelled to her as she carefully and deliberately sashayed over to us.

"I'll go and change," I said weakly.

"No time!" snapped Susan, apparently without opening her mouth.

"There isn't," said Dennis, taken aback. "If we don't go now we lose the car, and my bosses are waiting. I dare not let the car go without us."

He and Desmond looked at each other – Dennis in consternation but Desmond blank, as always in an emergency. He expected others to rise above such inconveniences.

Dennis did. "Either we all go *now*," he said, looking at me, "or we all stay."

Obviously it depended on me. My last evening in Manila, my one chance to see Manila's high life – either I went as I was, or not at all.

I went. No great problem. I was never going to see any of these people again; I had my job back – if I were careful. Nothing lost, I decided, I would enjoy an evening out.

We arrived at our destination; Dennis and Susan had not spoken a word. It was not a hotel, but a private house, which incorporated a ballroom. It was also not magnificent, of the type with one hundred-foot chandeliers, or anything like that, but the residence of a multi-millionaire who had designed his house on local traditions.

He welcomed us; this was Dennis's supreme boss and his personal home. All the women, of course, were in full evening dress, as were the men. The women wore traditional Imelda-type evening gowns with balloon sleeves and full length, sheath skirts. I was alone in wearing traditional local 'folk-song' blouse with European slacks.

We were greeted and we sat. The women looked speculatively at my homespun blouse. Their etiquette was totally strict and formal – *dress was formal.*

Although I felt my dress (or lack of it) shamed Dennis and Desmond (Dennis for putting the wrong message out; Desmond for relaying it), I felt constrained to offer my host an explanation. On greeting, the wives, as all Manila wives do, felt that good manners demanded they should put me – ill-dressed as I was – at my ease. They immediately went overboard, praising my choice of blouse. "How unique of you to wear one of our local products"... "Why didn't *we* think of that?" they asked each other in total admiration of my hand-crafted garment.

"Well, thank you," I smiled. "How much I appreciate your kindness. This blouse was the first thing I just had to buy on my arrival in Manila – only here have I seen such exquisite embroidery!" But I was *cross*... the past ten days and ruined holiday cut deeply and I forgot (yes, *deliberately*) the rule: *Do not tell tales.* I submit; I apologise... but I don't regret a thing.

I then explained to the assembled table (twenty of us) how it had occurred. "I fear I hurt my back," I said, "on arrival, having undergone a *spinal fusion*. I thought it had been one hundred percent successful, but unfortunately we went to the new Mercato Centre and became involved with the Marcos entourage. Having left the hotel at nine am, after an hour's drive we then walked from ten am until two pm – at which point I asked for a coffee break." I now had the undivided attention of every person in the room. "None was forthcoming, however," I continued, "so we walked and shopped until four pm, by which time I had slipped the disc that had only recently been fixed! I then had to stay in my room, on my back, for ten days until this evening, when I was told to change from evening dress to casual wear. I hope you will appreciate, therefore, that I meant no disrespect to your hospitality – I merely did as I was told." There... that was off my chest!

The women, all Manila born, pampered society icons, were horrified.

"You *walked*, non-stop from *ten* o'clock to *four* o'clock? *Six hours* on your feet? Why?"

I smiled weakly. "We were shopping," I said sweetly. "At least, Susan was... I did not feel up to buying anything."

There was total silence from my three companions. Dennis and Susan retired to dance a few steps on the dance floor and then indulge in a private, quiet but furious row. I don't know where Desmond went – nor did I care. Left alone with my host in my wholly unsuitable attire, I succumbed first to the sympathy of the women and then to the knowledge of the men at the table – many of whom were 'into gems'. I am sure they were strictly on a commercial level, but that evening, to put me at ease, they explained the geology, the geography and the history of the land; how it evolved, where and how the minerals lay – you could still collect precious and semi-precious stones from the ground as well as gold and silver, if you knew where to look.

Altogether, it turned out to be a most fascinating and enjoyable evening. My hosts from Manila and their wives had gone out of their way to put me at my ease – having obviously made a major social error, which they acknowledged had not been intentional, and my apology had been graciously accepted. (I gathered afterwards that, whilst the ladies from Manila had arrived in their full evening dress – traditional – Susan had not gone down well in her plunge neckline and very little else, however delectable.)

Finally, Desmond, Dennis and Susan, at the conclusion of a seven-course meal and endless conversation, came to collect me. The evening ended and Desmond and I, with Dennis and Susan, were driven back in total silence.

I had ordered a taxi back to my flat, which Desmond insisted on accompanying. Having reached it, my sterling colleagues took over, putting me to bed as I relayed to them the details of my accident.

"Never will I move again," I told them. *Just get rid of them!* I was due back at work on Monday, and I thought I could make it. I was still a delicate shade of unwashed yellow, but that would soon be cured after a turn on Repulse Beach after school.

"How *could* you?" mourned Elizabeth and Mary. "How could you treat Desmond so badly? He is *heartbroken*. Well, indeed, if *you* don't appreciate him, then give *us* a chance!"

Desmond could do no wrong in their books.

"But I've had enough," I said. "All I want now is to hold down my job, and it starts on *Monday*. If I am to keep my job, I stay here."

Desmond appeared. "If you stay here," he said, "I stay too. I stay here until you come back to my flat."

Mary and Elizabeth agreed with him – as I said, no wrong could he do – and he stayed put, obviously determined to stay for ever, which would cost me my job anyway, as a single teacher, so I finally agreed to return to his flat.

I did get back to work on the Monday, with some difficulty and a considerable amount of morphine; but I got back. And kept my job. However, I clearly had to take Susan and Dennis on board in future; it was patently obvious that Susan was used to (and had every intention of continuing) enjoying the undivided and devoted attention of both Dennis *and* Desmond.

When she deigned to appear, Dennis picked up the bill; money was no object. Desmond could (and did) demand the best and obviously Dennis made good use of his legal acumen. After the business of the day was concluded, Desmond enjoyed lavish entertainment and in turn showered attention on the beautiful Susan, who could do no wrong (provided Dennis picked up the bill, which after Susan's shopping marathons caused considerable strife on their return home to Taiwan). This had been their lifestyle for several years; I felt I would be skating on thin and very dangerous ice if I attempted to alter the status quo.

It seemed odd. Susan, at twenty-eight or nine, was in her prime. They had dealings with the flourishing Chinese film industry, and Susan had immediately been opted in as 'an extra', which meant even more petting and primping. She could knock spots off any woman in Hong Kong, but even though I was no match for her, she was not prepared to tolerate *any* competition. My motto had always been, 'if at first you don't succeed, give up', and I intended to do so now.

Desmond had put the phone down to say, as casually as he could (and without making direct eye contact), "Er, Susan and Dennis are coming over again next weekend; er… alright with you?"

"Fine. Oh… next week? I am a bit tied up next week… I might be late back in the evenings."

"Oh, that's *perfectly* all right," said Desmond, with unbecoming enthusiasm. "As late as you like… as long as you're *here!*"

The following Friday, Desmond rang me at my flat. "Well, they are here!" he said jovially, and obviously after several drinks. "When are you coming over?"

"We'll have another drink while we wait for you!" shouted Dennis merrily down the phone.

"Or three!" trilled Susan.

My phone rang the next morning. "Where are you?" Desmond asked crossly.

"In my flat," I answered helpfully. "You seemed to be having such a wonderful time, I left you to it. I did ring, but even if you heard it, you evidently weren't in a fit state to answer it."

Desmond rang again in the evening, very subdued now. "Are you coming over?" he asked. "We've a table booked at the Miramar." Then, no longer able to keep up the pretext of politeness, "And it's booked for eight, so make sure you're *here!*" he snapped. "Otherwise we go without you."

Although surprised, I merely said, "Of course."

At fifteen minutes to eight, he phoned again. "Where are you Binky?" he begged. "Aren't you coming?"

"Got held up," I told him. "I did say I might. I know you are all on vacation, but I still have to work, you know."

"But you *are* coming?"

"Well, I don't know, to be honest… I don't think so. I did *try* to get everything done in time, but as you said be there for eight or not at all, well…"

Finally, Desmond switched on all the power of the male version of *femme fatale*. "We *won't go* without you, Binky," he said earnestly. "Susan and Dennis have taken the trouble to get over here *especially* to see *you*, and it will of course *ruin* their *entire* weekend if I have to cancel this evening… but we *won't* go without you." A slight pause then, but I made no comment. "Look, if it's about last time, we really are sorry that you hurt your back, but we are only going out for a meal – there won't be any walking. *Please* come!"

Dennis came on the phone. "Er, Wendy," he said, a trifle awkwardly, "*Please*, do come this evening; we were looking forward to seeing you and… and Desmond won't go without you, well… neither would we, would we, Susan?"

"No!" I heard Susan mustering a considerable amount of enthusiasm; her stint at the film studio had obviously paid off. "No," she trilled again, "we definitely want you to come."

"Oh well, fine," I said. "I'll hop in the car; I'm afraid I'm not dressed and I definitely can't make it by eight, but I will come."

"Oh, any time you like," I was assured. "Give yourself time to get dressed," Desmond said hastily. Whatever else, it would certainly not be appreciated if he had to take me out in slacks and sweater in the evening! "We'll wait for you."

So we went out and between them, they would have charmed the birds from the trees; we had a most pleasant evening. I thoroughly enjoyed myself.

By this time I had settled into the routine (entirely Desmond's own, which I had fitted in with). He had explained that he lived in hotels, or the shared flat, but I had been fairly shattered to learn of his lifestyle; servants washed his clothes, which he left on the floor, and the wardrobe was packed full of clothes never worn.

He asked me to 'sort out' his suits; he had two dozen of them, and there were *three hundred and eighty* shirts, and evening ties, etc. I pointed out that he had a shirt for every single day of the year with a few spare – some were still in their wrapping!

"Would you sort them for me?" he'd asked sadly.

I cross-indexed them so that all he had to do was select a suit and next to it he would find a variety of suitable shirts, ties and accessories.

Still, occasionally, he would ask me to choose his outfit. As he did now.

"I'll be back for seven-thirty," he said helpfully. "And Binky... could we have something *special* for dinner, you know... whatever you like, but we'll make it a *special* evening?"

I was to learn that phrase. Well.

I got in early from work, having dashed round the shops to get what I needed. We would have gazpacho soup; I couldn't make it to Susan's *haute cuisine* standard, but perhaps, with practice, I might... followed by a soufflé and fillet steak... and a baked Alaska.

Hm. I lit the candles and waited. And waited. And... waited. Finally, at eleven pm I threw the lot in the bin and, exhausted, went to bed. Desmond didn't arrive. Next afternoon, I arrived back from school, all prepared. I would remain *calm*. I would not shriek; I would not storm. Having thought about it, I had decided quite clearly that I had no right to. I was here entirely by invitation, having no status whatsoever; if I did not like it, then I could always leave.

Still no Desmond. Clearly, he was too ashamed now, and too embarrassed to come home. I would be forgiving; I would *understand*, I told myself as I savagely kicked my neighbour's cat out of the way.

By the evening, I was genuinely worried. I had as usual misunderstood – he had probably had an accident and was even now suffering in hospital. (So why hadn't he phoned?) Well, doubtless he was suffering from amnesia, following concussion... *perhaps dead!* I should ring the hospitals, notify the police – even if I had no official status, it was the least I could do, would do, even, for a friend.

Something still told me this would not be a good idea... brilliant! *First* I would ask his flat mate... I'd give him one more night.

Saturday morning, I knocked on Tony's door. He was in the middle of breakfast. I explained the situation. By now, I was white with exhaustion, having not slept for the past two nights.

"Um... you know, Desmond can look after himself, Wendy," he said.

"Oh, I *know*," I said earnestly. But *no* one would disappear for three days... I mean, where would he *be?*"

Tony looked really uncomfortable, as well as faintly amused. "I expect he is at the Correspondents Club," he said. "It's where he always used to hang out. He hasn't been for some time though... well, not since he met *you*," he said, thoughtfully. "But, Wendy... you have to understand that this is what he has always done – in fact it's rather unusual that he hasn't done it before. But they are fairly heavy drinkers at the Correspondents Club – he's probably put up at the Hilton. He'll come home when he's ready."

"But he might have had an accident!" I fretted. "He could be lying at the roadside, injured, or... in hospital!"

"Not Desmond," said Tony with certainty. "No. But if you are worried, give him one more day and I'll find him for you, okay? But listen, you don't ring anyone; he won't thank you for it if you do."

Which was, in fact, excellent advice.

Sunday afternoon, the door opened slowly; very slowly. A bunch of roses appeared round it, followed by a bottle of champagne (the first of many), followed by Desmond.

"Please don't shout at me, Binky," he said weakly. "Whatever else you do, *don't shout...*" and he collapsed.

Next morning, he was back to his normal self; he certainly had the constitution of an ox. I had expected an explanation; an apology, but there was neither. He was off-hand, business-like, and worked late at Chambers, making it clear that it was not for discussion.

After that, it became a matter of habit; about twice a month he would disappear for two or three days and return glassy-eyed and unshaven, demanding breakfast – always the full English – and rise next morning perfectly well and back to normal. This, apparently, was part of his routine and no one was allowed to disturb it. All phone calls from solicitors, Chambers, etc. were to be ignored. Pleas from his clients, usually facing murder trials and needing urgent consultations, fell on deaf ears. Tony was used to ignoring them. I made sure I never answered the phone.

By now, I had been in Hong Kong for eighteen months. My colleagues all had established lifestyles – I was left out. Desmond did not expect, at any time, to be left alone in his flat, but he refused to accompany me to any of the school functions, social or otherwise. He also ignored all the Legal functions. As teachers, we were invited to all the many Army functions – the social life was hectic. The Legal fraternity was equally generous. The balls and social gatherings were never-ending. Desmond ignored them all.

I missed all that – the dancing especially. I had been used to going out regularly in the New Forest – the forestry and farming communities were equally social-minded and all the fellows I had been out with had always been assiduous in their wining and dining. The Tennis club at Lyndhurst had entertained the influential and wealthy – the grand Balls being held either in private houses or hotels and my aunt and uncle who organised the Tennis club dances made sure my sister and I attended them all. Once established, all the fellows I met and had been out with had joined in the social life with enthusiasm.

I wasn't used to sitting back and watching as everyone else enjoyed themselves; it was a novel experience and not one I enjoyed. Still, I only had two options: I could stay – and tolerate the situation, disgruntled as I was; or I could leave Desmond and return to my flat. But everyone was now well established in Hong Kong, so more than likely that would mean staying in my flat for the remainder of my tour. I would certainly find other partners if I wanted to attend functions – there were always stray fellows looking for someone, but certainly no one I especially wanted to go with.

So I accepted the present situation. I had known Desmond was considerably older than I, but he had degenerated from dining out on a regular basis to staying in our flat every evening. I had insisted on going out *at least* once a month, just to make sure the world was still going round, so we ended up going out once a month – but certainly regularly – and that was to be my entertainment. There were massive recriminations if I attempted to accept theatre trips – even films were forbidden. I must be going out *to meet someone*. Why else would I want to go out?

I was invited by colleagues, my flat mates, acquaintances – all quite innocently, but it would cause such trouble for me that I inevitably rang to say I couldn't make it, and finally gave up altogether. We stayed in.

Dennis and Susan came over regularly. The status quo was maintained; because I arrived late (due to the pressure of work) and left early (the pressure of work), I agreed with everything and kept out of Susan's way. I was enjoying Hong Kong; it had been an experience. I had never had a relationship before – one didn't in the seventies. I had been wined and dined, engaged and disengaged, but this was my first experience of being treated as half of an old married couple. I would miss Desmond, but I was beginning to look forward to going back to my home in the UK, my dogs and my garden and being able to *go out* – theatres, dances, whatever – however superficial it may be. I would never meet anyone that I wanted as much as Desmond, but I was certainly beginning to feel like a rabbit in a cage.

At school, everyone began preparing to return to the UK. Elizabeth had met up with a lawyer and would be staying on in Hong Kong; Mary had won another contract to Mauritius. I wrote to Hampshire, reminding them that my three-year seconded contract was coming to an end. They sent me a list of Deputy Headships available, which I could choose from. The packing cases arrived. I ordered three small ones for my own belongings, mainly Chinese rosewood furniture we had all ordered when we first arrived in Hong Kong. One large case I sent over to Desmond's flat for my huge carved rosewood eight-seater dining table.

Desmond arrived back and found me packing.

He sat down suddenly on the sofa. "What are you doing?" he gasped.

"Packing."

"Packing? *What? Why?*"

"My tour ends in July," I told him. "I've sold my car, but everything else needs to be packed up for the Navy to ship home."

Desmond was white and shaking (genuine, but I never could work out whether it was rage, frustration or temper).

"Do I mean *nothing* to you?" he asked, his cheeks awash with tears, which he bravely ignored. So did I.

"Do our three years together mean *nothing* to you?"

"Yes," I said. "They mean a great deal to me – which is why I have stayed with you, even though I have missed going out. No theatre, no sailing – you turned down all the invitations Mary, Liz and I were offered; they went, I stayed at home."

"We've been to Taiwan," he protested, becoming more annoyed by the minute. "I took you to Manila and Macau…"

I agreed. "I enjoyed that," I said, "and I appreciate it, but it was business. You had to go and I came with you, but yes I enjoyed it" (even if I did have to put up with Susan). "But," I continued, "you've made it clear from the start that you don't want marriage, you don't want any responsibility and you don't want any commitment. Fine. But I have a very nice house, almost paid for, and a promising career; I have worked hard for both – from scratch – and I am not prepared to give them up. Either I sell the house or I'm going to have to go back to the UK and look after it. You knew that."

I was in full flow. "As you have said many times, you purposely own nothing – you have a far greater salary and you can afford to rent the flat, rent the furniture… rent everything. Anyway, it's the end of my tour and too late now to apply for another tour in Hong Kong; I have no option now but to go back to the UK."

For the first time, all Desmond's arguments failed to impress. As I'd said, the die was cast. My car was sold; I was awaiting a job in the UK; my tour in Hong Kong had reached its conclusion. Nothing to be done.

Susan and Dennis arrived. Susan was ready with her plentiful helping of scorn: "You're just walking out on Desmond," she drawled.

After three *years?* "It is not a question of walking out," I informed her. "I have responsibilities; they take me back to the UK."

In fact, we had a very quiet weekend. We went out for a luxurious meal and, for the first time, Desmond and Dennis didn't try to outdo each other in a drinking contest. They drank wine with the meal and a brandy afterwards. Dennis didn't end up eating the flowers on the table for a drunken bet made by Desmond, and didn't fall off his chair when Desmond refused to pay up. Even back at the flat they had a *sober* drink and didn't try to out-drink each other with as many American cocktails as they could make up from the *Barman's Companion* until they both fell off the stools and into bed.

For Susan and Dennis it was a thoroughly boring weekend for which they blamed me and left early, giving me reproachful glances as I drove them to the airport. There was an uncomfortable silence in the flat after they'd gone. Finally I said I'd better get back to my own flat and complete my packing.

"You're not really going to leave me are you, Binky?" said Desmond.

But for once there was no alternative that even he could come up with.

Halfway through the week he rang me. "I can't stand it any longer – can I come over?"

"I really am busy," I told him. "The packers are coming for the cases at the weekend."

"You must come out with me – at least this evening," he urged.

He came straight over. It *would* be nice to go out again and I was looking forward to the evening. He walked into the sitting room and looked round. "Where are the girls?" he wanted to know.

"Out shopping. Picking up last minute gifts to take home; they'll be back soon. Why? Do you want to say goodbye?"

"No, no." Desmond shook his head. "I just wondered... look, are you still determined to go? I would have thought..." he said bitterly, "... you would have realised how much I rely on you. The flat is empty without you and I am so miserable." The look he gave me did, indeed, convey his misery. "Not too much to ask, I would have thought," he went on, "to give *some* consideration to me."

He continued in this vein for some time; it was becoming tedious, and he was fast losing his unhappy, contrite persona to the angry, resentful one when we heard footsteps clattering up the stairs and the voices of Mary and Liz. Suddenly the door burst open and at that moment, almost as if on cue, Desmond's diatribe of injustices ceased and he dropped down onto one knee.

"Marry me, Binky... marry me!" he cried, tears rolling down his face. "I can't live without you," he continued brokenly. "*Marry* me..."

I just stood there and gaped while Mary and Liz reined in to a halt, mortally embarrassed at having walked in on such a highly emotional scene.

"No, no," said Desmond, coming very slowly back to his feet. "It doesn't matter now. Nothing matters now... except Binky's answer?"

He looked straight at me; I was forced to give an answer in front of all three. It made no difference. "I can't," I said. "My contract here is at an end; we've all got to go home, Desmond."

Desmond followed me into my sitting room, having first noticed, with great satisfaction, the impressive effect he'd made on Mary and Liz, and their reproachful glances in my direction as I left the room.

Still, we went out later and had a wonderful evening. Desmond could not have been more attentive. We arrived back and he happily returned to his own flat, confident that he had played his part well.

Mary and Liz, however, set upon me in earnest first thing next morning. "How could you, Wendy?"

"Yes, how *could* you? Desmond... *Desmond* going down on his knees to propose!"

"Of course *you* wouldn't have noticed, but he was in tears... *Desmond!*"

"No. You don't understand," I told them. "He was being Desmond... he was *ordering* me to stay until he heard you coming up the stairs. The whole thing was stage-managed."

"Oh, for heaven's sake, Wendy!"

"Yes, for heaven's sake... well if you turn him down after that, *neither* of us will speak to you again!"

"How could you do such a thing after *three years*? That is just *unforgivable.*"

The atmosphere in our flat after that, you could cut with a knife. I stayed in my room, my thoughts going round in circles until I could stand it no longer, and finally rang Desmond. "I appear to be in the doghouse all round," I told him, "after that show you put on in my flat."

"Me? Put on a show?" laughed Desmond. "I told you, I want you to stay; I *intend* you to stay. I'll come and pick you up in half an hour."

He collected me and we went out. He made no attempt to deny he'd planned the whole display.

"You've quite made up your mind to go?" he asked.

I explained, yet again; I had no option.

"In that case," he said decisively, "the offer's genuine. No, I didn't want to get married, but if that's the only way you stay, then that is what we'll do." (No question of asking, now.)

But that really wasn't the problem – although the offer was certainly a shock. "I *have* to go back to the UK," I told him. "Either I sell the house, or I go back and live in it... it isn't intended as a threat; it's a fact. As I said before, I can still come out to Hong Kong – after all, I get three months vacation – and you are even freer. We don't have to get married, that's not the problem – we could commute. But the fact is that my security and future are in the UK while yours are in Hong Kong."

He insisted that he'd always intended returning eventually to the UK but, having no ties there, had always put it off. Now, he said, he wanted to get married. Quite definitely. And he wanted to work in the UK – he could always look up his old chambers, find a job there. I could teach as I chose, but now he had decided it was time he returned and eventually retired in the UK. Would I think about it?

I would indeed.

I was not at all sure about this sudden change of heart after all those years as a happy bachelor. But I was only too keen to persuade myself that it was genuine. I went back to my flat and discussed it with Mary and Liz. They were over the moon. There was absolutely nothing now to prevent the marriage... but of course they had known it from the start... admit it, I was just a bit difficult at times. Not trusting enough, they concluded, but everything's fine now.

So the cases had to be unpacked. I wrote (albeit with great misgivings) and gave up my seconded Deputy Headship – they couldn't hold the post for me and I certainly could not get everything rearranged and be back in the UK in time. I would have to take a temporary job in a Government school in Hong Kong for a term to pay my mortgage.

At the end of term, Liz, Mary and I drove down to the Registry Office and Desmond and I were married. Not without incident, naturally. Not one, but three typhoons descended that day and all Hong Kong battened down the hatches. The Registrar refused to turn out. No taxis were out.

"Cancel it," I said.

"No," said Desmond.

So I drove everyone in my (sold!) car, and Desmond managed to get hold of another Magistrate to marry us. Liz and Mary had arranged a small reception for us afterwards at the Mandarin. Just to complete the day, Desmond unfortunately could not attend his own wedding celebration; he had, he said, to be in court. Naturally. Everyone understood, but it was only later that I discovered he hadn't been in court in his more usual capacity of Prosecuting Counsel. No, he was on a drink-driving charge himself, which was why he had been unable to avoid it. God knows whose car he'd been driving, but at least it hadn't been mine.

I took Desmond home for the first time – to see my house and Southampton, and to remember London.

Before I could put the key in the door it opened, and Mother fell out. "I've put the potatoes on, Wendy," she gasped, helpfully. That was her sole contribution to social life. I had no idea what had been going on for the three years I'd been away. I had dashed home every summer, for the whole six weeks vacation, and spent it frantically cutting back the two-foot high lawn, pruning the sixteen-foot roses to ground level, trimming sixty-foot hedges down to their normal sedate six foot, and then racing back again… exhausted.

But Mother had deteriorated. Greatly.

Behind her loomed my sister. I couldn't imagine what she was doing there – nothing useful, that was for sure. But I introduced her anyway. Desmond was at his best in these situations. As usual, he charmed both, like birds from the trees – they ate out of his hands.

"We must take you out to dinner," gushed my sister. "Perhaps we could take you to the Royal Winchester Golf Club one evening? Wendy tells us she has been playing golf in Hong Kong!"

Desmond graciously intimated that they may, and Thelma bowed her way out backwards. He then surveyed his new territory, without enthusiasm. The house was 1930s built, with four bedrooms and stood in a quarter of an acre in a row of similar houses. A typical suburban residence. On one side was Doctor Brooks, now retired, and on the other, an Army officer, also retired. I felt it was adequate if Desmond wanted to live there. If he wanted the house to himself, then it was about time, after fifteen years, that my sister took over the care of my mother. I certainly had never managed to persuade my sister to take her, even for a day – but then I didn't have Desmond's persuasive powers.

But he enjoyed his stay, and so did I. The summer was hot and he lay out all day on the sun-lounger while I cut the lawns, trimmed the hedges and brought the place generally back under control. My mother pottered happily in the kitchen, preparing and serving meals to her heart's content.

In the evening, Thelma and Dennis took us out – to the golf club, for golf and dinner; out to the forest for drinks – Dennis was in his element. "This is *my* golf club; the Royal, of course, I think I may say, is the premier golf club in the county... I suggest we have *this* wine with the first course... a nineteen-seventy-three from the south side of the vineyard, I would say (sniffing delicately)... a little suggestive, but not pretentious, I feel..."

Desmond drank. As long as the label was expensive and someone else was paying, he didn't care. I just wished I'd been invited out like that when I'd been at home – I had been carefully omitted from all invitations to the Royal Winchester – now, it appeared, I was eligible.

There was no work at all for me in Hampshire; if I came back now, I would have to take my chance with supply teaching to keep my mortgage payments up. I had less than £1000 to pay off before it was bought outright and became mine. If necessary, it would be worth working an extra year in Hong Kong, to make sure of it. Once the house was paid for, I was prepared to do whatever Desmond wanted. I had bought the house for £8000 in the sixties and was surprised to hear it was now worth almost £200,000. It now needed decorating throughout – but well worth the effort. My male colleagues had been dashing home – even for a fortnight – to make sure they had a property to return to. Some had been devastated to find that whilst they had been working themselves to death in Hong Kong, trying to carve out a career for themselves, property prices had doubled, trebled and quadrupled and they were completely out-marketed – unable even to put down a deposit on a starter home for their families.

I, however, was master of the situation; I had done exactly the right thing and poured all my money into a deposit on a substantial property when prices were low – I now reaped the benefit. I presented this to Desmond like a puppy with a bone for its master.

Desmond grudgingly agreed. He was obviously assimilating all these experiences to relate to Susan and Desmond. *How boringly provincial Wendy was – always concerned that bills were paid on time; buying a home.* Not like Susan and Dennis – the Big Deal; the Sting – how to trick your way to success. Frankly, there was no way I could support Desmond in Southampton, or London, come to that. Finally, though I had not the slightest regard for my sister or her husband, I felt I had to say that unless Desmond returned their hospitality, we should not go out with them. Fine he said, so after that I refused all their invitations. I was not prepared to face the embarrassment of a partner who couldn't and wouldn't pay his way.

We had some pleasant excursions in London. We tracked down all the most exclusive restaurants – known only to the most discerning, where Desmond was greeted warmly and pampered with the most expensive wines and food. This he paid out for willingly; he was more generous when entertaining women.

Now that we were married, Desmond had moved out of Tony's flat. He had no furniture other than bits and pieces that had been left behind, unwanted, in the old flat. He begged me not to send the rosewood furniture home. He already had an eight-seater teak dining table and chairs and I pointed out that he hardly needed another. But, as he explained, the teak was so battered now it was no good any more, and there was plenty of room in the huge, luxurious apartment on the Mount, so it stayed.

Having settled everything to his entire satisfaction, Desmond settled into a routine. Every evening he relaxed in the flat watching TV, or sitting on the balcony that ran the full length of the flat, to watch the sunset over the South China Sea, overlooking the tiny uninhabited islets.

Still, twice or three times every month he would make a point of asking me to select his outfits. Always one of his Savile Row suits, bought on a trip to London, with a suitable shirt, tie and all accessories. Then he would order in something 'special' for dinner, that I must prepare myself – being out of the range of the cook boy – and that meant another drinking session. I had no idea why it obviously gave him so much pleasure to think of my dashing home, picking up the food, preparing it and then sitting waiting for it to burn, or get cold – either way, thrown away – but for some reason it did. At least I always knew when he was going to be out… and little things certainly pleased little minds!

At the end of three or four days, the door would slowly open and the inevitable bouquet of roses would appear – followed by champagne, followed by chocolates, followed by Desmond (usually in that order; the latter being unshaven and bleary eyed, ready to collapse on the couch). He certainly got an uninhibited, wet but genuine welcome from Susie Chow, who was the only one now to really appreciate Desmond.

I couldn't get used to the phone ringing. They were mostly calls from solicitors, getting more and more desperate – where was Desmond? Did I know he was due in court tomorrow? Let me know where he is and I'll find him… but all I was allowed to say was, 'I don't know.' If I could have given an answer, I might well have replied, "Almost certainly at the *Bottoms UP Club*," but it didn't seem the thing to do.

Susan and Dennis arrived to see the new flat. I was instructed to get back early from school – they would expect me to be there for drinks, and they wanted to dine out early. As hostess, I naturally flew home and was back at six to await them. I dashed into the bedroom, changed very quickly into evening dress and was back in the sitting room in minutes.

"Where the hell *is* Susan?" Dennis said crossly, not noted for his patience. Eventually Dennis disappeared to find out.

"She's lying down, exhausted by her afternoon's shopping," he informed us. "God knows what she's spent if she's exhausted herself! She says she's too tired to go out this evening. We'll stay in."

I changed into slacks and top and went to see what food might be available. Fortunately, I had got salads in – no use asking Chu Lee to provide anything at short notice.

I was not yet used to the art post I had taken, which involved lumping great packs of paper and card and vast amounts of pottery ready for firing; I felt more like a stevedore than a teacher as I cleared the Art class off the table and put out in its place the best china, the wooden bowls from Manila, the candelabra, my Chinese flower arrangement, lit the candles… at last the table was ready and I could sit down.

Dennis came back with Susan; she'd had a rest and was ready to go out now, he announced. In Susan sailed, radiant in one of her newly acquired gowns and twirled for admiration.

"Fantastic!" enthused Desmond, coming to life at last. "You look a million dollars." Turning to me, he lost some of his enthusiasm. "My God, Binky – you can't go out looking like *that!*"

Nothing to be done but smile prettily… well, bare my teeth prettily. Nip into the bathroom, change, slap more make-up on the black, under-eye circles, and emerge. Gather up the unwanted food and tip it in the bin. No problem!

We had a wonderful evening out. The wine (and spirits) flowed, and it was hilarious – at least it seemed to be… well, Desmond, Susan and Dennis found everything hilarious until finally, at 2.00 am, the restaurant tactfully suggested we leave.

Back to the flat – and the huge bar. Dennis was generously dispensing large drinks all round. I had to be sober for school in a few hours time.

"Oh my God, Wendy – a large white wine," sneered Susan as she handed it to me.

Desmond gave me a disgusted glance – I was obviously the wet blanket of the party.

"I'm sorry," I protested. "But I have to work tomorrow; I have to leave at six-thirty, it's four am now and I can't arrive at school hung over and definitely the worse for wear!"

"Oh my God!" said Desmond wearily. "Well, go to bed then, if you must… of course, we *do* have *guests*…"

Eventually the liquor won and they all collapsed, to rise and greet the following day in the afternoon, ready for another session.

I began to get the impression I was definitely a fish out of water, and a very provincial one at that. They stayed for a few days, completed their business with Desmond, and then left. There were one or two calm evenings, albeit on my own, but sitting out on the verandah watching the blissful Oriental sunset. In any case, why pick an argument when I would shortly be back in England *without* Susan and Dennis?

Just before they left I said, somewhat gleefully, that I expected they would miss their trips to Hong Kong in the future. Dennis looked at me uncomprehendingly – and then in total disbelief as I told them smugly, "I'm going back to the UK. Desmond is going to find chambers in London – but I *have* to go… my house is there and it won't look after itself for ever!"

Dennis and Susan both looked questioningly at Desmond.

"Good God, no," he hissed as he walked past us into the bedroom.

Dennis grinned back at me, now comprehending. I felt cold to the pit of my stomach. I had known, of course, that Desmond never had the slightest intention of going to the UK to live. I had managed to get a Government post, but I wasn't used to teaching art to four-to-eighteen-year-olds and, physically, I knew I couldn't last. But the mortgage had to be paid. Either that, or sell it… and it was clear that Desmond owned nothing, paid nothing and cared less. Still, I was working; it would have to wait until the vacation to be sorted.

Suddenly, I was told we had been invited out to have dinner with a business acquaintance of Dennis. To my surprise, it turned out that they lived in very shabby surroundings in a tired-looking apartment block. However, we were made a great fuss of; an American couple with a small child, they entertained us. Dinner consisted of meatloaf, potatoes and carrots – very plain and ordinary.

"Sorry there's no wine at the moment," said our young host quietly, "but you do understand?"

Clearly Desmond didn't. He liked his wine; dinner without it was unthinkable.

The couple tried to make conversation, while Desmond did the opposite. Frantically, I searched for a topic, a compliment… but frankly, there was little to compliment them on. Finally, in desperation, I remarked on the delicious meatloaf. "You know," I said, "I have tried to make it several times, but either it goes dry and crumbles, or else it's all soggy and collapses. This is perfect and it's delicious… could I possibly have the recipe?"

Desmond stared. If it had been put in front of him at home, he would have exploded and thrown it straight into the bin.

"Of course," said the girl, "I'll go get it right now."

When she came back, the ice having been broken, she began to chat. "Of course," she said, "things have been so difficult since the accident."

"Accident?" I repeated.

"Oh yes. That's why Desmond is here – so good of him to come *himself*; we do so appreciate it."

The floodgates were wide open; they could not stop talking. The young fellow was, or had been, a rep for his firm. Driving round Taiwan, he had, not surprisingly, had an accident. He had crashed a couple of vertebrae and needed a spinal fusion. Unable to drive, there was no income.

"Still," he beamed, "I am covered by the firm's insurance. I have to go back to America for the operation and I don't know whether I'll be able to drive after that, or even walk well enough to work." Still smiling, he continued, "But at any rate, there will be enough compensation to cover all my expenses and if necessary, set myself up doing something else. Dennis assured me of that, and of course, Desmond is going to handle the legal side of everything for us."

So *that* was why we were here…

"But that's the operation I had," I told them. "I did exactly the same thing."

"Really?" They were excited to hear this. "Tell us about it – how much compensation did you get?"

"Nothing," I told them flatly. "It wasn't diagnosed soon enough and by the time I was able to claim, it was too late… you must be sure to claim straight away," I stressed.

"Oh, that is why we invited Desmond here," the young man replied. "Now, tell me about the op – is it as painful as they say? But anyway, you've had it, and you don't have a limp…"

"Well, no," I said, "but I was a guinea pig; I had to accept that if I had the normal procedure – that is, repair and be in plaster for six months, I might…" I stopped. I was so carried away, I was about to say 'never walk again, or at least not without a disfiguring limp'. I shut my mouth.

"… be a long time getting back to work," I managed, after a pause.

The couple were far too excited to notice Desmond glaring at me ferociously across the table. He began to talk loudly and clearly, praising the meal, praising their child whom he had failed to notice until now. "A delightful meal," he enthused, "thank you so much… must go now…"

At home, I asked, "So what will happen to them? It's going to cost a fortune to ambulance them home – you notice he couldn't even get out of his chair the whole evening. Will there be enough compensation to start him off in another career? I told you, without immediate hydrotherapy, he will never walk properly again…"

"Will you keep *out* of my affairs," roared Desmond. "It's none of your business! I wish to *God* I had a wife like Susan – she understands business."

I shut up. He was furious, and he was right. At least I had made it clear that the young man certainly had cause to worry, but with American style compensation, I assumed all would be well.

A couple of months later, we were invited out to a grand dinner, Chinese style. It was such an unusual occasion for me to be invited out anywhere officially with Desmond, I greatly looked forward to it. It was held in the sumptuous Mandarin Chinese Restaurant. I was well used to Dennis's lavish entertainment, but this was exceptional. We were served a fifteen-course meal; over three hours of course after exotic course, each one with a different wine and brandy and liqueurs thrown in. Sharks fin soup, followed by the turtles which we had previously seen swimming in their tank; fish from their tank, then snake from theirs (thank God no monkey or dog, due to our European sensitivity), caviar, and heaven knows what else.

Desmond partook of all with enthusiasm. Various toasts were proposed – all of them to Desmond, who stood to accept each one with becoming modesty. The toasts grew more and more exuberant until the last speaker rose and, finding himself unable to focus on Desmond, let alone remember what he had been going to say, finally subsided and concentrated on getting his glass from table to mouth.

My young companion on my left had been most attentive, trying to fill my glass at every opportunity, but I had work the next day. I was still rather confused about Desmond's much celebrated achievements; he had been uncharacteristically modest and retiring when I quizzed him about it. "But what has Desmond done?" I asked my companion.

"Didn't you know?" he asked me incredulously. "Damn clever, *damn* clever! Well you see, there was this young chap, been with the firm *years* – started straight from school – no qualifications, but by God, he worked hard... did well, too," he said thoughtfully. "One of our best workers. Been promoted to executive level... top money, of course, *top* money – makes you work hard, but my God, pays well when you do."

I listened attentively; no doubt he *would* get to the point?

"Anyway," he went on, "just as he was about to take over the desk job... got married too, and had this child... thrilled about it, he was. And we were all glad for him, of course... *glad* for him... where was I? Oh yes, anyway, just as he was about to take over, he had this car accident – got a report on him. Poor chap... *poor* chap," he repeated, looking morosely at his empty glass which was swiftly refilled.

"Never walk again, they said... never walk... not properly, anyway. Just about to take over a desk job, too." He shook his head sympathetically.

"I think I met him," I said, "in a block of flats down the marsh."

"That's him!"

"Oh well," I said proudly, "we went to see him and he told us that with the compensation, he would be able to take up a desk job again."

"Oh no," said the young fellow, clearly shocked. "No, the compensation would have been *massive*. Would have cost the firm *thousands*! No, Desmond went out to see him personally. Persuaded him to sign the forms for compensation, making sure of course that he didn't read the small print and he got nothing... *nothing!* Can you believe it?" Grinning like a Cheshire cat, he went on, "He didn't read the small print! He signed it all away."

Roaring with laughter, he banged his glass on the table hysterically. "Saved the firm thousands! *Thousands*," he repeated. "My God, that man is good – *that's* what we are celebrating."

"So what happens to him?" I asked, horrified. "He was presumably sent back to America?"

"God no," said the fellow. "He couldn't walk."

"So what happens to him now? He has a wife and small son."

"Dunno," he replied happily, "but it saved the firm a fortune." He looked at my face, and his grin slowly evaporated. "It's *business*," he said kindly. "You don't understand, that's business. Have another drink; as Desmond always says, if you can't take the heat, *stay outta the kitchen!* That's what Desmond always says... he's good," he said dreamily, "damned good."

I went home thoughtfully. It explained a lot. Yes, Desmond was clever; apparently devious and unscrupulous too, but clever. It explained his position as the leading QC in Hong Kong, why everyone deferred to him, respecting him in law, but very little else. No friends and no hobbies. Just law – and certainly nobody could beat him at law. I saw now why Dennis paid all the bills, accepted his word in everything and why there were frequent visits whenever there was a legal problem, which Desmond could always solve... and always to their advantage.

Still, there had been an improvement. The drinking bouts had stopped. Desmond had discovered yoga. I toyed with the idea of joining myself – at least then I would see more of him. I was swimming, but not every day as I had been able to do on the Island. Yes... perhaps Yoga?

"Definitely not!" said Desmond firmly. And then, with unexpected tenderness, "You might hurt your back."

Such thoughtfulness almost brought tears to my eyes. This, from the man who, when I was lying in bed with Asian Flu, was surprised when, after three days of alternate shivering and then burning with a temperature of 103°F, I tottered through the living room to get to the kitchen for a drink of water, and shouted (quietly... I had a headache), "You are just about the most selfish, unfeeling and brutish man I have ever had the misfortune to meet up with!" Anxious to appease my fury, he leapt up in great concern and left the apartment, rushing back later, triumphant.

"You see, Binky, I did think about you; don't worry about a thing, Binky. I've been to the Hilton and had my breakfast – I am just fine – no need for you to get up at all today."

There was no more drinking, but certainly he arrived back later in the evening two or three times a week, after his unaccustomed exercise. Then, after such exercise, he rang and said much though he appreciated his yoga (and he was sure it was doing him good... and I had said he should take more exercise), he was falling behind with his work. "Not to worry, Binky," he assured me, "I'll skip dinner – don't wait up for me – I may be home late."

After the third episode – not to wait dinner, he'd skip it, he'd be home late, perhaps very late – I responded by questioning him. "Oh," I said, "working late at the office, are we?"

"Yes," he replied smugly, "I am." And then an isolated thought struck him; "No, no," he said angrily, "I don't work in an *office!*" With measured dignity he then said, "I am working late in chambers." Then, crossly again, "I have told you before – don't meddle in my affairs. You obviously do not understand the first thing about business, so leave it to those who do... anyway, whether you like it or not, I am working late and that's that!" He slammed the phone down.

The next time, he was more defiant. "I am working very late tonight. Obviously you don't understand in the least and since it puts you in a mood when I am late, I will be staying at the Hilton, so you need not worry at all about me."

So, once or twice a week he would overnight at the Hilton rather than cause me any disturbance and arrived home late, somewhat flushed and breathless on the other days.

However, a couple of months later I had a lovely surprise. Desmond came home with an invitation to the Legal Annual Ball. I had never been invited to any of their functions before – Desmond always refused point blank to go, whether obligatory or not. This was totally out of the blue and definitely one of Hong Kong's top functions.

I dressed with care. Desmond was attracted like a bee to honey (you could see his eyes water) to the lowest décolletage (the lower the better, and backless evening dresses), but he would not allow me to be seen out unless I was covered to the neck, wrist and ankles. Even so, I had on a skin tight sheath, hand made in Manila; halter neckline, but certainly up to my neck, with exquisite hand embroidery falling in a cascade down the length (to the ankle, of course.)

We'd arrived at the Hilton. All the dividing doors had been thrown back. The full length of the conference floor was one long room with rows of enormous chandeliers. The dance floor was in the centre, surrounded by huge tables to seat twelve to twenty, sparkling with silver and crystal settings.

We queued, were announced and we progressed in state to walk for what seemed like four miles on one-inch thick, crimson carpet to our table, and sat down. Gradually the room filled up. I was introduced to the other guests at the table. They were curious; they hadn't seen me before... why did I not persuade Desmond to join their round of activities? Invitations followed.

"No." said Desmond, shortly. There was no further conversation. Suddenly the huge double doors at the far end were flung open to admit a woman. Everyone was now seated, so all eyes turned. She was announced and walked through, confidently and poised, if a little surprised to find that she was apparently late. She walked the full length of the room until she reached our table and stopped. She had eyes, however, for only one.

"Desmond..." she said, and held out both her arms to him in pleasure.

Desmond stood up. She looked at him and registered surprise to realise that his table was full. Surprise turned to shock when Desmond made the formal introduction: "Wendy, meet Anne," he said. "Anne, meet Wendy... *my wife.*"

She gasped and drew back. Her hands, outstretched in greeting, dropped to her sides. Her face turned ghastly white and she faltered and swayed. Two of the escorts at the table rushed to her side but, recovering, she pulled herself away from them and straightened up, brushing their supporting hands away from her as though they were so many flies.

Stiffly, like a marionette, she turned and propelled herself slowly back up the considerable length of the room to the double doors, where the flunkeys were waiting, with great interest, to let her out again. Every eye was upon her, every careful step of the way. She walked through the doors and they closed behind her.

Every eye then swivelled to our table. The men at the table gazed at Desmond, aghast; the women regarded him with avid curiosity. Desmond silently picked up the menu and studied it with the greatest concentration.

"I think I'll have the duck!" he said conversationally.

After the meal, everyone milled around the dance floor, some talking in groups, others drinking, many enjoying the dancing. Desmond obviously was *not* dancing. After a while, a young lawyer came up and asked me if I would care to dance. "No," growled Desmond. I was mortified... I had leapt to my feet and was in the middle of saying 'I'd be delighted' (until Hong Kong, my life had revolved around dancing). Chastened, I sat down again.

The evening passed.

At this time there was much publicity and consternation in Hong Kong. A young, ambitious constable had returned home in disgrace. He had retaliated by accusing the Chief Constable of Hong Kong of corruption, and the whole force of bribery and corruption. The accusations were dismissed and ridiculed; everyone was relieved, the general consensus being that the man deserved to be ruined and disgraced. However, unabashed, he stood his ground and refused to give way. Indeed, he offered to name names and proceeded to do so. Then a few more disgruntled officers resigned, returned to the UK and backed his story. They were disillusioned and bitter and prepared to sacrifice their careers now that someone had taken the initiative. Gradually, their attackers began to crumble. There would be an enquiry; the police fired back there would not.

Finally, it became obvious there was a problem. An inquiry followed and there was overwhelming evidence that Chief Constable Goaber practically ran a syndicate in Hong Kong, crushing anyone not prepared to submit. In fact, it was said that if, in your first year as a police officer in Hong Kong, you did not clear a million pounds, you were likely to be investigated for not being sufficiently corrupt. Goaber went to prison with several other high-ranking policemen.

Desmond was coming home white-faced and obviously worried. The drinking had stopped, as had the yoga. He was preoccupied and tense. I came back one afternoon to find the room full of top ranking police officers. Desmond asked me politely – in front of them – to leave. They were in *private consultation*, he said.

I took Susie Chow for a walk.

The following evening, the room was full of well-dressed Chinese. They were sitting around; there was no sign of Desmond. I offered drinks and they accepted. They admired the jade ring and bracelet I was wearing. What stones did I most like? I launched off; it was my aim, I told them, to get a local stone from each place I visited whilst in the Far East. I had collected a black star sapphire from Bangkok and turquoise from Greece before I came to Hong Kong.

Those were just semi-precious stones, they laughed. Now that I was in Hong Kong I should collect opals from the Philippines… rubies… but *best of all*, diamonds. All ladies like diamonds. I told them that as a teacher I was of somewhat limited means, at which point Desmond returned.

"Your wife," one of his guests said, "likes jewels." Then, turning to me, he said, "We now get you many jewels – remember opals and rubies and diamonds!" They all enthusiastically joined in the 'opals and rubies and diamonds' in chorus, which made me smile happily.

Short-lived. Desmond turned to me in fury. "I have told you," he said, "*keep out* of my business affairs! Can't you find something to do?"

I apologised to the room. I had no idea it was another private conference. "I merely offered to fetch drinks for your guests. I'll walk the dog." Susie Chow was very surprised.

Gradually, everything was settled. The disgraced police were renounced and those that remained kept their heads well down. So did Desmond.

There was trouble again with Susan and Dennis in Taiwan. The American companies had made a fortune there. Now the Taiwanese wanted them to leave. They came over, as life there was becoming increasingly difficult. There was a 'situation' at the airport. All Americans were having their luggage carefully scrutinised, sometimes confiscated. There were more worried consultations. Private, of course, and poor Susie Chow wasn't used to such strenuous exercise.

There were no financial problems. Apparently. Susan came back happily from her daily shopping and as I had just come in from work, twirled enthusiastically for my benefit.

"I'm just altering the price tags," she told me. "Dennis would go berserk if he knew what I'd *actually* paid for them."

I picked one up in silver lame. "Wow!" I said. The price was two hundred – in the seventies, a fantastic price.

She snatched it from me. "I haven't altered it yet!"

Not surprisingly, Dennis told us Susan had insisted on dining out in the most expensive night club in town. "Her new dress..." he explained.

We gathered in the living room for drinks. Susan showed off the silver lame. Not exactly a strapless evening gown; more a gownless evening. Desmond's mouth fell open. "You look a million dollars, Susan," he said. "But then you always do," he worshipped. "I wish Wendy could look like that."

"Wendy *could* look like that."

"Wendy," I said, somewhat bitterly, "can't afford two hundred for an evening dress."

"What?" roared Dennis. "*Two hundred pounds?* That wasn't what you told *me!*"

Not surprisingly, Susan turned on me a look that would have felled an ox at forty paces. "Not *this* one," she said scathingly, "another one." But looking at the dress it was clear that it was expensive and certainly not a sale or reject item.

Dennis was truly furious and hustled Susan away to their room, from where their raised voices and recriminations could be heard clearly. They finally reappeared, both flushed and furious. However, the legal negotiations had apparently gone well and Desmond and Dennis were celebrating. But I had well and truly put my foot in it and Susan was obviously hell-bent on revenge. Worse was to come.

Negotiations having been completed, there was a problem – legal documentation had to be drawn up, but it was considered too confidential to entrust to Desmond's secretary, who did all the typing for several other barristers. Finally, it was settled. Susan had once been a *Private Secretary*.

"Typist," said Dennis succinctly.

"Private Secretary!" snapped Susan.

"Anyway, she can type," said Dennis.

So Susan was dispatched to the spare room – being already in disgrace (there was to be no more shopping), to type out the legal documentation that Desmond had prepared. Two days later she emerged, having completed an eight-page document. She handed it over to Desmond, who checked it and passed it to Dennis for his approval. Dennis then checked it and gave his approval. Then Desmond handed it to me to check. Dennis demurred – this was strictly a private document.

"I know," said Desmond, "but it has to be correct. A comma in the wrong place, and the whole thing would be ruined. A legal secretary I could trust, but Susan isn't a legal secretary." He hardly liked to admit that, if it wasn't checked by his secretary, I had to check through all his documents. Neither he nor Dennis could spell.

Silently, over Susan's glowering body, it was handed to me. Three pairs of eyes bored into me as I read it through. My heart sank to my boots. "Fine," I said eventually. They relaxed. "Except for one thing – you've spelt *principal* the wrong way throughout the document."

It was on practically every page. There was much consternation. Undoubtedly the fault was Desmond's – he had written it. Grandly, and without hesitation, their full fury fell upon Susan. She should have corrected it. Was she or was she not a secretary? And if she were not sure, had she never heard of a dictionary, for God's sake?

Desmond, in the wrong, was incomparable. The full weight of blame was placed fairly and squarely on Susan. I suggested Tippex, but this was treated with such savage scorn, I hastily retreated. There was nothing else for it. Their return to Taiwan was postponed and Susan was banished (shades of Rumpelstiltskin) to the spare room in disgrace. She may not emerge until it had been typed correctly.

I felt that Susan and I would never be really friends.

There was no more shopping, but finally the task was completed and they returned to Taiwan.

Susie Chow had been delighted by the developments. I had been turned out of the sitting room so often for *private consultations*, she now looked forward to daily treks round the block. In any case, I had needed time out to think. I could not get the woman at the Hilton Ball out of my mind. I should have felt jealous, I concluded. But I didn't. I could think only of the appalling situation she had been put in and frankly, I admired the way she had carried it off.

For Desmond I could only feel disdain. So, he'd had an affair and wanted to end it. Surely he could have told her on the phone... hardly gentlemanly, but an easy option. Could he not have taken her out to dinner one last time and broken it gently? But no, in Desmond's book, why waste money on a dinner when you no longer want the goods? To borrow his favourite quote, *If you can't stand the heat, get outta the kitchen!*

I had been warned over and over again. Desmond was not the marrying kind... "Desmond brings a new woman home every night." The constant stream of women that wore out the lift at Tony and Desmond's flat... everyone's surprise that even Desmond had settled down at last – well obviously he hadn't, nor had he the slightest intention of ever doing so. And quite clearly, his activities were of necessity private. He did not wish me to be involved. Nor did I want to be.

It was pleasant to come back every day and walk Susie Chow in the clear evening air. As I rounded a corner, a small terrier hurtled out of nowhere and attempted to sink its teeth into my ankle. I had changed, as always, into a loose kaftan for the evening, and the dog missed its target, catching its teeth in the hem, thereafter hanging on grimly. Susie Chow, though sweetly gentle and affectionate, was not an ex-sampan dog for nothing. Casually but firmly, she swung round and sank her teeth in the little dog's rear.

"Gee, hell!" said its owner. "Come here, Trixie."

Oh my God… an American! After Susan and Dennis, as far as I was concerned, the only good American was a dead one. Plus, what had I heard about Americans and *compensation*? And I had ruined their obviously valuable, certainly *pedigree* dog.

"I am very sorry," I apologized, hopefully. "I am afraid Susie Chow was surprised and frightened (frightened? I had made her day!). She is a stray I picked up and I'm afraid I haven't yet had the time to train her (I'd had her a year, but she was as trained as she would ever be).

"Hell, no," replied the American. "My dog attacked you. Are you sure you're alright?"

Reassured, I gabbled that yes, I was quite sure.

"So your dog's a stray, too? Well, I've had this one a coupla weeks, but I'm not sure I can keep her much longer. Felt kinda sorry for her," he confided. "Got run over in the street, so I took her to the vet and then kinda got attached to her."

Typically American; pick the dog up, spend money on it on a casual impulse and then drop it. "So what are you going to do with her?" I asked, concerned, as we swung down the ramp towards the road together.

"Dunno," he shrugged.

I looked at him, aghast.

"Oh no," he said quickly. "I wouldn't have her put down. But I need some advice – and *fast*." He sighed. "Well, it's like this; no matter what I try… she was obviously half-starved when I picked her up, but everything goes straight through and she isn't house-trained. I'm renting the apartment and I can't let her ruin it."

Relieved, I explained that dogs locally were fed on the left-over scraps of their owners, mainly rice and very little meat. "You've probably been feeding her on tinned dog food?" I wondered.

"Why yes," he agreed. "Uh, what else?"

Susie Chow, I didn't tell him, had refused to be parted from me that first day I brought her back and, when refused the bedroom, had curled herself up against the bedroom door on guard, and of course had deposited her hasty and over-rich meal immediately outside the door. It had been unfortunate that Desmond had been first to emerge that particular day… and barefoot.

The next day, the American was waiting for me.

"Well?" I asked.

"Wow! Too right…"

"You'd been feeding her titbits," I said, not intending any accusation.

"Well yes… treats," he admitted. "You see, she's had a real hard time and I guess I just wanted her to know she was welcome."

"Well, no more," I said firmly. "A nice light meal with a little meat in it, no more. And then take her out straight away and regularly, until she passes it through; then praise her and let her know she has done well."

"Oh, I will," he replied fervently. "I sure will. I guess if I can just get that sorted, she'll make a swell pet." He paused. "I'm here on contract," he added, "so I have to get it sorted before I take her home."

I was greatly relieved; most people who took in strays just left them in the street when they left.

After that, he was waiting for me at the foot of the ramp when I came down to walk Susie Chow and we discussed progress. The two dogs were now inseparable… Susie Chow had a *friend*.

He told me about his house he had just bought in LA. It sounded to me like a chalet-type building, although he called it something else. It had its own swimming pool and a huge, bare garden. He explained that a team of Japanese gardeners looked after all the estate gardens but, being new, he had to decide how he wanted it designed.

We discussed houses, plants and gardens. "My contract finishes soon, as well," I told him. "I'm looking forward to going home to mine in the summer; it's difficult trying to keep it up together, being so far away." I explained I hadn't intended staying here so long.

"Kinda homesick, I guess," he said.

"Yes," I said, surprised. "Yes, I suppose I am." Then I told him about my house – not as large as his, just four bedrooms, but a pleasant back garden on two levels with a carp pool containing pink and white water lilies, a rose garden in front and a magnificent magnolia tree.

He wasn't that interested, but he let me ramble on. "I'm fed up," I concluded, "driving to work in an air-conditioned car, working in an air-conditioned school, and coming back to an air-conditioned flat."

"Apartment," he corrected. "Yes, I know what you mean… guess I miss the fresh air too."

"Though you should see the *mist* we get in the Forest," I said.

I began to look forward to the evening walk with Susie Chow. It was getting close to the summer holidays and I was finding full time art tiring. Teaching art was fine, but it involved climbing round the school, hanging pictures, and mounting and arranging them *after* school. Some days I was on my feet from 8.00 am to 7.00 pm, snatching a meal when I could.

As a primary teacher, I had been standing and sitting as I chose. My back had obviously made a full recovery in spite of everything, but I was working harder now than before the op. And I had come to Hong Kong to recuperate! Still, the art post came to an end anyway in a few weeks time and, if I stayed in Hong Kong, I would have to look for another, easier, post. I had been offered a music specialist one – by the recommendation of my present Headmistress, but I pointed out that although I liked music and was a competent pianist (I had waxed lyrical to my American friend about my beautiful *Steinway* baby grand, and how I missed it), I had absolutely no qualifications. I had reached the standard, but refused to have the anxiety of taking exams in that as well. I would have to decide.

My American friend was equally looking forward to going home.

We stopped one evening below the ramp while I untangled Susie Chow from Trixie.

"I'm going home," he said suddenly. "I leave for LA in three weeks."

I swung round in dismay. "Oh?"

"I'm finished here, he said. "A little earlier than expected, but – guess I'll be glad to get back, y'know!"

No more evening walks. No more chats about the dogs… no more anything. I was disappointed – no, it was more than that, I was devastated. I hadn't realized how I had depended on our meetings.

"Say… uh, I got a good job, and I've got a great little house back home – you've seen the photograph. We both like the same things and we, uh… get on well. I'd hoped to have more time, but I have found out about you – I know you are here with someone," he said hurriedly, "but everyone says you are only seen alone, and… well, you said things hadn't worked out as expected?" He looked directly into my eyes and I was transfixed; I didn't know what to say to him.

"So… uh, will you come with me?"

After a bit, he said kindly, "Your mouth's still open."

I closed it.

Another shock; I stood rooted to the ground. I looked at Susie.

"Oh, she comes too," he said hurriedly. "This isn't a proposition, no way," he said. "I've got the house; I've got the job. I want a wife; I want a family – the lot." He looked at my stricken face. "Guess it's kinda taken you by surprise."

Oh, the thought... a beautiful house, gardens; a *home* and a wonderful, kind American to take me there... dream on. I dreamed on.

"Now," he said, "you will think about it, won't you?" By now he was fairly confident of his ground. "See you tomorrow," he said. "Perhaps we could go out somewhere afterwards and talk?"

I nodded dumbly. Fortunately, at that moment Susie, thoroughly fed up with *too much* conversation, took off forcefully for the lift and I shot off unexpectedly after her, into the lift. The doors closed and I went up in a dream.

I went through the hall and into the sitting room. There was Desmond, pacing up and down like a caged tiger. "Where have you *been?*" he roared. "*Who* was that man? Don't tell me," he said helpfully, "you've been meeting him every evening *behind my back!*"

"I've been walking the dog," I said, "every evening."

"You lie!" he bellowed. He had flown into a temper every time I had been seen having coffee with, talking to, or just passing a man, so far. Now there was a tangible presence – he was genuinely beside himself with fury.

"You've been seeing him every day," he growled. "Don't argue... (I hadn't opened my mouth) ... I asked Chu Lee."

Chu Lee simpered in the background. He was glad he had managed to get me into trouble – Desmond wouldn't notice *his* misdemeanours for a bit.

"*Who is he? What's his name?*" he fairly howled.

"I don't know," I said, calmly. "He did tell me, but I have forgotten. His dog's name is Trixie. We walk the dogs together. I don't trust Chu Lee," I said firmly, determined to cook his goose once and for all. "I know he would fry her and eat her, given half a chance."

Chu Lee coloured, backing away.

"Tell me one more time her lead is broken," I shouted at him. "If you think of coming back without Susie, don't come back at all!"

Chu Lee's head shook furiously from side to side.

"You don't walk her," I said to Desmond, "so every day I come back and make sure she is walked before you come home."

Desmond, wrongfooted, was not a pretty sight. He strode up and down the room, thumping the table (my table) every time he passed, and thumping one fist into his palm. "I'll *kill* him!" he shouted. (Desmond would not have been able to swat a fly unaided – he would call his servant to do it). "*I'll find him; I will deal with this*," he raged, and strode out, slamming the door behind him.

I lay back on the settee, dreamily. A home in LA, someone nice and kind, who liked dogs and who liked *me*. Of course it was impossible, I knew that, but what a wonderful dream. What had he said? 'I've a home, I've got everything, and I know what I want… you.' It was like someone putting a warm soft blanket around me and giving me a hug. I was lost in a dream, not entirely sure that I was about to give it up.

Where had Desmond gone, I wondered? I had no idea where the fellow lived. There were four apartment blocks, twenty-five storeys high. I had no idea which apartment he occupied. I didn't even know his name; his Christian name I knew, but nothing else. Desmond couldn't possibly find him.

I'd reckoned without Desmond in the temper he was in. In that mood he'd have found a needle in a haystack. He came roaring back in an hour later. "A *consultant!*" he thundered triumphantly. "You said he was a *consultant!*"

"Yes," I said. That was what he had told me; I hoped he hadn't lied to me… why should he?

"Worked in the hospital," he sneered. "I suppose you thought he was a *brain surgeon.*"

I was surprised. Yes, he had said he was a consultant; I'd assumed he worked at the hospital.

"Ha," he sneered again. "He is an *engineering consultant!* That's what he is!"

"Well, I didn't ask him," I said. "I just knew he was a consultant."

Desmond was finally calming down now, having obviously triumphed over his opponent. He looked as though he'd gone ten rounds with Frank Bruno and won, but knowing Desmond, it would only have been a verbal battle. I looked at him; he was jubilant, having totally destroyed the opposition. A bit like Susie Chow, I thought; they say owners take after their dogs and vice versa, and Susie was just the same. A gentle and exuberantly affectionate animal – give her a bone (as Chu Lee managed, surreptitiously, to slip her) and she would retire to her basket. Holding it protectively between her bared teeth and growling furiously, she would become more and more hysterical until she foamed at the mouth. She would be like that for days at a time – in fact until I managed to retrieve it.

At first alarmed, especially in Hong Kong – the home of rabies – and staring in the face of a maddened dog, I'd had no option but to don protective clothing. Wearing a leather jacket and leather gauntlets, I'd faced up to her and taken the bone from her by force. Once I'd challenged her and took hold of the bone, she would drop it and immediately rush around with her tail wagging furiously, belly on the ground, ingratiatingly licking everything in sight.

Chu Lee certainly wasn't prepared to face up to her. Desmond hid behind his newspaper, insisting, "It's *your* dog, Binky, deal with it." Poor Susie Chow; as a stray, she desperately wanted that bone, would snatch it away from anybody else, but hadn't the least idea what to do with it when she'd got it. She couldn't even take a strip of meat off it; just held it between her teeth, refusing to eat or drink until finally it had to be taken from her by force.

Desmond was much the same. Dog in a manger. I was just a possession; he didn't want me, but would fight to the death to make sure no one else would take his possession away from him.

Tomorrow, I thought, I will see my American, and yes… I would like to go out and *talk*. I had now come to terms with the situation and was prepared to *think it over*. Next day I walked Susie Chow. There was no American. Nor the next day… or the next.

Desmond was triumphant. He arrived home with a bouquet of roses, the champagne and the marrons glace. We would go out to dinner, he purred. I had worked until late (end of term), taking down all the pictures throughout the school, collating and distributing them after school, getting home tired and dusty… all of which was entirely beside the point. Desmond, having relaxed at home all day, was prepared to entertain. He exerted all his charm, which was considerable when he put his mind to it, and we went out and dined expensively and luxuriously. He ordered the Swiss chef to do his 'special' – a hand-made Swiss Chalet in various chocolates, filled with cream and ices, and which had to be sculpted in advance. He was in his element.

I wondered about finding out where the American lived. I owed him an apology at least, and I desperately needed to offer an explanation and find out what *had* happened. But... face it, the whole thing was impossible. I had met him – we had both been attracted – *walking the dogs!* Laughable.

I was married. I had already made a complete hash of that. Now here I was, contemplating going off with someone I didn't even know. Ridiculous. Certainly my American friend had now realized the same thing and thought better of it.

But then I came down in the lift – and there he was. "I'm sorry," he said. "So very sorry. I had *no* idea what the situation was. I am completely in the wrong. I'd no idea, *no* idea at all." With that, he turned from me and walked quickly away.

Stunned, I stared after him. No idea about *what*? What had Desmond said? I was totally at a loss. Frankly, I dreaded to think what Desmond had said, but as the American would have put it, *it sure was effective.*

Totally confused, I walked Susie and went back. I could hardly look him out now. He'd had the opportunity and accepted the situation. I supposed I had better leave things as they were; I seemed to have caused quite enough trouble as it was. Anyway, he had made his apologies and left.

Desmond was charming and attentive. I hardly recognized him when, a couple of days later, he said, sheepishly, "Er, Susan and Dennis have asked if they may come over for a few days – if you don't mind, of course."

Good heavens; I was being *asked!* "Not at all," I said, impressed, as if I had an option... but it was nice to be asked.

They arrived. It was now end of term. Then I'd go *home* and sort everything out.

I drove out to the airport to pick them up. They gaped incredulously when Desmond opened the door for me and thanked me sweetly for the use of my car. He suggested the Golf Club.

"Great," said Dennis.

"I'd like to play golf," said Susan.

"You can use Wendy's clubs," Dennis said immediately and automatically. "Oh, er... that is, if Binky doesn't *mind*."

It meant I couldn't play. They would go round without me – I would have to watch from the eighteenth. However, not to be outdone in sweetness, I smiled back. "Of course not," I said.

"It means leaving early," pointed out Desmond. "We'd need to leave at six; would that be all right, Binky?"

Susan and Dennis gazed at him in consternation. Hastily, Desmond took Dennis aside for a whispered consultation. Susan and Dennis both turned round and stared at me; then at Desmond with renewed respect. Susan's look was speculative; it would appear that she had an opponent almost worthy of her skill.

In fact, the next evening was the Staff Outing. A block booking had been organized for the theatre, followed by dinner at the Peninsular. The Peak School was, of course, on the Peak – the ultimate location. The Governor's house was there – all the Royalty of Hong Kong, mainly the Jardine family, lived there, and the children attending the Peak School were the elite of Hong Kong.

I had taken all the art work down ready for the end of term; now there was the Open Day and obviously it all had to be set up again for their appraisal. I had intended staying late to get it done – now I had to be back by six. I would miss the Staff outing which, though officially was *un*official, meant a distinctly black mark if I were absent. Ah well. It was worth it to avoid more upset, but I would need to be up at the crack of dawn the following day to get the display up in time.

Knowing Susan, Dennis and Desmond's itinerary, they would be knocking back cocktails in the flat until the early hours and I probably wouldn't get to bed at all. I really began to think I'd had enough; it had been a hard year. And next year I may as well take the Music post but, frankly, on a strictly temporary basis.

However, at school I made my excuses as best I could; it did not go down well, but it was the end of term – and I was leaving. For good. Anyway, I shot off, drove as fast as I dared and hared into the flat at five-thirty pm. A fast shower, quick change (formal dress would be needed) and I'd be ready by six on the dot.

Dashing into the bedroom, then the bathroom, I stopped dead. It was empty. But then it was the *bathroom*. I went back slowly to the bedroom – empty. Sitting room – empty. Susan and Dennis's room – empty. Into the kitchen to ask Chu Lee what was going on. Empty. To put it finely, *the flat was empty.* Chu Lee had obviously been given the evening off.

Stunned, I sat down to think. Obviously Susan had thrown a tantrum and insisted on leaving early. They were playing the PGA Open Championship there and all the big names would be present; Jack Nicklaus, whether he played or not, would be there... Greg Norman? At any rate, all the names Desmond had been full of for weeks. He had invited them all back to dinner – a couple had even accepted and he was over the moon. For once he had ordered a 'special dinner, Binky', and actually turned up for it. Susan and Dennis had come over to meet them, and obviously were not prepared to wait for me to get home.

The phone rang. Ah! Apologies accepted, Desmond, I practised in my mind – No, I don't mind at all!

It was Jerry, Deputy Head of Peak School. "Wendy, are you coming tonight?" he asked. "Only the Governor and his wife have arrived. *Everyone* is here and word has got round that you aren't coming. You really *must* come."

It meant, of course, that my reference was at stake. Having had nothing else to concentrate on but my career, I had made sure that whatever else, I always had impeccable references – which had got me my plum job in Hong Kong.

"I can't, Jerry," I said. (Far too late to try to gatecrash now; it would only make things worse... think of something better...) "The thing is, Desmond has one of these big murder trials on tomorrow – you know what it's like, these trials and things," I said vaguely with a sigh. "He is going to be up all night going through the papers and I will have to stay up all night with him, supplying fresh coffee. I am so sorry. Please give my apologies to everyone, but *do* explain that *duty* comes before *pleasure* – always."

"Good one," he said. "Will do. I understand, leave this to me."

"Oh thank you, Jerry," I said with feeling.

"Remember... you owe me one."

"I will," I said. "Oh, I will." Thoughtfully, I replaced the phone. Finally, it hit me. I'd had enough. Enough was enough. I had tried. I had been stamped on, patronized, condescended to and generally treated as a dogsbody. I obviously wasn't wanted – my golf clubs were preferable to my presence – but I was not allowed to leave. Fine. I would now deal with the new situation.

I carefully set my alarm for 2.00 am. Then I wallowed in a foam bath, dried, made myself a sandwich and went to bed. I did not even feel my head touch the pillow.

I awoke, refreshed, when the alarm went. I dressed and put my make-up on – well, *slapped* it on, carelessly. Wearing the gold sheath dress with the décolletage neckline that Desmond would not allow me to wear, gold high heels and my long diamond earrings, I poured myself a glass of sherry and turned all the lights out apart from one low-level bulb in the corner. Then I arranged myself on the sitting room settee. And waited.

They were back early. Golfers, I knew, did not appreciate heavy drinkers. They preferred to eat and drink lightly in the clubhouse, requiring clear heads the next day. Desmond was first in. "Ssh," he said. "Ssh, Wendy will be asleep."

Susan giggled. "Well, we are not," she retorted. "I need a drink."

"So do I," agreed Dennis. "I'll be barman."

"I bet Wendy will be *just wild* when she knows what she's missed," Susan said.

"Well if you hadn't left early," I said from the darkness, "I *wouldn't* have missed it!"

"Binky!" "Desmond switched on the main lights.

"You left *early*," I reproached them. "You didn't wait for me," I continued mournfully. "I came back early, but you'd *gone*."

"I can explain that," gabbled Desmond. "We *had* to leave at six, or we'd have missed all the big names!" Desmond was wronged... and as usual, became irritable. "I *told* you we had to leave at six. Susan *is* our guest," he added righteously. "It was her *one* opportunity to meet them all."

By now he had come round to the settee where I was laid out in all my glory.

"*What the hell...*" For once he was speechless. Then a torrent: "*Where the hell have you been? Who have you been with and what the hell are you wearing?*"

I smiled sweetly. "A dress," I said, simply. "Why?"

He spluttered to a stop... and calmed right down.

"Where have you been Binky?" he asked quietly. "And who with?"

"Theatre," I beamed at him.

"Theatre?" he repeated, totally sidetracked.

"Theatre." I was not known as The Queen of Drama for nothing. I'd had to give up the drama teaching I so enjoyed, and absence makes the heart grow fonder as well as more determined.

"Which theatre?" he asked, disconcerted.

"Can't 'member... but lovely play, beaut-i-ful play," I enunciated, dreamily. "*As You Like It!*" I said suddenly, shooting out an arm to Desmond. The sherry at the end of it slopped onto the floor. "*As You Like It*; definitely."

"I'm sorry... we were late," said Dennis hesitantly, "and went without you. Honestly... (sensing disaster ahead,) honestly, we couldn't wait any longer."

"But *after* the theatre!" Desmond shouted. "Where have you been?"

"Didn't I tell you?" I exclaimed indignantly. I couldn't keep it up for long and had to relax into sobriety. "This evening I was supposed to attend the Staff Outing – which this year was at the Festival Theatre, then on to a reception, hosted by the Governor and his wife, since their children attend the Peak School." There was silence; certainly the Governor's status was way above that of any of the celebrity golfers.

"You asked me..." I continued with my indignant tone, "you *asked* me to be here when Susan and Dennis arrived. And *was* I here? I was *here!* Didn't go to the staff outing? No..." I said bitterly, "...I was *here!*"

Desmond, Dennis and Susan looked at each other aghast.

I wasn't finished yet. "So... said I couldn't go... got back here instead. *Early.* Gave Susan my golf clubs, so *she* could play golf, and when I got *back*," I said, dramatically throwing my arm wide to show how I had given up golf, my evening, *everything* for them, "you'd *gone!*"

"But why are you dressed... like a... like *that?*"

"School rang," I said indistinctly, taking a sip of what was left of my sherry after the dramatic movements. Now having an enhanced audience, I rambled on. "*So*... School rang and said I should be *there*. So I went."

I now had their full attention.

"Binky, you're drunk!" uttered Desmond uncertainly.

"Not drunk," I said. *Not Drunk.* Had champagne. Lovely," I sighed. "Governor ver' nice... *ver* nice."

"You're drunk," Desmond repeated. "You didn't go *out* like *that?*" he asked angrily.

"Why not?" I demanded to know. "*Why not?* Why shun't I? My best dress..." I smiled at them disarmingly. "They *liked* it!" I pronounced with great satisfaction.

"I'll bet," Dennis said, appreciatively.

"Well, when they rang and said I really should attend, I decided to wear this. I haven't worn it before," I added thoughtfully. "I don' think Desmond likes it, but since Desmond wasn' there, I wore it. It went down awfully well."

"I *would* like a *drink!*" said Susan from the bar.

"Still," I said brightly, "I have to get up early in the morning. I have to go home in a couple of weeks time," I explained earnestly. "Next term I have to find another job – definitely on a temporary basis," I confided. "But, since I gave up my *seconded* job to marry Desmond, I have to work here, *for a bit*, until I can get a more permanent one, to secure the mortgage." I yawned. "Anyway... you know..." I shrugged. "I *think* I had too much champagne tonight; ver' tired... ver' tired. Think I'll go to bed... G'night."

I heaved myself erratically off the settee, slewing my décolletage neckline at an impossible – and improper – angle. Desmond sprang to my assistance – not to help, though, but to make sure the neckline wasn't entirely lost to gravity.

"Leave you to the bar," I said grandly, pushing Desmond firmly away. "As usual, eh? Drinks on the house? Feel free!" I aimed somewhat uncertainly for the hallway, to the bedroom. They followed like sheep. I turned and, flying out an arm, pointed at them. "I must get some sleep so don't keep me awake," I implored. "I have to be up early tomorrow... six-thirty *sharp!*"

They cowered behind me. No question of a further two hours drinking cocktails, discussing their successes. They'd met the golfers, eaten with them, played with Wendy's golf clubs. Now go back and celebrate... this time, *NO!* And never again.

Next morning I was up early and out. I prepared the display for the Open Day and, at last, could relax. I had totally ruined the weekend for Susan and Dennis – which delighted me – and I fully intended that their discomfiture would continue.

For the rest of their stay, I was included in all the arrangements and everyone steered well clear of me.

Desmond was most attentive.

Five

Iwas back home with Desmond for a traditional, English Christmas; I would show him! Out we went for the ceremonial Christmas tree. I had hoped that Desmond, for once, might have been just a *little* bit interested in planting it, but no. He sat and shivered pathetically (and noticeably) in the house, whilst I went out collecting buckets of earth and then hauled them inside. Having got the tree to stand more or less straight, it was out with the traditional decorations.

"Would you mind moving to the side?" grumbled Desmond. "I can't see the television."

I switched on the tree lights – they looked fantastic. I glanced round, delighted. "Look, Desmond," I urged. There was no response. He was apparently engrossed in his programme. Still, the festoons went up across the room.

"Coming for a walk, Desmond?" The common was just across the road. The holly was full of berries – ivy, mistletoe, they were all there for the picking. No answer.

I decorated the hall and stairway with holly and hung ivy and mistletoe round the six-foot square Venetian mirrors; they looked wonderful. Desmond went to bed.

After that he made it clear that he hated England; hated Christmas in England; hated the English weather – in fact, just generally hated England and the English.

"Would you like to go to London?" I suggested.

No, it was too cold; too damp. He thought he might be starting a cold – he'd never been so cold in his life. He was suffering... nobly, of course.

"I only came because of you, Binky," he said as he sat shivering in the best armchair.

"Desmond," I said, "it *is* England, and it *is* December. The central heating is up to eighty degrees Fahrenheit, but it has to be said, in England we simply don't expect to be sat indoors all day in just a short-sleeved, Aertex tennis shirt. If you're cold, I do suggest you might consider wearing a sweater." Mother and I were both in cotton dresses and perspiring freely. So was Desmond.

"I've got a temperature, I think," was all he said.

I further turned up the thermostat; to ninety-five degrees.

Christmas Day, and I surveyed my pile of gaily wrapped boxes under the tree. They were all for Desmond; I had bought half a dozen presents, splashing out, as this was possibly my last Christmas in the UK before my house was finally sold up. I had bought and wrapped presents for my mother to give him. Her cataracts were now so bad that she couldn't shop, or even see to wrap them. Even so, she insisted on paying for them, so they were her very own gifts.

Thelma and Dennis, my sister and brother-in-law, came over and brought gifts. We sat and unwrapped them ceremoniously. I hadn't quite known what to do about Desmond; he had been 'too cold' to go out and buy any. However, he didn't seem to mind that he was the only one opening presents, and no one else appeared to notice.

We sat down to a huge Christmas lunch with all the trimmings. Desmond did take over at that point to serve the wines – one gathered they did not entirely meet with his approval, but he was too polite to say so – and then he went heavily into the sitting room to wait for coffee and liqueurs.

Boxing Day, and Desmond was sitting morosely in the sitting room. "Why don't you have a proper fire?" he asked. "Why have a fireplace and no *fire?*"

I explained that I had bought the house just before moving to Hong Kong and there'd been no time to attend to it. I'd had a couple of gardeners in from Exbury House – Lord Rothschild's estate (I had taught their children) – who had landscaped the garden, installing the carp pond, specifically for easy maintenance, just before I left. There was a huge Adam fireplace but, working full time, I had installed a gas fire in it. It could be removed, I told him; yes, we could have a real fire – it would look cheerful.

Of course, the first time it was lit, smoke immediately billowed out into the room. Desmond, choking and purple with fury, slammed out of the room and went upstairs. It soon settled down, and when he returned, there was indeed a Dickensian log fire roaring away merrily. The heat was overpowering and I had to turn the thermostat down to make it bearable. But Desmond had lost interest; he decided to go into the dining room and read.

After that, no one knew quite what to do about Desmond. He wandered the house – idly, but ostentatiously drawing a finger along the white paint of the dado – obviously checking for dust, but fortunately finding none. My mother's sight may have been failing, but she still managed to keep the house clean and tidy.

Then to the French windows looking out on the garden. "God. Rain, rain, rain," he groaned. "This awful bloody weather!" Finally, he announced he must ring up Hong Kong and check with Chambers that all was well. No one was unduly surprised when he put the phone down and announced he must "return *immediately*." A case had blown up; his solicitor had ordered him back *now.*

"Sorry, Binky," he said. "I did try. I came back especially for you. Of course, I think I've got another cold… this freezing weather, but I don't mind, you know I'd do anything for *you*."

"I'll come to the airport," I told him. The new term was due to start in a few days time.

"So you'll follow on? Take the original return flight?"

"I don't think I can," I said. "Looking at the house – I'll have to ring school and tell them I won't be back. It'll take me a few weeks to get it up together and then I'll have to see about selling it."

"Anything you say, Binky," Desmond replied with little interest.

Coming back to the house alone was surprisingly pleasant. That awful atmosphere had gone. In any case, all the Christmas decorations had to be stripped and packed away, which Desmond would have hated. Once done – redecorate.

I enjoyed shopping for paints and wallpaper. I would start on the dining room. Out went the furniture, off came the wallpaper, in came the ladders and trestle tables. This was what I most enjoyed.

To my surprise, once started, I felt disinclined to continue. Eventually, I was putting up one sheet of wallpaper and then sitting down for half an hour's rest; another sheet – another rest. I'd never get it done at that rate. Obviously, I still hadn't quite recovered from my bout in hospital; my back continually ached and I was too tired to work a full day. No problem. I would visit the doctor for some painkillers. Then finish the house and get back to Hong Kong.

The doctor greeted me with surprise. "Haven't seen you for years."

I explained my problem… I hadn't had any back problems for years but then there were the two bouts in hospital and probably I needed a tonic…

"Probably," he said. "After four years, perhaps a quick check-up?"

His face gave nothing away as we settled ourselves back at his desk. "Ah," he began, "well, your back's fine. No problem there. The problem's in the front – you're about five months pregnant."

"Oh no," I said firmly. "No. *That* can't be right. You see, as I told you, I had a miscarriage in November, and Desmond and I have been living separately ever since. Not possible."

"Afraid so," he said. "I can think of only one explanation – that you lost one of twins. Did you have a clean up op afterwards?"

"No. Because I'd had a miscarriage and it wasn't thought advisable, or necessary."

"Then that's it," he stated.

I was still reeling. All set to sell my house and go back to Hong Kong. I had already decided I would need to take up my career again – no more taking stop-gap jobs that didn't interest me – and insist on a Head of Department or Deputy Headship and if necessary, be prepared to *wait* for it and let Desmond (for once) pay my expenses. He clearly admired Susan who spent her way lavishly through her yuppie husband's cash reserves, and Desmond clearly despised my bourgeoisie habits of boringly paying my own way. That would stop – as of now. Now, I had to re-think again; but before I could get any further, the doctor continued.

"You will go into hospital *today*. You have two options – you can either go ahead and hope for the best, *or* you can have a test to see whether or not the child is damaged, as you lost one twin. You would also, of course, find out the sex of the child."

I went home in a complete daze. Eeny meeny miny mo – now I was pregnant; now I wasn't. Now I am; now it might be damaged… or it might not. If I have a test it could cause an abortion; if I don't I might have a damaged child to contend with.

Finally, I went into hospital and was asked if I had come to a decision.

Yes. I had.

If the child was damaged, I would have an abortion. Desmond was clearly totally uninterested in even a healthy child. If I had a damaged one, it meant giving up my marriage altogether, as well as my career, to look after it – with no income to do so.

If, however, it was healthy and the test didn't cause an abortion, then I would have the child – and Desmond could go jump in the lake.

The test results came back. A little boy – perfect in every way. Suddenly I was elated and everything fell into place. I would stay in the UK and redecorate the house; collect Susie Chow from quarantine – how she'd hated it, but she could now run to her heart's content in the garden, and as a good sampan dog she would soon have a baby in a pram to guard, night and day. She would be in her element and so would I.

I rang Desmond with the news. He was quite calm. "But you *promised* you would follow on," he said. "You have let me down, *badly*."

"But," I replied, "I have *explained* why."

"I have been very *patient*," he said. "I have been here *alone*, with *no one* looking after me. I have been very unhappy. You *promised* you would come back as soon as you'd sold the house."

"It's too late for me to travel now, anyway," I told him.

"Check into the London clinic," Desmond urged, "and then get a flight straight home. *Unaccompanied*."

It took a while to sink in. "But there's nothing the matter with the child," I told him. "It *was* an option, but not now."

Desmond had obviously prepared for this. "If you have *any* feeling for me at all, Binky, you'll do this for me. If you have a child, you'll give it one hundred percent – there'll be nothing left for *me*. You have made me very lonely and unhappy; the *least* you can do," he said, beginning to lose patience with the caring approach, "is to check into the clinic, deal with it and *get on the next flight home*. You will, of course," he added hurriedly, "pay for it yourself. Entirely your own fault of course. *Entirely*. Just check in, Binky and get back to Hong Kong – I can assure you it will never be mentioned again," he finished magnanimously.

I put the phone down. I'd had enough shocks for that day. But as far as I was concerned, my marriage was now over. Still, I reasoned… not a bad plan. Desmond didn't want to leave Hong Kong; I didn't want to leave the UK. I could have the child and bring him up in the UK – most teachers took their children to school with them. I had three months holiday a year – I could even take a term off now and then and commute to and from Hong Kong.

I had my house valued. It was worth two hundred thousand and I had less than a thousand to pay off the mortgage and then it was mine. I had some investments I'd put away that were doing well, and there was a lump sum saved in my deposit account – and I was in an excellent profession. In fact, the future looked rosy.

I put myself on the supply teaching list and gradually, offers of work came in. At first, as I knew well, one had to 'work one's way up' from the bottom. Most schools had their own 'standby' teachers – those within easy reach who didn't want to teach full-time, but had taught previously at the school and would pop in at the drop of a hat and do a turn. But the inner city schools, where no one wanted to go, had to rely on the official list. Youngsters straight out of college had cut their teeth on these schools; if they survived, they were teachers. If not, they left – and weren't.

I found the going tough. I had been well and truly softened up. Having been used to a routine, now I would find myself driving out to the east of the country, negotiating country lanes to find tiny, tucked away schools to teach a class of six-year-olds in the morning, then spend my lunchtime driving cross-country again to teach ten-year-olds music in the afternoon. North the following day to find a school and teach ten-year-olds pottery and south again in the afternoon to take a class for football practice.

In the evenings and, mostly, in the night, were the never-ending phone calls. "Binky, please come home. I miss you." And, if I did bother to hold any conversation, "How *dare* you leave me on my own? What am I supposed to do? I've no one to look *after* me!"

This I very much doubted. He would of course ring during the evening when he was home from Chambers and brooding about his hard life. The fact that the time difference meant the calls reached me at two or four in the morning was entirely irrelevant. In the end, I made sure that all the doors were closed before retiring, so that I could sleep through it. Then one morning I was awoken by a sound like a fire alarm. It was so penetrating that it was impossible to ignore it. When I answered, it was the GPO. I was told that my husband was worried about me and had asked that in future they 'bleeped' me to make sure I answered. Was there no peace to be had?

I did answer, but it was always the same. "When are you coming home? I can't manage without you."

"What," I said, "and have the child there – in Hong Kong?"

Silence.

"The only reason I don't want the child," Desmond eventually found his voice; "is because you would, I know, give it one hundred percent attention and there would be nothing left for *me*. You do understand that, don't you?"

"Oh yes," I agreed wearily. "I'm only wanted back *unaccompanied!* Well that is not going to happen. Goodnight."

But the phone calls continued, until finally, I snapped. I had groped my way downstairs at three in the morning and that was the last straw. "Very well!" I barked, irritably. "I'm on my way – I'll come back!"

There was a stunned silence.

"Wha... what did you say?" stammered Desmond, hardly ever at a loss for words. His phone calls had become so perfunctory, so automatic, simply to make sure that I had disturbed nights until I buckled, that he had difficulty coping with a new idea.

"I'll come back," I said. "I'm exhausted. I can't cope with heavy teaching *and* being woken up every night. You want me back in Hong Kong? Okay, I'll come. Tomorrow. I'll get a taxi to the airport. I'll be there the next day."

There was wild confusion at the other end. Desmond's far-off voice said hoarsely, "She's coming *back*, Now!" More rustling and banging could be heard, then Desmond again, having probably dropped the phone in his bewilderment.

"Er... perhaps we ought to *think* about this, Binky. Of course, I'm only thinking of your health, er... are you sure you ought to travel? Perhaps it would be as well..."

"No," I interrupted. "No. You've made your point. Over and over again. I'm going back upstairs now to pack my suitcase. I'll be on the first plane out tomorrow."

Putting the phone down, I had the best sleep I'd had for ages – and again the next night. Finally, the phone rang, but now at a convenient time.

"Where are you, Binky?" asked Desmond sadly. There were no extraneous noises now in the flat. He was obviously alone and genuinely unhappy.

"Well, you see," I began, sweetly, "I had to check things with the doctor and, as he pointed out, only a *fool* would ask me to get on a plane when I'm seven months pregnant – and only a *fool* would do so!"

Again there was a silence. But Desmond was undaunted. "Does that mean you're not coming back?"

"It does," I told him… and hung up.

At the hospital they were becoming more and more concerned. "I don't think you are taking your situation *seriously* enough," I was told.

I explained that I had coped, just, with the teaching, but not with the constant disturbed nights.

"I think I must have a word with your husband," said the consultant.

"He's in Hong Kong," I said.

"I know, but this is important. I'll call him. You will need to come into hospital for the rest of the pregnancy and then on strict bed rest. The child is now wedged in an impossible position."

I listened carefully, as he launched into a detailed, no-holds-barred explanation.

"It will certainly need a caesarean section, but the trick now is not to have a miscarriage. Since you are here on your own, I have no alternative but to explain the situation and discuss it with you directly. Now, there are four main positions requiring a caesarean – and yours is the worst. At the first sign, I have exactly fifteen minutes to get to you and operate *and*, hopefully, save the child. Your chances are rapidly decreasing. You will need to stay in the ante-room so that you can be rushed into theatre at a moment's notice.

"I can appreciate that your husband wants you home; I will explain it to him. There must be no more late phone calls, and *you* must now go home quietly and calmly, get packed up and come back into hospital prepared to stay for the duration. There is no question of you travelling anywhere. To put it plainly, I have a window of ten minutes to operate – fifteen at the most. Now, even if you were allowed on a plane, which I doubt, the flight would almost certainly precipitate the birth. Even if you happened to be over Bahrain, who boast the most sophisticated hospital in the world, it would take the pilot twenty minutes to make an emergency landing. Bahrain would certainly have all facilities on standby – on arrival you would be rushed directly to a first class hospital with a consultant surgeon second to none and given the best possible care…

"*But*, it will have taken you twenty minutes to get down, twenty minutes in the ambulance and at least ten to prepare you for surgery. You don't have fifty or sixty minutes, so – get on that plane and the only way you get off is in a *box*!"

He looked as grim as his words had sounded. "I am sorry to have to put it to you like this," he apologized, "but you are here and on your own and, frankly, you have no options left." His expression softened a little. "Don't worry," he said. "I will ring your husband. He obviously does not understand the position; I will explain everything. Just you go home, get packed up, and I'll deal with everything."

Well. Thoroughly cowed now, I agreed. I rang the schools – no more teaching. I rang my latest school and assured them I would be back teaching for them in September. "I'll have had the baby by then," I said cheerfully.

"Are you *sure*? You can *guarantee* you'll be back?"

"Oh, definitely," I told them. I *was* sure. It meant no pay for the whole of August, and one way or another, I had to be working by September if I were to keep up the mortgage payments.

I packed a suitcase. I was used to that. I had always packed my suitcase in half an hour flat at the end of Christmas and Spring terms. I reckoned to be on a flight the following day and on a beach, sunbathing by the afternoon. It had been one of the 'perks' of a single and successful schoolteacher.

That evening the phone rang – again at a 'UK-friendly' time. This was Desmond at his very best – the renowned Silver Tongue of the Law Courts.

"Oh, Binky," he breathed. "I am *so* unhappy. I cannot *live* without you. I *have* tried, but it's no use – I just miss you *so* much. Now, don't say a word – just *listen* to me…

"I am your *husband*. You promised to love and *obey*; now I am asking just that you *trust* me. I *am* your husband and I need you here, *now*. I have been *alone* so long – I have been *so miserable* – no one to cook for me, no one to look after me, the place is filthy – the servants are all over the place…" His fury was mounting, but he stopped short, remembering where he was. "Anyway," he carried on, bravely, "never mind about *me*, I am just thinking about *you*, always, Binky. Just get a taxi – don't bother to pack – just come to the airport as you *promised* you would, Binky, get on the next flight and I'll be waiting for you."

I felt cold to the pit of my stomach as he went on, breaking the heavy silence at this end of the line – I was totally speechless.

"Don't listen to *anyone*, Binky." A gentle tone now. "Just listen to *me*. Everything will be *fine* – just you get on that plane and I'll meet you at this end. Don't listen to *anyone* – doctors, hospitals – what do they know? *Nonsense*, Binky," (I hadn't even spoken). "Get in a taxi *now* and *please*, Binky, *come back to me*!"

I put the phone down and called for a taxi immediately.

"The hospital," I said.

It was very pleasant to be waited on in hospital. A bit isolated, all on my own in a tiny room, but it was my own. It had to be tiny – it was right next door to the operating theatre and there was an endless succession of patients being wheeled in and (hopefully) out again.

But gosh, it was hot. Over 33°C now, every day. I was concerned about the house. It had not been looked after for six years and – unless watered – the gardens established by the Exbury House team would be ruined. But finally I was forced to acknowledge defeat. I could do nothing but wait.

After that it was just plain boring. Days, weeks, a month went by. I rang Desmond. He was very quiet and uttered the occasional half-choked sob as he endeavoured to hide his loneliness, his unhappiness – that I had caused him.

"I've decided to call him John," I told him brightly.

"Ah, my second name," said Desmond.

I realized it was – I just liked the name; it was no-nonsense, you couldn't shorten it or mess about with it.

"Not Desmond?" he queried.

"Definitely not Desmond," I said flatly.

"Then I'd like you to call him Paul as well, then."

"Paul? Why?" Actually, I quite liked the name, now I thought about it.

"I've always like the name Paul. Just for *me*, Binky. Will you?"

"Yes," I agreed. John Paul – yes, they went well together.

"And *Mary*," he added.

"*WHAT*?" I roared.

"Now Wendy, listen. This *is* important to me; it's the Donnelly family name and it's been handed down to the first-born, regardless of sex – it's an Irish tradition."

"I'm afraid I have to go now," I said. "I'm feeling very tired."

No way. No way was I going to inflict a name like *Mary* on the poor, unfortunate child; I felt we had enough troubles to endure, without adding any more misfortunes to the list.

Six

The days passed.

I was wheeled out with the other unfortunates to the verandah, where we lay, like a pod of beached whales. The temperature rose; so did tempers. Having been defeated, there was no further word from Desmond.

Weeks passed.

I awoke at 2.00 am, in some discomfort. I rang my emergency bell. "I would like something for my indigestion," I told the nurse. "Something must have disagreed with me – I've never had indigestion before…" I was totally unprepared for what followed.

Within seconds, I found myself being thrust through to the operating theatre, trolley dispensed with (I hadn't realised I had been lying all that time on a trolley disguised as a bed) – it was whipped away and I was transferred to the operating table. We waited. Seconds later, the Registrar appeared… in his nightie, it appeared – just a green gown covered him.

Blearily, I looked at him.

"You've *started*," he said.

"I have indigestion, I think."

"Oh."

We waited. Then discussed the problem.

I had awoken, I told him, with a pair of nutcrackers squeezing my stomach. As I had treated brazil nuts in the past, so they were wreaking revenge on me now. Clench, release; clench, release. "Indigestion," I said. "Haven't had it before, but then I've never been confined before."

We waited. Nothing.

An hour later, the surgeon returned. "All seems to have quietened down," he observed.

"Please may I go back to bed?"

"You may. Thankfully, so may I, *but*, you are due for the chop next operating day," he told me. "No more fooling around!"

I began to protest – it was only indigestion, after all. That's all it was. But I was speaking to air; trolley-borne again, I had been wheeled back to my room.

On Tuesday (next operating day) at 9.00 am, I was rolled in, unprotesting, to the theatre again. Would I accept a rubber mouthpiece through which to administer gas?

No. I would not!

"In the interests of the child," murmured the anaesthetist and before I could agree, a mask was forced over my face.

What only seemed like moments later (09.35), I re-emerged and somewhere in my delirium thought at least I should enquire about the results of my labours.

"He's fine," I was told.

I tried to focus – at least to check it had two eyes, a nose and mouth, but failed miserably amidst a sea of fog. "Wonderful," I said, and sank below the pillows again.

Some time later, I awoke. Delight! I was in a large, airy ward, with a cot beside me.

And a beautiful child lying within. Success at last!

I had occasionally managed to say one or two words to the ward members when I'd been wheeled out of that miserable, dark, ante-room onto the small grass courtyard where we had lain together, like sea elephants, all gasping for air in the soaring temperatures which had reached thirty-four Fahrenheit. Now they greeted me enthusiastically; they were so kind and generous. "How have you been?" "So glad to see you finally got out of that dreadful room – a dungeon, no less." I agreed, happily.

I was told I must stagger out of bed and trot round to see my son. "Good Lord, of *course*!" I told them, and eagerly leapt from the bed. The sister caught me in time. I had quite forgotten about being on my back for two months – the sudden rush of oxygen, plus the stitches, newly implanted, had brought me down to ground level with a bump.

With more care, I tried again. This time I made it to the foot of the bed. The baby was perfect! Not at all as I had expected. He lay there happily; not a wrinkle, not a crease. A perfect complexion with rosy cheeks and dark curly hair. Bright blue eyes stared at the world as he gurgled away in his cot. This, then, was my son, John Paul Desmond Donnelly... I was impressed.

The next day, I tottered round a few other cots to admire my neighbours' children. My mother and sister arrived to inspect the new addition.   We all agreed he was far superior to any of the other children. To begin with, he had the complexion of a smooth peach – unwrinkled, rosy-cheeked and... even a slight suntan! A beautiful child.

"Hm," the surgeon had said. "Clearly a Caesarean – no wrinkles, but slight touch of jaundice."

Nonsense – he had a perfect Mediterranean suntan!

We continued with our mutual admiration society until the fifth day. 1976 had been an unusual year; for the past two months the daytime temperature had remained at well over 30°C. My mother told me the lawns were brown, and concern was rising as the ground cracked and split – we were on dry soil and the neighbours were concerned for the foundations.

I couldn't care less. I had survived and so had John Paul, in spite of all the macabre predictions. As far as I was concerned, all was well in my world. I had my home almost bought and paid for; I had my new son; I had half a term's employment in September, albeit in one of the toughest schools in Southampton. It would be hard going, I knew, but I would cope – as I had always done, up to now. The mortgage would be paid, Desmond would fit in somewhere – I foresaw a great future.

I woke up next morning full of the joys of spring – although it was high summer. In fact, even that seemed to be easing – it didn't seem so hot today, although everyone else was still complaining. The rubber sheets, obligatory in that ward, had finally been relinquished. We were suffering enough from heat exhaustion – the hated rubber sheets had been removed after much protesting. By midday I was really cold. Of course I had been used to Hong Kong temperatures and we had for the last month only been issued with one thin sheet for cover. I now requested a blanket.

The nurse, surprised, supplied it. "Everyone else is begging me to let them take their one sheet *off*," she said cheerfully, "but decency necessitates they have at least a sheet to cover them!"

I dare not ask for another; something may be wrong. I decided to practice my new walking ability – I was now allowed to walk as far as the ward doors. I would try my luck. I knew the public phone was just outside the door, and made it. I rang my mother. Could she ring Thelma and get me a blanket?

"Surely the hospital supplies them?" Mother was mystified.

"Just do it," I told her. "Of course, the weather has changed and after Hong Kong, I am really feeling the cold."

"It's still baking hot!" she exclaimed. "Are you sure you're all right?"

"I'm fine. Just ask Thelma to bring me a blanket; I'm freezing here."

By the time Thelma arrived half an hour later, I was lying curled up in my one blanket, teeth chattering with the cold. The nurse had insisted that I get up and I had reluctantly left the warmth of the bed and now sat in a chair, shaking uncontrollably, huddled in my blanket. She took my temperature and left... hurriedly. She came back with the doctor, who confirmed my high temperature and ordered half-hourly supervision. I was returned to bed.

Thelma disappeared, in conference with the doctors. They were coming back to my bed at five minute intervals now and becoming increasingly concerned. Finally, the doctor consulted with the nurses and when they left, I saw they had placed a card above my bed: NIL BY MOUTH.

"My God," I said to my sister. "All I've been getting is drugs so far. I've only seen that notice over the cages in the zoo! Does that mean they don't intend to feed me any more?" But by now my teeth were chattering so much I could hardly speak. I had no idea one's knees could really knock together, but as I was shivering they were literally knocking together like castanets.

Finally, I could stand it no longer. "Thelma," I begged, "please, please, *please* go home and get me a hot water bottle! I don't know what's going on, but something is wrong and I'm obviously going to get no help here." The curtains had been drawn round my bed and – as far as I could tell – I had been abandoned.

My sister left, hurriedly.

Now the doctor came, accompanied by another, for a second opinion. He took my temperature. He turned away from me and a low, terse conversation took place. A decision was made.

"Call the Registrar, please, Matron!"

She hurried off.

Five minutes later the curtains parted, for the surgeon. "Causing more trouble?" he asked cheerfully. He took my temperature and his face dropped. "My God... how long has she been like this?"

"Since this morning."

He turned to the young doctor in a fury. "*Why wasn't I called?*" he demanded to know.

The young doctor wilted and offered some weak excuse which the surgeon brusquely disregarded. Then they all marched out, leaving me alone again. Immediately, the curtains parted and my sister appeared, with a carrier bag.

"Look," she said, "I've been home and both Dennis and I are worried about you. What would happen if, you know... the worst?"

I stared at her. By now I was shaking so much I could hardly think, let alone speak.

"Dennis has given me this," she gabbled, thrusting a paper at me.

I looked at it in disbelief; it was a printed Will form.

"It's quite legal – Dennis collected it from the Post Office. It leaves everything to us. That *is* what you'd want if... anything happened to you, isn't it? Of course we would look after John Paul – we would take care of everything."

I was so impressed, if I had been capable of speech I would have thanked her. I was deeply impressed. My thoughtless, elder naughty sister, finally showing some care, some interest... some thought for my welfare and even that of my new son. It was about the first time she had even shown she *cared*. As it was, I just stretched out one shaking hand and snatched the paper from her. She handed me a pen – she even had a pen ready – and I signed it, thankfully. At least someone was there, looking after me.

Then she brought over the carrier bag and after burrowing through layers of insulating blankets, she finally retrieved a glowing hot water bottle and gently slid it beneath the sheet against my back. Oh! Bliss! As I leant against it, I could feel the shaking subside – and a warm glow suffused my whole being. And for the first time that day, my muscles relaxed.

At that moment the curtains were roughly thrown aside and the registrar strode furiously through, followed by a small army of doctors and nurses, headed by the formidable Matron. Thelma gave a squeak, snatched the hot water bottle away and in one stride had backed out through the curtains – I had never seen her move so fast; in a flash she was gone and to my heartbroken dismay, so was the hot water bottle.

Instead, the nightmare procession bore down on me. First, the irate surgeon. Followed by a group of crestfallen housemen... followed by a severe Matron... followed by half a dozen nurses carrying clanking pails. My sheet and blanket were unceremoniously torn away from me and a rubber sheet was placed beneath me. And then, in spite of my shrieks and entreaties, two nurses emptied their buckets of ice cubes on to it, rolling me on top of them. Two more nurses then emptied their pails of ice on top of me, then the sheet was wrapped round me and the corners securely fastened so that I was totally encased in *ice!* By which time, I was speechless; I just wanted some peace – to die with a little dignity.

The Registrar's face was grave as he addressed the houseman. "I didn't," he ground out between gritted teeth, "get her through that Caesarean to then lose her through *your* stupidity!"

To my surprise, once I had settled in amongst the ice cubes, the shaking and the muscle spasms stopped and I was able to relax. I was cold, yes, but the awful shaking had finally ceased.

I smiled gratefully at the sea of faces surrounding me. "It's stopped," I said, happily.

The Registrar took my temperature. "It's moving," he said.

There was an apprehensive silence.

"Down," he added.

Everyone breathed out. They waited for a few minutes, but now I was comfortable. In a room temperature of 34°C, lying in a bed of ice cubes was a definite option. I began to relax. My temperature continued to go down and finally the Registrar left, after barking his terse instructions to Matron. The young houseman was dismissed in disgrace.

Eventually, I was allowed out of the melted mess, dried off and settled back into bed. I had been appalled to be handed John Paul for feeding in the midst of shaking to pieces in my bed of ice cubes – one presumed for his Last Supper, assuming I wasn't going to make it. First things first, I suppose, but I had to admit that at the time it was not high on my list of priorities.

Still, all was well that ended well. The curtains were whisked back and I was back in the war again – albeit now that *both* John Paul and I were in Intensive Care and I was in a room of my own.

"But *why?*" I asked my new nurse. "*Why* douse me in ice cubes when I was freezing to death?"

"You had a temperature of a hundred and six degrees," she answered.

"Is that bad?" I asked anxiously.

"Well," she said, "put it like this – there isn't a temperature of a hundred and *seven* degrees!"

"There isn't…?" It took a while for the penny to drop.

"It was rising all day," she said, "and nothing would bring it down. One degree more, and that would be *it*. The Registrar decided that was the only way."

I couldn't see how it was possible to have a temperature of 106°F and shake with cold. *Odd*. I never did find out.

My sister came in and, of course, we laughed like drains over the hot water bottle. "Silly me," she giggled. Well, yes – it had been par for the course; in fact it had been too good to be true. Trust my sister, the one time she had ever displayed any feelings of care or thoughtfulness towards me, she had damned near killed me – now *that* was more her style.

John Paul's jaundice was finally being brought under control. There was some concern that he was steadily losing weight but, as was pointed out, I had been fed solely on drugs since his arrival, so that was all he had been receiving also. Hopefully, I could now begin to have some food, and less drugs, and things should improve.

Finally the day came. My new son and I returned to my own (nearly paid for) home, to be greeted by an ecstatic Susie Chow, just released from quarantine. She ran round and round in circles, delighted to have her family home. Had I been able to, I would have joined her.

John Paul had arrived at 9.35 am on 20th July. Due to the temperature hiatus and a subsequent further ten days in Intensive Care for us both, it was August before I arrived home. School began 3rd September… so far, I had only been allowed to walk a few steps. I still walked bent double, unable as yet to straighten up.

My new headmaster rang. May he come and visit? There was consternation… of course, I was out of hospital, I had told him. Problems? Of course not. Was I up to taking on a 'challenging' class of twelve-year-olds? Of *course* I was!

Of *course* I wasn't! But I had dipped alarmingly into my savings and if I were to keep up the mortgage payments, I must get in the six weeks work I had been offered.

We had it all arranged. The doorbell rang; my mother answered it and showed the Headmaster and his Deputy into the sitting room. I half-rose, banking on their good manners.

"Oh please, don't get up," they said.

"I'm so sorry," I said as convincingly as I could make it, "I didn't hear the doorbell – do sit down."

Problem solved.

Was I fit to take over? A tough class... I may have had second thoughts... (I certainly had). But, to be perfectly honest – and here they both smiled winningly and with total insincerity – they doubted they'd be able to get anyone else if I let them down. They had come to plead, beg, entreat – but make sure I turned up on 3rd September.

Reassured, they left. I half-rose again, but my mother – on cue – saw them out, giving me time to stagger to the front door where, straightening up with an effort, I managed to wave them off the premises upright. Round one to me.

Now, I had exactly four weeks to get myself on my feet. By the 3rd, I was just able to drive the few miles to the school, teach until midday, home for John Paul's feed, back to school in time for afternoon classes, home for 4.00 pm, stay on my feet until 8.00 pm, fall into bed at 9.00 pm. Up for midnight feed, back to bed until 4.00 am feed, up for 8.00 am feed and off to school again.

That I could manage. The class I could not. Thankfully, there was never a full house. At least six were always absent for court appearances, truancy, or mischief which would result in *future* court appearances.

Mischief consisted of torturing neighbours' cats – for example putting them on bonfires with Guy Fawkes; nailing planks across the local, friendly, Indian-owned tuck-shop and then throwing lighted torches through the letterbox, watching while the fire brigade rescued the family from the upstairs windows, and also torching any cars dared to be parked in the vicinity. It was tough; it was very wearing and I still couldn't stand up straight. I was no longer able to feed John Paul and, since he began to lose weight alarmingly, was finally reduced to bottle feeding.

The Headmaster watched with increasing anxiety, but I was determined to complete the six weeks. Failure to do so, kind and helpful though the staff were, would mean they could hardly recommend me for further work, which I now needed desperately.

As we neared half-term, an appointment for a teaching position at one of the two most prestigious schools in Southampton was advertised. A vacancy for a teacher at a C of E School, requiring a Divinity specialist; Art and Craft abilities would be appreciated, music an advantage. I knew I stood a good chance after my Hong Kong reports, but would my present Headmaster let me down? Nothing to be done about it; I applied – and was offered an interview.

Not only was I a specialist in Divinity, but also in Art – plus I had held down a Specialist Music post in Hong Kong. They were delighted. I explained about John Paul. No problem, I was assured. He may attend their play school as well as their crèche (it was next door to the University where most of the children's parents attended, either as students or tutors). It would be a temporary appointment for one term and, providing all went well, it would then be made permanent. There would then be a vacancy for a Deputy Headship.

I returned to my own school on cloud nine, and went straight to my Headmaster to offer my most heartfelt thanks. "I do appreciate you putting in a good word for me," I told him. "Obviously I didn't let on how unfit I was… you have watched me, I know, and I have been struggling. I haven't been the teacher you were entitled to expect, and you have covered up for me. Thank you."

"Well, no, you haven't," he agreed. "My deputy and I realised that when we visited you at home, actually. But you were so determined to make it, we had to let you try. To be honest, we didn't think you *would* make it, but we take our hats off to you – you certainly stuck it out. We gave you a superb reference for effort – if not ability!"

A nice man.

I now had six weeks left of the term, and a three-week Christmas vacation – over two months before I was welcomed back as a permanent teacher again, plus an assured future in the 'University' primary school. He would go straight into the crèche, on to the pre-school, and then into primary school with me. Our futures were assured. The mortgage would soon be taken care of, the house was safe and my savings replenished. The future was rosy.

My new Headmaster had enquired when John Paul would be christened. "We have to get his name down," he explained. "Being so near the university, there is great difficulty getting a place here. And you *are* slightly out of our catchment area. The standard here is, of necessity, unusually high, but with your husband a lawyer and yourself a top-grade teacher, there will of course be no problem!"

I had the rest of the term to organise that, I told him. No problem. John Paul's name went down on the waiting list for a place at the school, and for next term in the crèche for teachers' children. I hadn't thought about the christening; to be honest, I had merely been concerned with survival until now.

But now things were different; I had a future again. Clearly, I would be staying in the UK permanently now. With a regular salary, I would be able to travel with my son to and from Hong Kong – but only to *visit.* A pleasant future stretched ahead. First, though, a courtesy call to Desmond to tell him of my – our – (John Paul's as well) good news.

Desmond listened. It began to dawn on me after a little while that he was less than pleased. "And what about *me?*" he enquired coldly.

"How do you mean?" I asked him.

"I have been *neglected,*" he replied bitterly, "and *very* badly treated. I thought I had a wife, companionship, someone to *look after* me. And now you are clearly planning to *stay* in Southampton... I need you *here*, Binky!"

"No way," I told him. "You made it clear you didn't want to get married in the first place. You were right and I was wrong. And it didn't work out. Fine. I've got my job back, a future for us both, and I'm not giving it up.

"I couldn't, even if I wanted to," I explained. "This will be the last permanent contract available in Southampton – my last realistic chance of security. Hampshire are providing no more permanent jobs – miss this one and there won't be another opportunity."

"Then I'll come to Southampton," said Desmond. "My son *must* be christened as a Catholic, and I intend to come back to the UK to ensure that he is."

"Impossible," I told him. I had overlooked the fact that there might be a problem; to be honest I had clean forgotten Desmond *was* a Catholic... it had certainly been of no consequence to him before.

"My son, *my* son," wailed Desmond. "To think you could even *consider* doing such a terrible thing to me, Binky; do you do these things *deliberately* – just to hurt me? The Donnelly's have been staunch Catholics for generations, Binky. No! At all costs, he must be christened in a decent Catholic church."

"I had no idea you felt so strongly about religion," I said. "I hadn't thought…"

"You hadn't *thought*," he said sadly; "but then you've never thought about *me*, have you Binky? You've never taken me into the slightest account… well, I am prepared to give *everything* up for you, Binky. As I always do. As I have said, I always intended retiring to the UK – you didn't *honestly* think I intended staying in Hong Kong for the rest of my life, did you?"

I protested. "But I thought you had given up the idea of working in London; we went there, but nothing came of it, and you clearly *hated* my house, Southampton *and* the thought of working in London!"

"My happiness doesn't matter!" said Desmond grandly. "My son *must* be christened as a Catholic. If it means I have to finish here and work in the UK, then so be it. Of course," he added hurriedly, "you will have to arrange everything – *everything*, but get it arranged, and I'll be home for it."

I put the phone down in a trance. Did I really want my son christened in the Catholic Church? Did I really want Desmond home? I discovered I really had not the slightest feeling for Desmond… no, that wasn't right – I had not the slightest regard or respect for him. Frankly, I didn't trust him *and* I now had a son to consider. I was freelance no longer. On the other hand, it was a simple choice – did I bring my son up as *our* son, with a father and a substantial income, which meant I could spend time at home with him, which I dearly wanted to do (though clearly I would have to continue supply teaching… I couldn't rely on Desmond to keep us) – or did I embark on teaching as a full time career, dumping John Paul, at a few months old, in a crèche to be brought up by strangers while I pursued my career, with occasional visits to his father in Hong Kong? How important was my religion to me? More to the point – how important was my son?

I rang Desmond again. "There's very little time left to decide," I told him. "In six weeks, John Paul has to be christened, and I start work. If you are *absolutely* certain that you want John Paul christened in the Catholic Church, it means you *guarantee* and *give me your word*, which I will accept, that you will return to the UK, be here for the christening and undertake to oversee his religious education. I am not prepared to become a Catholic," I continued, "but I will accept that John Paul is brought up in the faith provided you are here to oversee it – in other words, you will return to the UK on a permanent basis."

"Of course," declared Desmond grandly. "You just make the arrangements, Binky and I'll be back for the christening. I'll find suitable Chambers – in fact, I think old Humphrey has a place. Of course, had you *asked*, taken the *trouble* to find out, I had put some thought and effort into it already!"

"Very well," I said. I put the phone down and rang the Headmaster.

"Your husband is a Catholic?" said my new Headmaster. "Ah, a problem... but we can overcome that."

"And John Paul is to be christened as a Catholic," I added.

"That, I can't accept, Mrs Donnelly," he said. "Places here are at a premium, as you know. You are out of the catchment area – I can cope with *that*, but there is no way I would place a Catholic child in the crèche or, indeed, find a place here in a C of E School! It simply can't be done – in that case I would have to accept your resignation."

I put the phone down, sadly. But the die was cast.

I rang the church and arranged for the christening. When I rang Desmond to tell him the date I explained it had cost me my chance of a permanent teaching post or, indeed, of any future in the teaching profession in Hampshire.

For once, he was impressed. He took it quite for granted that it was one of my wifely duties, and – at last – I appeared to be giving some satisfaction.

"Of course, of course," he interrupted me, "no need to *go on* about it – only thing you *could* do, of course," he gabbled. "You should never have accepted the post in the first place – the whole thing is entirely your own fault; you should have asked me *at once*. I shouldn't have to *tell* you these things!

"Anyway," he finished grandly, "I *forgive* you. Just make sure the arrangements are made and *my son* is christened as a *Catholic* as soon as possible!"

The date was set. We laid out refreshments in the house for our return, although in the time available it had only been possible to arrange a simple ceremony with Thelma, my mother and a couple of acquaintances. I dared not invite anyone else if Desmond was there; he did not appreciate company – unless it was Susan and Dennis, or his drinking cronies.

The day came. No Desmond. Finally, a phone call – he had missed his flight, he would be there as soon as possible, but *go ahead* with the ceremony. Off we went to the Catholic Church. It was deserted. Eleven o'clock came and went. Where was the priest? We had no idea. The church was freezing, the service had been due to begin at 11.00 am, and it was now almost 12.00. No Desmond and no priest.

I came to a decision. "I'm not staying here," I told my sister. "I've done what I promised to do; I'm not happy about it at all and I'm certainly not prepared to catch pneumonia on top of everything else – I don't believe in omens, but this is ridiculous. Call it off; I'll explain to Desmond, and if he wants it organised, he can do it himself!"

"No," my sister said. "No, no. If *Desmond* wants John Paul christened, then we *must* stay." (Desmond's will was law as far as women were concerned.) She rang a bell in the church. A verger appeared and asked if he could be of assistance.

"We had a christening booked for eleven o'clock," I told him. "It's now twelve-thirty. Give my apologies and explain I couldn't wait any longer." I walked out. Immediately consternation grew and then things began to happen very quickly; my sister grabbed the christening robes, pulling me back; the verger darted off to find the priest; the priest rushed in, full of apologies.

I offered to come back – make another appointment when Desmond was here, but I was in a Catholic Church and they were not prepared to lose a client. The font was hurriedly filled with freezing water; a heater (one bar) was switched on, which had no effect upon the freezing temperature whatsoever, and the service was gabbled through as quickly as possible. But it was done. John Paul was a Catholic and we all went home.

Desmond rang. He was on his way (and in a very bad temper, by the sound of it). He was not remotely interested in the fiasco at the church. *Had* the child been christened or not? Yes? Fine, that was all he wanted to know. He then gave me the expected time of his flight arrival at Heathrow and I arranged to meet him.

With some trepidation, I caught the train to the airport. I was totally committed now; no job – no prospect of a job in the near or far future in Hampshire. And a Catholic child. I had no feeling for Desmond. Stuck in a marriage I no longer believed in, but I couldn't see an easy way out. Looking on the brighter side, at least I had my home, a resident husband and a beautiful son. Maybe I could work something out...

Desmond fell off the plane, hatless (he was proud of his Russian hat and refused to travel without it), coatless, and with a small case only. He was cold, shivering and *furious*. Clearly, he had been thrown out from somewhere – presumably by a returning, irate husband – after an unscheduled overnight stop.

I simply couldn't help it. "What happened?" I asked demurely. "What happened to your overcoat? Where's your hat? Where's the rest of your luggage?"

He was too furious even to reply. He stomped out of the airport. "Where's the car?"

"What car?" I asked. I'd been in hospital nearly three months, and then staggered straight out to teach – when and with what had there been any opportunity to buy a car? My sister had lent me hers to get to and from work for six weeks, but I really wasn't safe to drive, even now, and certainly not up to London.

"You mean you haven't even got a *car* to collect me in?" Silently, he stomped to the train. No seats. Standing, freezing, and glaring at the other passengers, he shook with temper and cold all the way to Southampton. It *was* cold, I had to admit.

In a furious temper he clambered out of the taxi. My mother opened the door with a greeting, but he pushed past her and went straight up to the main bedroom.

"I have John Paul in my room," I informed him. "He spent so long in intensive care, it was felt advisable to have him with me, in case of emergency."

"I'll use the spare room," Desmond quickly said.

"You'll want to see John Paul..."

"No!"

I could not help but look surprised.

"I'm *cold*," he said. "*Frozen!* I need a hot bath and some food. Good God – do I have to tell you *that*? Have you *no* idea? I want looking *after*."

"So how *did* you come to lose your coat? And *hat*… and *cases*?" I asked, discarding all pretence of tact.

"Oh, well… er, had an accident," he quickly replied, after which he refused to discuss his late arrival, was not the least bit interested in the christening, having confirmed it *had* taken place the previous day, and then demanded that the central heating be turned up and he be immediately waited on.

"Sorry," I told him, "the temperature stays at seventy degrees. If you are cold, put a sweater on. This is England, and if you are going to live here, you'd better start getting used to it."

There was only a bus for transport. I had in fact arranged to buy a car, due to the new teaching job, but that had all changed now. Desmond stomped off into town and came back with an overcoat, still complaining of the cold weather and the locals.

I carried on my routine with a new and demanding baby. Up at four-hourly intervals for feeding. Out walking with the pram. Local shopping with Susie Chow following the pram. Cooking and serving meals. Not Desmond's lifestyle at all. After a couple of days of thumping bad-temperedly around the house, he finally announced that he had booked a flight back to Hong Kong.

"But I thought you were now staying permanently," I said. "You were going up to London to arrange Chambers?"

"Got an appointment," he muttered. "No need for you to come to the airport; see myself off."

And off he went.

The following day he rang from Hong Kong. "Changed my mind," he said abruptly. "Couldn't stand the climate in England. And anyway, there is no work in London – not work I'd want, at any rate." That was it. The line went dead.

So now I had a Catholic child, no husband and no job. Nor any hope of a job in the future. My savings were almost gone and mortgage payments were due. On top of which, two thousand teachers had just been axed in Hampshire. Most had accepted early retirement; others had returned to domesticity, but put their names down on the supply list, prepared to pop in for a day or two at the school they had left, if the necessity arose.

Almost every school was now covered by at least one spare teacher. The only schools available for anyone out of town such as myself, and the newly available were the tough inner city schools, whose staff, if retired, would ensure they went elsewhere to teach. But still, I put my name down on the list, and I managed to get a morning teaching maths (fifteen miles east); an afternoon taking a class of five-year-olds (ten miles west), and off again the next day taking ten-year-olds for football before driving off in yet another direction for an afternoon's teaching elsewhere.

I was still getting up for John Paul's midnight feed, and again at 4.00 am, then awaiting a phone call to confirm the day's work, feed at 8.00 am, back for lunch and midday feed, out for afternoon's work, back home for 4.00 pm feed... and a (very) brief rest. Fortunately, the available work became less and less – but of course so did the money. And now my back was beginning to give out under the strain. My doctor expressed concern; so did my teaching acquaintances I met en route.

"But why is this necessary?" they asked. "I thought you were married?" "You should be at home with John Paul!"

How I would have loved that...

Finally, I had to face facts. Outgoings with John Paul were greater than incomings – repossession loomed. I went to a solicitor. "Either," I told him firmly, "Desmond helps me financially or I get a divorce. Even the work I manage to obtain, I only receive half pay for. If I am to be taxed as a married woman, and treated as a married woman, then Desmond, as the other half of the marriage and John Paul's father, contributes to his expenses. Otherwise, frankly, I would prefer to be single again."

"No problem," answered the solicitor. I left it with him.

There followed a furious phone call from Desmond. "How *dare* you consult a solicitor? I should be the one demanding a divorce from *you!* I have been very *badly* treated; I am *suffering* – you have *no* feeling for me."

I told him I didn't mind who divorced whom – all I wanted was a fair day's pay for a fair day's work. The divorce lawyer was unmoved; either Desmond contributed financially or divorce proceedings went ahead.

Furious telephone calls from Hong Kong followed. Proceedings went ahead. Finally, Desmond rang to say he was flying to the UK to sort things out. The solicitor advised against seeing him. "All he will do," I told him, "is talk over me and just insist that I do as he says;

there is little point in arguing with him and, frankly, I am too exhausted to take Desmond on – that is the reason I am employing a lawyer. Yes, he may come and I will listen, but it will make no difference."

The lawyer foresaw arguments and acrimony but I told him I was not prepared to tolerate this – Desmond had begged me to *listen* and *listen* I would.

He arrived bleak-faced. "I am *hurt… deeply* hurt," he announced. "Now you have *really* upset me. I have been *ill – very* ill, but I am not here to talk about that," he added nobly. "Just your stupidity; dear God, a first year student could tell you there is no cause for *you* to divorce *me. I'm* the one that's suffered – *I* should be divorcing *you…*"

I interrupted him. "I'm sorry – I'm afraid I have to feed John Paul now and then I'm off teaching."

"But I've come from *Hong Kong! All* this *way* to *talk* to you – we need to discuss this…"

"Later; sorry."

At 4.00 pm I arrived home for John Paul's feed and Desmond was waiting.

"Now, sit down and *talk*," he ordered. But of course, it consisted of him prowling up and down the lounge as though he were in front of a jury, discoursing on 'Why you should not have a divorce'. We went over the same ground – over and over and over again – while I dutifully listened.

"I have to give John Paul his eight o'clock feed now."

He had quite forgotten I was there; he was so carried away with his own monologue. I had been up since 6.00 am. I told him when I came back: "I'll wait for his midnight feed and then I'm off to bed."

Off he went again… how badly treated he had been… how lonely… how misunderstood…

"Twelve o'clock," I declared. "I'm going to bed."

He stopped, mid-stride. "But I haven't finished yet," he blustered. "Now listen to *me…*"

"Night!" I said, and left him to it. I was gone when he rose next morning at his usual 10.00 am. But he was ready for me as soon as I got home at 4.00 pm.

"I don't think you realise the *importance* of this," he began. "I'm a *poor* man, Binky, a *poor* man – and I've been very *badly* treated. Now the least you can do if you *must* have this divorce is to agree that you don't want any money from me. That would cause me *hardship*, Binky, and I *know* you wouldn't want that."

On and on he ranted. I was too tired to follow his arguments – they were pointless – but by midnight the following night he had quite convinced himself that he had really been badly treated; I *may* have a divorce if that was what I *really* wanted – anything, absolutely *anything* he would do to please me, but of course I must understand he could not be expected to *pay* anything.

Evidently pleased with his new approach, he continued, "Indeed, *you* should be paying *me* – *I* am the one who has been badly treated and, well any first-year law student could tell you – you've no *grounds* for divorce. But if *that's* what you want, Binky, then *that* is what you shall have... *anything* at all to please you!"

"Midnight," I said. "I'm off to bed."

"Well, I'm glad that's cleared up," Desmond replied and stomped happily out of the room.

When I got back at 4.00 pm, he had gone.

Then came the furious letter from my solicitor. Fortunately I had a day off and went in to see him.

"What's *this*?" he stormed. "What *is* this? I've a letter here from Desmond stating that you have agreed to no maintenance from him?"

"Absolutely not," I said wearily. "I told you, I am neither prepared, nor equipped, nor fit enough to discuss divorce settlements with a lawyer of Desmond's calibre. I said I would listen, and I did – interminably – and I am now exhausted. Frankly, his talk was just a load of rubbish which, as a divorce lawyer, I expect *you* to be able to deal with."

I could feel a degree of anger rising. I continued: "And I would suggest you tell him that he is more than welcome to come back here at any time to *talk*, and I will always be prepared to *listen* – but *nothing* else! I am paying a divorce lawyer to supervise divorce proceedings and I have no intention of interfering."

Mollified, the lawyer sat down.

The divorce went through smoothly on the grounds of unreasonable behaviour, which obviously incensed Desmond, but it went through and I was awarded maintenance payments of £450 a month.

I gasped with relief; at last I could relax – the house was safe. I could work as and when available, but no need to be charging around the countryside desperately searching for the toughest jobs in the county. And even, perhaps, some time at home with John Paul now. My mother had been delighted to note his first proper smile, his first sit-up, his amusing antics – now I could see them for myself and not hear about them second hand. More importantly, I might even get some *sleep*.

I could envisage a future again.

My first *single* cheque arrived; this time for the full amount – no tax deducted for the privilege of being *married*! No big deal – the days taken off going to see my solicitor and attending Court hearings had cost me dear – but it was worth it.

At the end of the month, a cheque arrived from Desmond – for £250. I waited to see if any more came, but none did. Still, my earnings had made it up to my pre-marriage salary, so there was enough to cover the mortgage.

The following month I received £250 again; and after that, varying amounts from £100 to £200 – in fact, whatever Desmond chose to send. But it kept the mortgage going. All work had now dried up; in any case, the little second-hand Metro I'd bought wasn't up to it. Neither was my back. I was being ordered frequent spells of bed-rest by my doctor and I was forced to take his advice.

Then, the school where my sister taught, needed a specialist teacher to take over a new class. The Head Teacher pulled a few strings and I was offered a term's appointment. So now I was working full-time; John Paul was on his feet and almost ready for play-school, which would leave me free. On top of which – if the venture were successful – I would obtain an excellent reference.

The money from Desmond had stopped completely, but there was no time now for solicitor's appointments. It was more important to get the teaching contract completed.

Completed successfully, the Headmistress recommended me for a Deputy Headship at a school seven miles out of Southampton. She also managed to get a place for John Paul in her school – out of the catchment area, but an excellent school.

Having established John Paul at his school, I was faced with the problem of leaving him there and driving the seven miles to my own school. Could he stay with my sister? Help her in her classroom the few minutes before school started? No. She could not possibly accept any responsibility. It only meant dropping John Paul off at school at eight-thirty and driving on to my own school, but I couldn't leave a five-year-old on the pavement waiting for school to begin. Taxis refused to transport an unaccompanied child to school… Reluctantly, I had to turn the job down. Back to square one.

I was really cross. Had Desmond sent the money the Court had ordered, even for a few months, it would have enabled me to employ a helper – just to get John Paul safely to school – and I could have continued my career. Very annoyed now, I returned to my solicitor and complained that the money had simply not been sent. Various legal appointments then followed and I had to forego supply work so that I was available for Court Hearings and all the other appointments concerned with them.

At the first Hearing, Desmond's solicitor turned up without statements of income – without any information at all, in fact. Desmond had been taken seriously ill and no information was forthcoming. It was adjourned for six months, during which time no money arrived and there was no response from Desmond. There were further appointments and another Hearing ensued. The money would now be paid, I was assured. The alternative was to get a High Court Hearing which would be detrimental to Desmond's career.

We arrived at court. My mortgage was now at risk. I was very fraught – everything depended on Desmond. His solicitor arrived and spoke with my Counsel. He had a personal note from Desmond which he had been told may be handed only to me, personally.

My Counsel consulted me. Perhaps a reconciliation? He suggested that, either way, a *personal* note from Desmond sounded encouraging and could do no harm. He agreed I may be handed the note. I unsealed and opened it; it was a badly written message on cheap, lined paper. The heading said it was from 'Ching Lee' and in pidgin English, it read:

Me velly solly to tell you – Massa, he velly ill – he dying of cancer and have just 3 week to live. Please Missee do not ask Massa for money, he dying but we in office no likee tell him – so you no askee for money.

It was signed by some Chinese, presumably from Desmond's Chambers.

Too silly, of course, but it had all been very fraught and having that thrust underneath my nose so unexpectedly was the last straw. Blindly, I stumbled into the Ladies and sobbed my heart out. Eventually, my Counsel's clerk came and thumped on the door. They were ready for the Hearing – but I was incapable.

My Counsel explained to the court what had happened. I was questioned, but it was quite useless. The Magistrate was sympathetic and castigated Desmond's solicitor for deliberately 'nobbling' me before the Hearing, but there was little he could do. The Hearing was adjourned again, by which time I should have composed myself and be in a position to present my case.

Needless to say – no money from Desmond.

I was determined I *would* get a Court Hearing and there were more appointments and discussions with my solicitor. Another Hearing date was eventually obtained. By now John Paul was attending school and showing promise; I was out of work, had 'signed on' and was receiving some State benefit.

I took John Paul to see the film, *Clash of the Titans*. He was entranced. I had made sure I would not make the usual teacher's mistake of trying to teach him myself – leave it to the school, I decided. I'd paid various helpers to come in and mind him when I'd been working, but it mainly rested on my mother – and as her sight deteriorated, she relied more and more on the 'Schools' programmes which she allowed him to watch on TV. But no one had taught him to read.

After the film, we went with the other children into the Corner Shop, where he spied a comic book, *Clash of the Titans*. Desperately, he begged for it.

"But you can't read," I told him.

He begged and begged, until finally I bought it and that night, sat beside him talking him through the pictures and telling the story. Each night after that, he wanted the same story. Every day, we acted out the story in the garden – I played all the girl parts, he, of course, was the hero, Perseus.

Then, as I came upstairs one evening – he had been in bed some time waiting for the story – I heard his voice… *reading*:

"And Per-seus came over the moun-tains," he was declaiming carefully, "thr-ough the mist to find the boat Danae had hid-den in the str-eam. Per-seus came and hel… helped Ap-hiro-dite… Ap-hiro… but *who*," he asked, as I came in through the door, "who is Ap-hiro-dite?"

I had felt cold, to the pit of my stomach, as I came up the stairs.

"Well," I said, as I sat down by the bed, "if you're going to learn to read, there are a few rules you need to know first. Her name is Afro-di-tee – Aphrodite."

"Oh, *now* I know who *she* is," answered my son, happily.

So at five, he was now reading Greek Myths and Legends; obviously I had another problem to tackle. Out of work, I offered to help on a voluntary basis. I noticed he sat with his hands held behind his back most of the time. I asked his young teacher why.

"Because," she replied, "no matter what I give them, he always finishes far quicker than the others, so I've taught him to sit with his hands behind his back while they finish."

I checked his reading book, *Johnny Appleseed* – a first, simple reader; this for a child reading Greek Myths and Legends, having taught himself to read out of desperation, since no one else was prepared to. I checked his writing book. In impeccable writing, he had copied out his reading book (unheard of – total time-wasting exercise).

Johnny Appleseed, he had written carefully, *goes up the hill.*

I turned the page and read: *Johnny Appleseed comes down the hill.* I turned over: *Johnny Appleseed goes up the hill again* – and on the next page: *Johnny Appleseed comes down the hill again.* And then afterwards, still carefully written: *I hope he brakes his neck.*

That was it. I'd seen enough. Each day he came rushing out of school and ran round and round the block, almost with steam coming out of his ears. A model child, I was told; never puts a foot wrong. At home reading myths and legends… at school going out of his mind with simple reading. At home counting, sharing, dividing, playing with numbers… at school going out of his mind counting *three* lettuces –

colour *one*, leaves *two*... then sitting with his hands behind him, to hold him back.

I had a word with his teacher. "I have the same trouble with all teachers' children," she smiled sympathetically. "They all think their children are brighter than anyone else's."

I had to agree; after all, I'd had the same problem, but this was exceptional and I could not accept her dismissal.

I tackled the Head. "A good teacher," she said dismissively. "Leave it to her."

So, there was no job for me in Hampshire, no money forthcoming from Desmond – and now... useless schooling here. Time to go?

I waited for the Court Hearing. If Desmond could be prevailed upon to pay the maintenance ordered by the Court, I would try and find a way out of the problem. If not, frankly, house or not, we would have to find a life elsewhere.

However, I met my Counsel for the Court Hearing, who pointed out that unless Desmond paid, as ordered by the Court, it would mean a prison sentence. Faced with that, he *must* pay. We went inside. The case was due to be heard at 2.00 pm. Desmond's solicitor arrived. He was calling a very important witness, he told us; but he hadn't arrived yet.

The Magistrate was clearly impressed. "If he's that important, we'll wait," he said.

We waited. Two-thirty came and went. The Magistrate looked enquiringly at Desmond's solicitor.

"A *very* important witness," his solicitor announced. "Flying in *specially* – from Hong Kong!"

Desultory conversation ensued. "Of course... flights unreliable... long way... problems landing... blah, blah, blah..."

The clock ticked on; it turned 3.00 pm. The Magistrate began to get restive. "I cannot wait any longer," he declared.

Desmond's solicitor stood up. "In fact," he announced, "*Desmond Donnelly* himself is flying in!"

Well, that was final; no one dared argue further.

Three-thirty came and went. I think we all knew what to expect by now. I certainly did and had given up by 2.30. Another trick; really, it was better than *Perry Mason* – and just as *hammy*. Even the Magistrate was embarrassed, and so he should have been – he had been made to look a complete fool.

Desmond's solicitor was duly castigated, which he accepted, subdued and cowed, but obviously enjoying Desmond's joke.

I had come to court to beg, either for some of the money I was owed, or, if Desmond continued to plead poverty, to ask if my rosewood dining furniture, that Desmond had kept as *something of you, Binky*, (and valued by Harrods at £21,000), might be returned to me – at my expense, of course. I had bought it, with Liz and Mary, before our teaching contracts had expired, and Desmond had piteously begged if he may have them in his flat whilst I continued to teach in Hong Kong. But they had been bought and paid for long before the marriage, and I still had the receipt.

The Magistrate gave everyone a good dressing down for wasting valuable Court time, but clearly a clever joke had been played and those in legal circles had appreciated it. From my own point of view, though, there was obviously no money forthcoming. "But what about my furniture?" I asked my QC. At least if I brought it back I could sell it – I was now seriously in debt and the house was forfeit.

A message had come from Desmond, through his solicitor: Desmond considered the furniture to be his own. In vain I produced the receipt.

"Come back to court if you want to argue about it," I was told. Clearly futile against Desmond. So the furniture had gone as well. Clever Desmond – beaten everyone in court *again*. "*If you can't stand the heat, stay outta the kitchen!*" Case over.

The fact was, Desmond Donnelly, QC, of Hong Kong was now a thief as well as a murderer, but of course, being a Queen's Counsel he was totally above the law – no one could touch him, he was inviolate.

I went home and wrote to my ex-Commanding Officer in Hong Kong, explaining my position. He was sorry to hear of the circumstances, but only too delighted to welcome me back as a single teacher. If I were prepared to be in Gibraltar in ten days time, there would be an 'Excellent-graded' school for me, requiring a Deputy Head for the following term, plus an equally 'Excellent-graded' school for John Paul.

We arrived in Gibraltar in two days flat. Glorious sunshine greeted us. We had been booked in temporarily at the Rock Hotel.

We duly presented ourselves at our respective schools. We caught the bus at 7.30 am outside the hotel; I dropped John Paul off at St. George's and then ran most of the way to get to St. Christopher's on time. I was distinctly apprehensive at leaving John Paul at a school I didn't know, but I had met the Headmaster, and his teacher, who were both friendly and welcoming – one foot wrong and we'd be *out!*

The playschool recommended by my sister, to get me back into teaching, had been disastrous. Run by over-qualified teachers – they all had degrees in one subject or another – and attached to a teaching college, I had left him, as I thought, in good care.

It was my mother who had finally accompanied him there. "Did you know," she asked, "that as soon as he arrives, the known bully of the school sets about him? Last time, he broke a blackboard over his head!"

The teacher merely sat in the corner and made psychiatric notes.

I told the Head Teacher of the school I was at, and immediately, she found a place for him – under-age at three and a half – but instead of coming back to a silent, frightened child, when I collected him, he was rolling on the floor in hysterics over some game his totally unqualified, but gifted teacher had made up to pass the time while waiting for me to dismiss my class from the Middle School.

So now into the hands of Shirley Frist and Mrs Good or, as she was known – the children told me – Mrs *Bad*. If I found John Paul sitting with his hands clasped behind his back waiting for the other children to catch up, there would be trouble!

I needn't have worried. This was, of course, an MOD Forces School, and impeccable – as always. I ran all the way back as soon as school was over.

What now? No sign of John Paul.

The Headmaster came running out to greet me. "We showed him the computer room – the other children play games on them, but he is *programming* on his! Incredible. Where has he been? What has he been doing?"

I explained the problems I'd had with him at school, telling him that he'd been trained to sit with his hands behind his back to stop him working ahead of the other children. He showed me into the school library. John Paul was rolling around the floor in hysterics.

"He's just discovered Asterix," the Headmaster laughed. "By the way, no need to worry about collecting him – we give him the run of the library after school hours. He is of course totally trustworthy."

John Paul scrambled to his feet, dutifully putting the book back in its allotted place. "Please may I come back tomorrow?" he asked the Headmaster.

"Delighted to welcome you aboard," the Headmaster replied.

John Paul was thrilled. "I can come back any time I like," he assured me.

We had found a home; a permanent contract and salary assured; an excellent school and a happy, contented child.

After school it was back to the Rock Hotel, where John Paul quickly established himself as the hotel favourite. Abdul, our waiter, was his slave – *anything* John Paul wanted was immediately provided. Arriving back from school, totally exhausted, John Paul wanted to watch TV; I just wanted to collapse in a heap on a sun-bed by the pool – swim and sunbathe. In any case, the TV room was out of bounds to children, *except for John Paul,* Abdul assured me. "He know *exactly* what to do; I have told him he in charge of the TV room."

John Paul would show me in, importantly draw the curtains, usher me to a seat and switch on his programme. At the end, he would throw the curtains back, re-programme the TV and usher me out again, with Abdul beaming proudly at him as we left. Most impressive.

It is fair to say that John Paul had the run of the hotel; he visited all the floors, chatting up the residents and, in the evenings, would be asked to join them in the lounge, where he happily regaled them with his daily exploits. He would open doors for elderly ladies, and run and fetch for them, and in return he was made a great deal of fuss of.

At the pool, we met Vivian Peralta with her two small daughters, a little younger than John Paul. John Paul immediately took over, helping them into the pool. At ten months, he had been a proficient swimmer. Now he took over, and Vivian and I could relax. "John Paul will look after the girls," she laughed. "Now *I* can relax!" Up until then, she'd had to keep her wits about her to ensure the girls were safe, but when John Paul was around, she was happy to leave them in his hands.

And so the days passed pleasantly; the future looked rosy again.

For about a fortnight.

John Paul's Headmaster caught up with me on the stairs, after school. "We have an HMI inspection coming up," he said. "A full one."

Every four years Her Majesty's Inspectors instigated a full inspection of the schools, and this one was imminent.

"It's about John Paul," he said.

Oh my God. More trouble... "What now?" I asked wearily.

"I have referred John Paul to the educational psychologist," he informed me.

This was for disturbed children – statementing them for Special Schools.

"John Paul?" I asked incredulously.

"Yes... well..." he answered, "it's not just for *backward* children. But you see, I've been monitoring John Paul – he is way above average, so I have had him tested and his IQ is *way* up. In fact, he is officially listed now as 'gifted' but not just in one area – it's right across the board, English, maths, computers – you name it." He gave me a very serious look. "He is, not to put too fine a point on it, a genius, and... well, something has to be done about it.

"It means leaving Gibraltar," he continued. "He must have private schooling. He will be available for scholarships – it will mean Prep School and a top Public School."

I shook my head. "Out of the question," I told him. My only chance of saving the house before it was repossessed depended on a permanent salary. My savings had long since gone, and although my investments were good, they were not enough to keep me.

I was introduced to the panel of Inspectors. "It won't cost you a penny," they assured me. "The only thing you will need to be aware of is that all the major Public Schools will be after John Paul – it would be a feather in their cap, you see, to have him. Regard John Paul as a *pearl* – to be cosseted; absolutely everything has to be made ready for him."

"But my job here," I began to object, "as Deputy Head..."

"Is as *nothing* compared to John Paul!" I was told.

Desmond for a father! I had given up so much – career, savings, investments – there was little point in sabotaging John Paul's career now. He was all set for a brilliant future; as I had been warned – my career was as nothing in comparison. I could risk it all... but for what?

A destroyed child. The deed was done and there was only one way forward. He had a brilliant future and I was the only custodian... no, it could not be risked.

So, back to the house and to hope some supply work came in.

Seven

Finally, the end of the final year at Prep School arrived. No work had been available for months now – I dared not even look at my overdraft; although it was enormous, it was dwarfed into insignificance by the amount Desmond now owed.

I remembered the letters that Desmond had written – one in particular telling me jubilantly how he had finally accomplished his ambition and cleared over £100,000 that year – a fortune in 1980 – but he had always pleaded poverty in court. Now *that* was proof of income!

I had kept all his letters and rushed up to the spare room to get my hands on them. Gone. He had used his last visits to clear out all his belongings – ties, socks, spare shoes, etc. including his letters – all of them... gone. Time to give up on Desmond. My QC was still insisting, with a London High Court Order as well as a Hong Kong High Court Order, that he must pay maintenance or go to prison. But not Desmond. Everyone else must pay their maintenance, but no, not him. He was *above* the law.

Still, John Paul was now back on an even keel and producing brilliant all-round results. Then came the visits to Winchester, Bristol and King Edwards in Southampton. Everyone was impressed with him and each school expressed the opinion that *theirs* would be the best for John Paul and so arrangements were duly made for him to sit the three scholarships. A walk-over.

Then came a call from his Headmaster. Would I take John Paul to Charterhouse as well?

The schools arranged their Scholarships in series; they were staggered so that one could not sit scholarships in 'out of series' schools. It was Winchester, Southampton, Bristol or Charterhouse, which was held later.

No, I told the Headmaster; I would not.

John Paul was definitely a *home* child; we had been sent to Gibraltar, separated, and he had been sent to Prep School against my inclination and his wishes. Now, *somehow*, I'd get my job back and John Paul would either commute to Winchester or, as we both secretly intended, be a day boy at King Edward's in Southampton and have some sort of home life.

There followed invitations, then entreaties – at least *visit* Charterhouse, it could do no harm. It was pointed out that, in fact, I had no right to refuse an opportunity for John Paul at ten years of age – which he might well regret later in life and, indeed, blame me for not allowing him to achieve his full potential.

Very well, I agreed, we would *visit*. John Paul sat all three of his intended scholarships. Having got those out of the way, there seemed no harm in accepting the invitation from the Headmaster of Charterhouse.

On arrival we were shown round the School. I had to admit it was far more impressive than any of the others. The educational psychologists had insisted that the world was John Paul's oyster, but only if he was placed in an environment *of his own choosing*. I had been warned – all the top Public Schools would be competing for him. Put too much pressure on him and he would be burnt out by the time he was twenty-one. He *must* be allowed relaxation – encouraged in sport, music and the arts and not force fed on academia.

Charterhouse had it all; a building which housed its own art studio, it had its own craft and IT workshops, its own theatre (comparable to any in London), its own eighteen-hole golf course and its own river, complete with craft.

John Paul was over the moon. What a wonderful place! Better even than Neville's offer of a billiard room and golf course!

We were thoughtful as we came home. As we left, the Headmaster had suggested – to help make up our minds – that he sit the scholarship anyway. It would do no harm; he had already sat three.

When the results came through, he had passed with flying colours. Of course. But what now?

I was called in to see his Headmaster, to be told that I could *not* turn down such an opportunity.

Finally, I went to see the Headmaster of Charterhouse. "Frankly," he told me, "Charterhouse is the only school that can satisfy all the criteria the educational psychologists have pointed out to you. Here, he can be allowed the freedom to not only fulfil his potential academically, but also to develop his other gifts in the Arts – a *complete* education."

I had to agree.

"Now," he continued, "the only problem is that he is officially two days too young to take up the scholarship; you will therefore need to pay the first year's fees of £13,000, at the end of which he will be offered a full scholarship, so no more fees, no more expenses and an education that will give him the opportunity to explore all his gifts and achieve his full potential."

With all the educational powers – and they were considerable – exerting all the pressure possible, I felt I had no choice but to capitulate. It certainly was a wonderful opportunity for John Paul and, finally, there would be no more school fees to pay. Provided my bank manager agreed, I said, I would accept.

"It *is* guaranteed," (my final passing shot) I said, "that if I can find the initial £13,000 for the first year's fees, he *will* be offered the full scholarship?"

"Nothing can be *guaranteed*," I was told. "Of course, he may have an accident and suffer major brain damage; he could be ill and not turn up for the scholarship next year. It will be your responsibility to see that he actually turns up, in which case he will certainly be awarded a full scholarship."

Good enough. I went back to my bank manager and explained the position to him. If I could borrow another £13,000, I told him, everyone's future was totally assured. He had, on previous occasions, listened grimly to my assertations of complete faith in my future – money would *definitely* be coming in from Hong Kong… a London High Court had assured the money… a Hong Kong High Court had assured the money. None of it had ever arrived. Both of us had finally accepted that Desmond was above the law; what applied to the man in the street certainly did not apply to him.

But this was different, it seemed.

"Until you got married," the bank manager pointed out, "you always maintained a stable job – your investments were sound and the properties you bought all quadrupled in value. It was only after your marriage that everything fell apart. I consider John Paul, therefore, to be an excellent investment for the future, and now that he will be boarding, it will leave you free to pursue your own career."

He must have been aware that there was no potential for me to teach in Hampshire now – I would certainly have to travel further. But I went home on cloud nine; the future was not only rosy, but *assured!*

No more school fees. They had been rising at an alarming rate. When it started, with a third of the fees being paid by the scholarship, I could *just* make up the difference. Over the three years at Northcliffe, the two thirds I had to pay had doubled, and then trebled.

"Get over the first year," I exulted, "and no more school fees *ever!*" My house was valued at £200,000; no more having to drop off and pick up John Paul from school every day – often not getting home until 9.00 pm and then having to rise early again for the next morning's drive. It had been a very wearing schedule and now all I had to concentrate on was my own career. Success at last!

I explained it all to John Paul that weekend. "A wonderful opportunity for you," I told him.

His face fell. "Does that mean," he said, "even after I have finished at Northcliffe, I *still* can't stay at home?"

"Well… *yes*, but you were so thrilled with Charterhouse – your own golf course, sailing, swimming, theatres, art workshops – the lot!" I enthused.

We had been to King Edward's. Two years ago, it had decided to become a public school but it was still a typical, if brilliantly successful grammar school. One building of classrooms, the football pitch and two tennis courts.

John Paul weighed up the situation. "I'd rather have stayed at home and gone to King Edward's, actually," he said. "But can I *really* play golf and sail and swim if I go to Charterhouse?"

"Of course," I confirmed. Clearly, even he was impressed by the glowing possibilities.

He was feted and made a fuss of at school; a notable success for Northcliffe. Proudly, it was announced on Sports Day, "… and John Paul has won a Scholarship to Charterhouse!" Clearly an achievement for the Headmaster of the prep school, as well as John Paul.

My bank manager was also impressed; not to *worry* about the spiralling overdraft… he had complete confidence I would now get myself back into full time employment. In any case there was always the house… two hundred thousand pounds worth; I now owed just a few hundred on it and then it was mine – outright.

We had a few frights. Susie Chow finally succumbed – to cancer of the throat. She was in no pain, I was assured, but her days were numbered. I had watched her anxiously. John Paul had only agreed to board at prep school for the last term on condition that he was collected immediately his games match was over on Saturdays, and he could rush home to his beloved Susie Chow. I had been warned – all three criteria must be kept in place… his home, his mum and his *dog*. What would happen when he came home and found her gone?

Out of the blue, Tim, a friend had rung to wish me *Happy Birthday*. I told him of my dilemma.

"Not a problem," he said. "I do appreciate that it's probably the last thing you want, but you probably should get another dog to replace her… if it's that important."

It certainly *was* the last thing I wanted – nothing could replace Susie Chow. But I did decide on having another dog; it would have to be the right one, and it could only be a pedigree. What I needed was essentially a guard dog, but good with children and not requiring too much exercise, since I would be at work. The answer was a rough collie – trained over centuries to stand guard, but prepared to walk for ever if required, and excellent with children.

I rang the Collie Rescue Service. They had the ideal dog. Normally free to a good home, this one had fallen foul of an owner struck down with a terminal illness, whose boyfriend was ill-treating it, and because it was a pedigree dog was insisting on the going rate for the breed.

Tim drove me all the way up to Milton Keynes and could not believe that I handed over the full asking price. We then went over to claim the dirty, emaciated, pitiful creature tied up in a muddy corner without food or even water. But he agreed no one with any feelings could leave her there in that condition.

She cringed as we approached and would not allow Tim anywhere near her; a sure sign that she had been subjected to abuse by a man. She accepted my presence, but I couldn't lift her on my own. With difficulty, and some distress to dog and rescuers alike, we finally got her into the car.

Terrified as she was, the first necessity was to bath and de-louse her. Then the two of us were left alone in the house. I had Susie Chow's old lead and food and drinking bowls which would suffice for now. It was going to take a little time to gain mutual trust and respect.

Susie's end had been peaceful; the vet had given me the pills with which to euthanize her when the time came. She had haemorrhaged in front of the fire and crawled up onto my lap as I sat on the rug with her and fed her the pills with some warm milk. She'd curled up and gone to sleep... then I drove her to the vet.

Now I had to face John Paul.

The match had been successful, of course, and he had fallen into the car with a couple of friends to be dropped off – high jinks, horseplay and schoolboy jokes all the way home. I still hadn't been able to tell him the news. He burst into the house and charged straight through to the garden.

"Where's Susie Chow?"

"Susie Chow was very old," I said gently. "She fell asleep, and I'm afraid this time she didn't wake up. You know she had been getting more and more tired and... well, finally she couldn't stay awake any longer."

John Paul's face went white. "I see." There were no tears – but there never were with John Paul. He went straight up to his bedroom.

Later, I called him down for a meal.

"I'm not hungry," he answered.

He came downstairs later, wanting a drink. "There's a dog underneath the dining table," he said. "Hiding."

"I know," I replied. "It's a dog someone asked me to look after and, since Susie Chow isn't here, I said it could rest with us for a bit. It's been starved and neglected, so I've washed it, and agreed it could stay for a while."

"I don't want another dog," said John Paul.

"Oh, neither do I... as I said, it's just resting for a bit; then it will have to go. I wouldn't go too close; it's hiding there because it's frightened."

After a bit, John Paul went back into the dining room. "It's still there," he told me.

"It's very frightened," I repeated.

After some thought, he said, "Perhaps it would come out for some food?"

"I expect it would." A glimmer of hope...

"Actually," John Paul admitted, "I *am* quite hungry; I think if we had some food, it might come out."

"I'll get your meal," I said. "You could try."

I brought John Paul's dinner into the dining room and he watched as the dog crept nearer and nearer, finally settling at his feet as he dropped morsels of meat down to her. There was no need to worry about a mess on the carpet – as he dropped (most of) the meat from his plate in small pieces, it was gulped down voraciously.

"She's very hungry," he agreed.

"I expect she feels a lot better now," I said with encouragement as John Paul went into the sitting room as usual, to watch his favourite TV programme. Automatically, the dog crept after him, on her belly. Children she could obviously cope with.

John Paul sat engrossed in his programme. Akita – Silver Indigo Lady, to be precise – sat and licked his filthy football boots until they were clean.

We had a dog. John Paul's permanent and devoted slave, but – to the end of her days – a man-hater!

Now life was indeed perfect. During the long, hot and, of course, perfect summer, I spent time getting the garden back together. It was a town garden – only a third of an acre, but the two lawns at the back, on separate levels, and two similar at the front, needed attention. After the scorching summer of 1976, the ground clay had baked and cracked, but gradually they came back to their original pristine state.

The pond needed digging out; not a pleasant job. The water lilies had overgrown and silted up. The Koi carp, not much bigger than goldfish when I left for Hong Kong, were now twelve to eighteen inches long and gasping for air in the overgrown pond. It meant clambering in at the deep end, hauling out the fish one by one, cutting back the lilies to their roots, replenishing the water, and replacing the fish. I hadn't been able to do it when Desmond was there; he was not impressed by the sight of me in wellies, digging in the mud and hauling fish about – one had servants to do that sort of thing... *Susan* would *never* be seen performing such menial tasks, but I enjoyed it. It was fun just watching the carp lazing with obvious pleasure in the clear water, with just a few lilies to shelter beneath when the heron came to visit.

But now we had Akita, or *Indigo Silver Lady*. She was a lady, to the tips of her elegant toes, and also perfection. The scabby, bald skin had healed and she now had a lush, silky coat. A Blue Merle tricolour, she boasted an enormous white ruff, sleek black shoulders, grey body, black and white tail which fanned out majestically and, as her name implied, long, silver guard hair. A truly striking dog.

As she moved regally down the road to the Common – a mixture of forest and green – with her behind swaying seductively and her huge, silver coat gleaming in the sunlight, she was greeted with admiration and adoration by neighbours and strangers alike. The local children would stop and make a fuss of her, burying their hands in her heavy fur – the smallest being allowed to pull her ears and tail; whatever, she allowed them all to handle her without complaint and accepted the accolades of adults with dignity.

A strong dog now, she was gentleness personified. She only ever had three faults, all of which I felt were perfectly understandable and acceptable. She was a greedy dog and would literally eat anything. When cooking, she would hover beneath, and her one treat was to catch all the off-cuts from the roast as they were discarded. One had no need for a *mechanical* waste disposal system with Akita.

She was so confident now, I would be greeted with enthusiasm whenever she came upon me. She would rise onto her hind legs, which brought her front paws to my shoulders, and resting gently against me, she would fastidiously lick my face. The first time, I had been surveying the neglected carp pond; gazing into its murky water, I had been pondering how best to deal with it when, bounding through the French windows, she had espied me, covered both lawns in a few silent and giant strides, and placed her paws affectionately between my shoulder blades with all her new-found strength. Fortunately, I had been standing at the shallow end which was only two and half feet deep. The muddy water had risen over my wellies and I suddenly found myself knee-deep in weed-entangled, muddy water, surrounded by panicking Koi carp, but I soon dived out. She did catch me a few times at the five foot end, but I was a bit more careful by then.

Akita and John Paul were inseparable. His friends came regularly and they all trooped off to the Common. She was the pride of them all. The boys were trusted on their own on the Common, provided Akita was with them. She had accompanied us to end of term celebrations at Northcliffe, where she entranced parents and pupils alike.

One of the parents, an amateur artist, asked if he may paint her portrait. She posed for him beautifully. Out on the Common one day, I was stopped and given a book of poems written by a visiting London poet. He had watched as Akita walked on the Common and had been inspired to write a poem about her. I accepted the book graciously. My neighbour, a retired police officer called Bruce, from South Africa, introduced himself. He had noticed her walking with me – may he be allowed to walk her?

To complete my perfect life, and having given up trying to get work in Hampshire, I had enquired with local private schools and had immediately been offered a temporary contract for a year, replacing a Deputy Head at a local Girls Preparatory School. I could now begin to replenish my lost savings and make some inroads on my debts.

My neighbour then explained he had retired through ill-health in South Africa as a police dog handler. He had walked Akita and found her so obedient – may he train her? I had been impressed; he was the only man she had trusted so far. Although greedy to a fault, she would only eat food that I gave her personally; she would not even touch biscuits or treats from any other. But after I had walked a few times with Bruce, she had finally consented to leave me – on my command only – and walk with Bruce to the Common. Bruce was thrilled; there was, he told me, an activity centre in one part of the Common for the active adults. So he put her through her paces; she walked along two-inch wide planks on command, obeyed his 'Sit', 'Down', 'Stay', leapt without hesitation over six-foot fences – everything his police dogs had been able to do. May he take her to the Police Dog Training Centre to see if she could officially pass their test?

I agreed.

That Saturday afternoon he came back grim-faced and crestfallen. *She had failed!*

Impossible. "What happened?" I asked.

"This is serious," he answered. "The police are concerned about your dog."

Your dog. Not Akita. This *was* serious.

It appeared that all the dogs had been put through their paces, Akita among them. She was faultless; several of the dogs had been discarded as they failed various tests. But not Akita. Then had come the final tests.

Jumping through a ring of fire. She had never seen this before. 'Stay,' she was told at one end. She stayed. 'Come!' had roared Bruce and without hesitation she had sailed through the flaming hoop. Then came the *Gunman*. Bruce walked Akita who took no notice whatsoever of the gunshots fired at her. The gunman attacked again – this time with a padded right arm. He fired two shots at Bruce and then ran. With a roar, Bruce commanded her to 'Attack', proudly confident of his impeccably behaved dog. Akita thundered off – a streak of silver-grey lightning. With one bound she leapt onto 'Thief' and effortlessly threw him to the ground, her teeth firmly embedded in his padded arm. All the police officers looked on with admiration as this impeccable dog obeyed her orders.

"Come!" commanded Bruce, to recall her and collect his accolades together with Akita's First Class rosette.

Nothing.

"Come!" he yelled. Clearly she hadn't heard him the first time.

She had. But disobeyed.

The police officer 'Thief' was now rolling around on the ground in some discomfort. Several policemen ran to the rescue as Bruce continued to roar 'COME!' in desperation.

It took several police dog handlers, with poles and loops to finally and forcefully drag Akita off the 'Thief'. Even then, poor Bruce said, she made a final snap at the 'Thief' as he was led, shakily, away.

"I swear," he said, sadly, "she went straight for the jugular. He showed me her teeth marks," he continued. "Went right through the padding – left a complete set of teeth marks in his arm." He shook his head. "Had she been a police dog, Akita would have been destroyed."

Her behaviour, for police dog purposes, had been totally unacceptable.

"She obeyed me at all times," he confirmed, "but when she thought I was being attacked, she showed her true nature and went straight in for the kill. She is now officially listed as a 'Killer' – one of those dogs that, if their owner or anyone belonging to them is threatened, is prepared to, and *will* kill! Since she is a privately owned dog and – hopefully – will never be put to the test, I was allowed to return her to you, but with a strict warning."

I was shocked. But it was true; she *was* very protective.

We had a huge and beautiful Persian cat, who was also the pride of the neighbourhood. He would sit on the wall to be admired by passers-by. He was held in awe by all the local felines; no one challenged him. But *thick?!* As a plank…

One day, a moggy had appeared from the nearby council estate; it had attacked several dogs and all the local cats hid in terror. Not Sam; he continued to sit on the wall and sunbathe. The moggy attacked him and Sam, very surprised – not to mention indignant – took refuge under a car.

Akita, of course, had soon taken control of Sam; he was allowed upstairs and in the living room and dining room but, for some reason, *not* on the kitchen floor – presumably because that's where Akita's bowl was. Sam had quickly trained himself to enter the kitchen and leap from the door to the top of the fridge (where I now began to put his food) before Akita's jaws snapped shut. I have never quite known what would have happened if he hadn't made it.

I was pottering in the back garden when Akita came to me, barking. I took no notice. She crouched and barked furiously at me, but I had no time to play at that moment, so I ignored her. Or tried to. When the barking didn't work, she caught my skirt between her teeth and pulled.

"Stop that!" I told her firmly. To my surprise she took no notice, and then, with her teeth firmly gripping my skirt, she began to go backwards down the garden to the driveway. She was by now a powerful dog and there was no way I could prevent being pulled along. Besides, I had every confidence in her. Eyeing me firmly and wagging her tail like a huge flag, to show she meant me no harm, she continued to pull me – down past the first set of ornamental gates, through to the front drive. By now I'd got the message – something was wrong, but she still refused to let go.

Through the second pair of gates – now across the road. She stopped when she got to the car. Letting go of my skirt, she sat at my heel, allowing me to survey the situation. Sam was securely under the car, petrified and paralysed with fear. Now I could see the problem; the moggy that had been terrorising the neighbourhood cats *and* dogs, ambushing and attacking them, was poised, out of reach on a far wall, waiting for Sam to emerge. His back was arched in readiness for an attack.

I went to shoo the cat away, but it immediately sprang to attack me. I managed to avoid its claws, but it only retreated to its original position – ready to attack again. It had reckoned without Akita.

Akita flew at it. Where the moggy went, I don't know – it all moved so fast. (In fact, it was never seen again.) Now Akita returned to me and looked disparagingly at Sam, rigid under the car, totally unable to move. I talked to Sam and tried to reach him. Nothing. He was lost in his own world – no longer Chief Cat of the neighbourhood – he had been beaten.

I reckoned that, with his brain capacity, it was going to take him at least a week to work that one out. What to do? Sussing my inability to deal with the situation, Akita kindly took over again. She left my side and, belly down, wriggled herself under the car. She caught Sam firmly by the scruff of his neck and then wriggled back out. Keeping Sam's neck securely between her teeth, she allowed his hind paws to touch the ground and gently walked him across the road. Poor Sam; he hung from Akita's teeth – even strong Akita would have found it difficult to carry huge Sam off the ground – until they reached the pavement, then she let him go.

Sam just stood there, swaying, still unable to move. Gently, Akita prodded him with her elegant nose. There was no argument – not with Akita. She wanted Sam to walk. He tottered, one step at a time, being prodded all the way; up the drive, through the gates, until he reached the kitchen step. *Home!*

Sam's eyes opened. Recognition dawned – he'd made it *home*! *Safe!* Cautiously, he jumped up to the top step; now he was on his home ground. Suddenly, he realised he was also on the *kitchen floor*! Wildly, he jumped for the safety of the fridge-top. *Snap!* Akita's teeth missed him by inches as he landed.

Satisfied that order was again restored, her duty done, she accepted her biscuit treat as well deserved, which it had been.

The attacking moggy was never seen again. But Sam had suffered a massive defeat. Not a pugnacious cat, his dignity had been offended; he was mortified. Totally above herself with her achievement, Akita looked at Sam, now cowering but recovering on top of the fridge. Triumphantly, she raised her head and barked sardonically at Stupid Sam. Now on home ground, Sam retaliated. He swung one massive paw in a mighty left hook and poor Akita, quite unsuspecting, felt her head almost separate from her neck as it was swung round. I think she saw quite a few stars. Shaking her head a few times to clear it, she then hurriedly retreated to the sitting room.

Once again, order was restored. The pecking order was re-established.

My life was now beautifully ordered.

I started my new job as temporary Deputy Head in September. John Paul started at Charterhouse. He was disappointed at not being able to go to King Edward's public school in Southampton, but was torn between that and all the opportunities offered at Charterhouse. All was in order; he had his home, (saved by the skin of our teeth) his dog – sadly not Susie Chow – but a dog admired by all his friends – and I had my job back. I had promised him faithfully that, although he must board and there was no alternative, he would be home *every* weekend. That was guaranteed.

At the end of the holiday, we set off for our appointment to the shop at Charterhouse, to get fitted out with school uniform. John Paul was impressed. Not only full uniform – that he had expected – but also the traditional *tuck box* with his name engraved on it; a massive trunk – also to be engraved, a man's overcoat as well as sports blazer, etc. Finally, he accepted his new status – he was being treated as an adult. Time, albeit reluctantly, to leave home.

Finally, the start of the autumn term. We drove off in style to Charterhouse. John Paul was introduced to his 'guardian', an older boy, to show him his new room on the ground floor as a First Year. The parents were gathered on the lawn outside the Housemaster's room and we were given a most reassuring talk by Mr Blake.

I had to admit that I'd entered John Paul into prep school and now public school, with considerable trepidation – tales of *Tom Brown's Schooldays*, and *Nicholas Nickleby's* dreadful *Wackford Squeers*, haunted me.

"Dismiss such thoughts from your mind," we were told. "Forget the old days. My House, at least," laughed Dr Blake, "is certainly not run on those lines." He continued to outline his philosophy – how he ran Robinites House, how it had evolved over the years and concluded, "In fact, if there *are* any problems, I may even ring you, as parents, privately. Or, indeed, you may ring *me* if there are any problems that arise, and," he added in a confidential tone, "we all know that *small* problems, indeed misunderstandings, may arise which, if left, *can* develop into *major* problems.

"I do not allow that," he told us. "If I have the slightest problem I will probably ring you – in total confidence – and tell you what that problem may be. We will then discuss it, and ninety-nine times out of a hundred we will be able to resolve it there and then, and without your child ever being aware that there was a problem in the first place! We just pick up the phone – you or I – and I guarantee to sort it out in total confidence."

We all gave a sigh of relief.

He hadn't finished yet. "And there is no bullying allowed; obviously I cannot speak for the other Houses, but in Robinites I do not tolerate *any* bullying, and, again, if you feel there is a problem, a phone call will ensure that it is dealt with – and promptly. But remember, with a lot of boys together there *are* high jinks, naturally."

Well, all that had reassured me. Really, it sounded just like home from home. The educational psychologists had insisted the world was John Paul's oyster, provided three things were kept intact – home life, his dog, and his Mum. A home life had been considered essential, but balanced against that I *must* select, from all the schools, the one that would not only allow him to achieve his full potential but also provide the same home environment.

Obviously, I had managed to achieve all three objectives.

I drove home. The sun shone; the day was perfect. So was life.

I started work at my own school, teaching English and Divinity as specialist subjects to beautifully behaved, interested pupils, keen to achieve good results and pass exams. I thoroughly enjoyed it.

At weekends I collected John Paul – the original golden boy; a model pupil, I was told. I positively *glowed*. Now he was Captain of the cricket team, Captain of the football team, top of the class again. Akita, reinstated as a model dog, was walked by Bruce at lunchtimes. It was late now when I collected John Paul on Saturdays since I had to wait and watch the regular matches against Eton, Harrow and the like. Life was really very busy now…

After-match tea and John Paul being congratulated on his successes, driving home (picking up a comic and video on the way), providing a meal for a ravenous boy before driving back to Godalming for 9.00 pm roll-call. On Sundays collecting him from Church at midday, home with comic and video, Sunday lunch, then pick up his friends. He would then take them on the Common with Akita for a game of cricket or football, back for tea and TV, drive his friends home and finally drive John Paul back for roll-call at 9.00 pm. Drive home again – two hundred or so miles. I hadn't been used to such a lot of driving; I was certainly working every evening now until 9.00 pm, teaching or marking work at home – and from 8.00 am until 11.30 pm at weekends.

But it was very successful. There was still no money from Desmond. I rang the QC; I thought it must arrive now that the High Court in London as well as the equivalent in Hong Kong had ordered it to be paid.

"It *should* have been paid!" I was told.

"It seems to me," I replied sharply, "that Desmond not only considers himself above the law, but *is* above the law!"

There was no reply from the QC. Fortunately, the house was safe and practically paid for and, at least for the coming year, I had an income and was still making good inroads on my now massive overdraft.

Winter arrived and John Paul was home for Christmas. There were vast celebrations, with all his friends round. More congratulations – I was now used to arriving at the end of term armed with my half dozen carrier bags in which to transport John Paul's even more impressive trophies – the Maths prize; English prize; Art prize; Best All Rounder…

John Paul had settled in well at Robinites. I was back in the swing of teaching; it was success all round.

One night I was awoken by Akita. She stood at the side of my bed and barked. Clearly something was wrong. I got up. No smell of smoke. Nothing. I got back into bed. Gently, Akita caught the bedclothes in her teeth and backed away. They slid off. She then firmly grasped the hem of my nightdress. Resigned, I allowed her to drag me across the hall and into the second bedroom. There wasn't a sound, but obviously something, somewhere, was wrong.

I looked out of the window. There was a shadow creeping out of the garage. As I watched, it crept towards the kitchen door. Akita, having given fair warning, opened her mouth to bark and clearly considered herself capable of dealing with the situation.

"Shush," I told her. Reluctantly she obeyed. I tried to remember what one was supposed to do. *Not* turn a light on; *ring Police.* I crept downstairs, dialled 999 and explained the situation.

"Great," I was told. "We've been out after a gang of burglars – one got away; now we've got him. We will surround the house." Slightly alarmed by the prospect of a siege, I listened as the officer gave instructions.

"There's a small wood at the back of your house. We will form a circle. One officer will knock quietly on your front door when the house is surrounded; you will let him in and he will then go through the house to the back garden and cut off the approach."

"Ah," I said. "There might be a problem there. I have a dog. I have told her to be quiet – she is fully trained but there is no way she will allow anyone into the house. I am keeping her under restraint at the moment, but with some difficulty."

"Madam," the officer replied with dignity, "our officer will be a trained dog handler. I can assure you that he will take total charge once he is there. All you have to do is quietly let him into the house."

"Very well." I was crushed.

Five minutes later, I heard a muffled knock on my front door. Holding Akita firmly on a leash and threatening her viciously with a fate worse than death if she dared utter a sound, I opened the door a crack. That was it; there was nothing now between Akita and the burglar. She leapt out of the door, over went the police officer, out streaked Akita – round the house, and down the garden. On flashed an army of powerful torches as the ring of police saw her – as did the burglar.

Upon seeing this silver-grey wolf-like figure (her guard hairs had risen with her hackles and produced a silvery sheen), the burglar fled, clearing the seven-foot fence with ease, crashed past the police, through the trees... and disappeared. The police grouped round the house, disgusted. A car set off in pursuit of the burglar, but Akita had taken everyone by surprise. Finally, disgruntled, they left.

Next morning, two white-faced and obviously unhappy police officers knocked on my door.

"*Very* sorry, Madam," said one, looking at a demure Akita lying, with elegantly crossed paws, at my feet.

"*Very* sorry indeed," said the other, "but your dog, in front of several police officers, attacked the burglar last night; without any hesitation, it leapt straight at his throat. The dog is a killer – it must be destroyed, Madam."

I hadn't expected it, although Bruce had warned me. "Not so," I assured them confidently. "You may check with Bruce next door. He is a retired Police Dog Handler and has personally trained the dog – up to *full* police dog standards. You will be aware that part of the training is to attack anyone threatening me or my property by holding with her teeth onto the arm of the attacker. This is what she has been trained to do, and is exactly what she did. Your officers shone your torch on the thief simultaneously, causing him to shield his eyes with his arm. The dog, therefore, had no alternative but to grasp his arm which also happened to be covering his *throat*."

The two officers took a step back and surveyed the situation.

"Akita, *stand*," I said casually. Thank God, she stood.

"Sit." She sat demurely.

"Down," I murmured. She sank to the floor.

"Stay." Motionless as a statue.

The officers watched. "But she *did* go for his *throat…*" one began.

"Nice dog," said the other in admiration.

"Blue Merle," I said modestly. "Indigo Silver Lady, actually."

"She's beautiful," said the other, and bent down to stroke her. He obviously smelt of *dog* – they were both dog handlers – and Akita responded, allowing her ears to be tickled.

"Off guard, Akita," I said off-handedly.

Immediately, she rolled over to have her tummy scratched. Operation Save John Paul's Dog successfully completed. Both officers were now on the ground, one tickling her tummy, the other her ears. Akita threw one front paw seductively into the officer's neck; with the other she playfully punched the second officer's midriff. He reeled. *Watch it Akita – don't overplay your hand.*

They got to their feet, a little sheepishly. "We are dog handlers; that's a beautiful dog."

"And fully trained," I murmured. "Of course," I admitted, "she does tend to be a *little* protective. You will appreciate as a retired… *disabled* teacher (no need to mention I'd recovered and was back teaching full time), I live *entirely* alone and depend *absolutely* on my dog for security. I am," I said, "very nervous living on my own. *What* I would do," I continued virtuously, "without my dog to depend on, I really don't know."

"That *does* make a difference," said one of the officers, relief showing on both their faces. "We agree, it was a misunderstanding caused, doubtless, by the thief being blinded by the torch lights and with his arm in such a position, it appeared that the dog was going for his throat."

"We will *have* to give you an official caution that the dog *could* be dangerous, Madam, and *that* will have to be recorded," the second one said, seriously, but with a pleasant manner.

"Oh, quite," I agreed. "I will guarantee to keep her under control at all times and, in future, when we are out, she will be kept on the lead."

"In that case, it's settled," they agreed, now wreathed in smiles. They talked dogs for some time, still watching Akita closely, but she was impeccably behaved.

As they left, one turned back. "Don't forget," he hissed, "if she ever does that again…" he drew a forefinger across his throat.

"Quite understood," I said. They then left, waving until they turned the corner.

I turned and looked at Akita sunning herself, rolling on her back after all the fuss that had been made of her. Reprieved. But I'd watched her – as had half a dozen police officers – and she *had* gone straight for the jugular. And I had no idea whether I could have called her off, even if I'd tried. Bruce certainly hadn't been able to. I eyed her thoughtfully. Definitely she would need watching in future. But I was determined now… nothing further would stand in our way. All three elements were firmly in place – a superb dog, a secure home and an excellent job, which would bring me the necessary references to guarantee future employment, outside Hampshire, if necessary.

The summer term was approaching, after which the full scholarship at Charterhouse would come into force. My job would guarantee that I'd clear my debts eventually; clearly, Desmond *was* above the law. He had steadfastly refused to pay maintenance or submit any bank statements and merely ran rings around any Court Order.

But the future was assured.

The summer term came and everything was going brilliantly. John Paul was coming to the end of an incredibly successful year at Charterhouse. I had received a glowing reference for *my* year at my public school and I had practically paid the house off.

End of term was hectic; pressure was building up. I was working at school – I now had end of term reports, parent-teacher interviews – and was getting home late at night. Saturdays meant collecting John Paul from matches; Sunday, driving him back late at night, then preparing to start teaching again on Monday morning. All had now been completed, and it was the last week of term. I was ready to collect John Paul, and had my carrier bags ready for all his trophies.

The phone rang. "Mum," a small voice whispered, "Mum. I'm in *hospital*, Mum. I've been *beaten*, Mum. *Twice*. I don't want to stay in this place any more, Mum. Please will you come and pick me up and take me home?"

I didn't even recognise his voice. It certainly didn't sound like John Paul; it sounded like a frightened five-year-old.

"Mum, can you *hear* me?" the voice whispered desperately.

"What happened?" I asked.

"There was an accident," he said. "At the school. A cricket ball went through Dr Blake's patio doors – just missed him. It could have *killed* him," he said desperately.

"But where were *you*?" I wanted to know.

"I was coming back from class," he replied, "with some of the others. Just as we passed his study, a ball whizzed overhead – straight through his patio glass."

"But you were with others? How many?"

"About six of us... but they don't matter. Mum, *please* can you come right now and take me home?"

I'd heard enough. "Right away," I said. "But just let me get this clear... you were passing his study, *inside* the goldfish pool?"

"Yes," he whispered.

"Therefore you were on the path immediately outside the patio window?"

"Yes."

"With half a dozen other boys from your class?"

"Yes."

"And the ball went *with force*, though a plate glass window? So *all* the boys were beaten?"

"No, just me."

"Why just you?"

"They all ran away."

"Fine. Now listen," I said, "I'm putting the phone down now. I am then going to ring 999, report the matter to the police and get an ambulance to collect you. I'll be on my way, but I may not get there before the ambulance."

"Thanks, Mum."

I put the phone down, then dialled 999. There would need to be an investigation – John Paul would be home for some time, and I was going to be tied up with end of term activities for the next week. There were two parent-teacher evenings, sports day, etc.

I rang my Headmistress and explained the situation. I would not be able to get in for the end of term.

A wily old bird, my Headmistress, said, "Hold on… now *think*."

"Nothing to think about," I snapped.

"Now listen," she urged. "Has John Paul actually sat that scholarship yet?"

"I *suppose* so," I said. "He should have done so last week."

"You depend on it," she replied. "Everything depends now on that scholarship. If you take the last week off, you lose two months pay for the vacation. You can't afford to; I know it's tough, but if John Paul is in hospital, he's in the right place – and you will have to watch your back. Without that scholarship, *you* can't *work*!"

She was right; I needed to think it through.

I rang Winchester School. Of course, they had been delighted to offer John Paul a scholarship last year, but I had turned it down… they would be delighted to offer him a place immediately, but it would have to be a paid place… £13,000 per annum… no, there was no possibility of a further offer, the scholarship had been handed to the next pupil who had come second to John Paul… sorry, it had gone…

I rang Clifton College. The same.

I rang King Edward's in Southampton. They would be delighted to have John Paul. They would only be charging £3,000 per annum since they could only accept day pupils, having no facilities for boarding. This I knew. This was where I had originally planned for John Paul to go – within walking distance of the house I had bought specifically. I had looked forward to John Paul attending there as a day boy whilst I taught locally – a normal home environment. All gone.

I rang Hampshire Education Authority, discussing it with the Chief Education Officer. Although they would do their best, since this was an emergency, obviously, two sets of their educational psychologists had specifically recommended that John Paul did not attend secondary school. He needed specific teaching which he could only get at a public school. Once I took John Paul out of the school, he forfeited his scholarship – no other school would take him. Added to which, there was no work available to me in Southampton and I would be unable to travel to find any. Feeling defeated, I put the phone down.

I rang back and tried to explain to John Paul. Useless.

"So," he said, "you're *not* coming to take me home"

"If I do," I tried again to explain, "it could mean you don't go to school at all, and I'd have to stay at home and try and teach you myself."

At the time, that clearly sounded like an excellent idea to John Paul. "Okay," said the sad little voice. "I suppose I'll *have* to stay here then..."

"Give me some time to work it out," I pleaded. "I'll have it sorted out when I come to collect you on Saturday." One thing was clear – I was well and truly over a barrel.

My year at the public school ended shortly. I was relying on a superb reference to get me work further afield. The house would have to be sold; John Paul would not just have an incomplete education in the state school – but none at all, and I would not be able to travel to find work.

I finished the term and then drove out to collect John Paul. After a week, he still wasn't able to walk properly. His friends silently helped him into the car and he lay flat on the back seat all the way home.

I called out my doctor for a report. He came downstairs looking grim. "A severe beating," he said, "but I *think* no permanent damage. I will make a full report."

It took quite a while for John Paul to settle and relax in bed. Akita totally ignored me – and all her prior training; on no account was she allowed in the bedrooms. She pushed past me, leapt onto the bed and lay beside John Paul, her paw on his chest, her nose on his chin.

I left them to it.

A couple of hours later I went up with restoratives – double steak hamburger, chips, lashings of tomato ketchup and a carton of unpronounceable ice cream, John Paul's favourite. I doubted it was on any hospital's menu, but it was certainly on John Paul's. Afterwards, we chatted.

He had been walking back, from school, with a group of his classmates, past the narrow path skirting the Housemaster's patio doors, when the cricket ball whizzed over their heads and straight through the glass. The boys had stood for a moment, shocked. Then they heard their Housemaster roar. They fled – all except John Paul.

"Why didn't you run?" I asked him.

He looked up at me with an expression of surprise and horror. "Would you have *wanted* me to run away?" he asked.

"No, no, of *course* not!" I answered, quickly. I dared not say what I was thinking. "So you were just left standing, to take the blame, when Dr Blake came rushing out? You had nothing to do with the cricket ball?"

John Paul came to life for the first time. "If you even have to *ask* me that, then there's no point in discussing it with you," he said bitterly.

I rang the school and made an appointment to see the Headmaster.

"I was unable to stop and see you at the end of term," I said pointedly. "I needed to get John Paul to a doctor immediately."

"Of course, of course," he said. "Quite understand, in the circumstances, of course. A most unfortunate incident," he murmured as we walked to his study. "But of course, John Paul has been punished and we can put the matter behind us."

"Oh no," I told him. "I am certainly not prepared to put the matter behind us. I do not accept that John Paul was responsible. I have seen exactly where the cricket ball landed – on the other side of a forty foot room, having passed Dr Blake's temple – missing it by inches apparently – first having gone through a plate glass window. As John Paul has pointed out to me," I continued, "he is not prepared to argue his innocence – he merely requests that we use our common sense in the matter. An eleven-year-old, untrained in the art of cricket, would quite obviously be physically incapable of hurling a ball from a standing position – and there were at least six witnesses on the path directly adjacent to the window. So," I concluded, "I will require a complete investigation into the matter. I did not contact the police at the time – I was too upset." This was the only excuse I could think of at that moment.

The Headmaster murmured sympathetically.

"In any case," I went on, "I presume you will do that here."

He became more uncomfortable.

"You *have* interrogated the other boys at the scene?" I asked incredulously.

"Er, no," he said. "No, in fact… no, we haven't. John Paul took the punishment, you see…"

"The Housemaster, Dr Blake," I said, "rushed out of his study, understandably in a fury, then, *not* understandably, grabbed the only child left standing there, who was clearly incapable, physically, of having committed such a misdemeanour, apart from it being totally out of character. Then he whisked him inside and without any warning, or questioning, delivered a savage beating."

"Throwing a ball through a window…" said the Headmaster, "… Dr Blake *was* understandably upset…"

"Maybe," I answered, "but having delivered his punishment, he then demanded an apology!"

"But John Paul refused," said the Headmaster weakly.

"Wrong." I told him. "John Paul immediately told Dr Blake he was very sorry the window had been broken; very sorry the cricket ball had been thrown, but since he had nothing to do with it, he was unable to apologise for having done it."

"Well, much the same thing," the Headmaster said unhappily.

"And so," I continued, "he gave John Paul a *second*, and totally inexcusable beating, which landed him in hospital for a week."

"It was our own hospital," the Headmaster replied feebly. "But there were only two options for me, as Headmaster; either I believed John Paul, who has been here for one year, or I believed my Housemaster, Dr Blake, who has been here for fifteen years." He suddenly increased in confidence. "It has to be said, Mrs Donnelly, that I make a point of backing my staff totally and completely in matters of discipline… and I will continue to do so. John Paul has an excellent record with us to date. The boy has a brilliant future, Mrs Donnelly. You must put this behind you. I consider it over and done with now – it is in the past. John Paul has his future to consider," he added, more ominously.

"So there will be no police enquiry?"

"We at Charterhouse consider ourselves quite capable of conducting our own investigations," he said, unmoved.

Clearly, I was going to get no further. I could either take John Paul away – give up the house, keep him at home and teach him what I could – until at eighteen, presumably without adequate education or qualifications, he tried to get a job and I tried to get back into teaching whilst living in B&B accommodation – I either did that, or I accepted the situation.

Of course, it would have been very different had John Paul had a father. I was up against a very determined and powerful school; I hadn't yet realised just *how* powerful and determined... John Paul and I were beaten into submission.

I returned home. At least, for the moment, we still had that. Then, finally, I plucked up courage and rang Dr Blake. I was sorry, I said carefully, to hear about the accident.

"Indeed," said Dr Blake formally.

"But John Paul did take the scholarship paper?" I asked anxiously.

"He did, yes."

"May I ask how he did? It wasn't in his report."

"Immaterial," he answered grandly. "It has been discounted."

"Discounted?" I gasped. "Why?"

"On behavioural grounds," was the terse reply.

"But John Paul has said he had nothing to do with the incident," I protested. "It would have been a physical impossibility, and in any case, there were witnesses..."

But the phone had gone dead.

Furious now, I rang the Headmaster.

"I am sorry," he said, "that Dr Blake has reacted this way. But I have no alternative but to back my staff to the hilt, and he has made his decision."

Dr Blake was well and truly taking his revenge. There would be no scholarship, but John Paul had no alternative now but to stay at Charterhouse. I went back to the bank manager. He listened as I explained I would need further assistance.

"Mrs Donnelly," he said, at length, "you had a huge overdraft of £15,000 to begin with, and no permanent job. You borrowed a further £15,000 for John Paul's first year at Charterhouse – at the end of which, you assured me his education would be free there, and you would return to full time employment. Now, you may have noticed that the country is in the biggest recession since the thirties... I fear I have no alternative but to call in the loan now."

There was nothing for it but to sell the house. I now had less than six weeks to do it in if John Paul was returned to Charterhouse in September. The last time I'd valued it, the house had been quoted at £200,000.

The same agent came back. "A good house," he agreed, "but that was a few months ago. Nothing is selling now; I would have to advertise it at £150,000."

I was disappointed, but now I was aware, for the first time, of how desperate the present recession was becoming. But a buyer came the following day; he seemed impressed.

The agent rang me, thrilled. "An offer of £145,000," he gloated.

"Great," I agreed, "but you won't take it off the market, will you? They didn't seem very sure when they were here and they are *very* young!"

"First time buyers," he said confidently. "The best. Leave this to me."

I heard nothing. I passed the office window; the particulars of the house had gone.

"Yes, of course," said the salesmen inside. "It's been sold."

I rang the agent. "You've taken the details out of the window," I accused.

"Oh well, yes," he said awkwardly. "But Mr and Mrs B are *very* keen."

"Why has no survey been carried out yet?" I asked him.

"Get on to it right away!" he replied.

Another fortnight. I rang again.

"Thought it had been *done*," he said.

A few weeks left to September. The bank was demanding the overdraft be cleared *immediately*. I rang the agent. "Unless completion of the sale takes place next week," I told him, "I am taking the house out of your hands and instructing another agent.

"Really awfully sorry," he said. "But the buyer actually lost his job and so... well, he can't purchase the house."

It was re-marketed.

By now, it was clear I was in desperate straits; there was no option but to put my cards on the table. Six more potential buyers came to view the house. But these were different – these were the *wolves* – the speculators – out for a quick kill.

They circled carefully. The agent had clearly explained my position. They waited for one to weaken first, and put in an offer. Then they would see how long I could hold out, and better it. They soon discovered how long I could hold out. The new term was ten days away. Could John Paul make it in time or not?

Suddenly, one of the six put in a cash offer. £105,000. John Paul was delivered to Charterhouse in good time on the first day of the new term. There was no scholarship; I returned home.

The beautiful Steinway grand piano was the first to go. Wherever I was going, there would be no room for that. I went through the house. All John Paul's old toys; libraries of immaculately kept annuals, classic children's tales, sports equipment – John Paul had always taken meticulous care of his belongings, and I had stored them lovingly for the next generation. I hauled them all down and took them to the next car boot sale, where they were eagerly snatched up.

The house began to clear.

I had re-ordered my Chinese furniture, having given up all hope of getting Desmond to return mine from Hong Kong. I was determined I would keep these replacements. Everything else could go.

With days to spare, I managed to find a small house on the 'wrong' side of town, but with enough space to create an illusion of 'home'. We moved in and at last, I could clear my account at Lloyds – the manager and I were at least on speaking terms again.

John Paul was back at school. Still bitter; we had somehow managed to survive another Black Hole. "There's nothing else to be done," I told him. "My fault, I should never have accepted that wretched scholarship in the first place – we should have stayed on in Gibraltar, but it's done now and can't be helped."

"It *wasn't* your fault," John Paul had said. "If it hadn't been for the cricket ball, everything would have been fine."

"You just have to work through it now," I said. "I *know* you had nothing to do with it. Now you have to show your worth – *prove* you were worth that scholarship and that no way could you ever have done such a stupid thing."

"Thanks for believing in me, Mum," he'd said.

"I can't understand, though, why he should have beaten you the second time," I said. "Not after you had at least said you were sorry that it had happened – even though you couldn't say you were sorry that you'd *done* it."

He'd grinned. "I think it was *what* I said after the *first* beating."

"And what was that?"

"Well, after he'd pulled me in and thwacked me with the cane – and it *hurt*, Mum…"

"Yes?"

"Well, he just kept shouting at me – '*Now* what have you to say? *Now* what have you to say?' over and over again, standing over me with the cane."

"So, what *did* you say?" I asked curiously.

"I said: 'I hope that gave you great satisfaction.' So he beat me again. That did make him cross," he added as he collected up his books and prepared to go back to school.

Yes, we had pulled ourselves up out of the Black Hole.

The new house needed re-decoration throughout; the garden was just a sea of mud. Oh, for my beautiful carp pool! But I stripped the walls, re-papered; stripped the paint, re-painted; took up filthy carpets. And then came the pleasant time – choosing colours, matching fabrics, up and down the ladder – and from the ceiling down, it began to live. Up went the crystal chandeliers, the full length velvet curtains, and out came the rosewood dining table, the huge sideboard and the silver.

In the garden, the mud dried out and was dug, re-dug and prepared. Then lawns were laid. No room, alas, for a carp pool, but I had a miniature one instead, with tiny goldfish. Paths were laid and shrubs were planted; it was *home* and we were *civilised* again.

I welcomed John Paul for his first weekend in his new home. Would it do? Or having lost the most important one of 'The Three', would he do as threatened, and 'collapse like a pack of cards'? I drove up to Godalming on tenterhooks, trying out various explanations: 'You'll like the new house'… 'I'm very pleased with the new house'… 'It looks almost like Batemans'… or should I ignore the subject altogether and hope for the best?

He came out to greet me, without enthusiasm. "Have to go, Mum. The match is in five minutes."

I watched as he led his team out, to success, and was back as usual for match tea with other parents. Afterwards I drove him home. None of the other boys went home on Saturdays, but it was the only way he was prepared to board the rest of the week. We drove in silence. He was 'listening to the radio'. At home, was 'not hungry' and went straight up to his room with Akita.

After a while, I called Akita down. Reluctantly, she came, followed by John Paul.

"You're going to have to put what happened behind you, John Paul," I said firmly. "This is important. As the Headmaster said, you took the punishment and it's over, whether or not it was deserved. I sold the house; as I've explained – we just *have* to make a new start."

"I know, Mum; that's what Mr Attenborough told me... but I *can't*."

"Why can't you?"

"When I got back to school," he began, "before I'd even looked on the list to see what room I'm in now, Dr Blake rushed out and pushed me into his study. He stood in front of me and said, '*Now* you will apologise for that cricket ball through my window. You will write out an apology for me.' All I could say, Mum, was what I'd said before; I *said* I was sorry the ball had gone through his window – I told him that, over and over – but I *can't* apologise for something I haven't done!"

I felt a chill down my back. "So what happened?"

"My *punishment*," he said, with a weary sigh, "for not apologising, is to clean the lavatories out every day. I have to get up two hours earlier – at five am now every morning, and clean the lavatories out before the other boys come down to use them at seven."

"Clean the *lavatories*?" I gasped.

This, for a child who had been fussed over and waited on by my mother while I went to work – had then gone on to prep school against all of our wishes and been waited on there, and then on to Charterhouse. To date, no one had even shown him how to wash up a cup and saucer. I simply couldn't imagine how he had managed as a twelve-year-old, being confronted with the evil smelling lavatories for which the school was famous, and having to *clean* them. Parents delicately avoided the issue and the boys merely got used to it, and now John Paul had been given a mop bucket and cleaning materials and told to 'report at five am.'

"How did you manage?" I asked him.

"Dr Blake comes down at seven am to inspect it," I was told. "It wasn't good enough, so I had to do it again. I am not allowed breakfast until it is clean. Didn't really matter, I wasn't hungry after I'd done that."

Hardly surprising.

I thought about ringing Dr Blake, but the position was clear. The battle lines had been clearly drawn, and I was totally over a barrel now. I could take John Paul away – any time I wanted – but then we simply lived at home until the money ran out, and John Paul ended up without education altogether. *If only* we'd stayed in Gibraltar! But no use looking back – the die was cast.

"Can you do it?" I asked John Paul.

"Oh yes," he said. "Actually, when Dr Blake wasn't looking, the Head Boy came down and ordered a couple of my friends to help me. None of them knew what to do," he giggled. "It was quite fun, really. Ed tipped over the bucket and Tom slipped up on the soap I'd left out… anyway, we *did* it. When Dr Blake came down after breakfast, he had to admit it *was* clean and he was surprised. Ed and me and Tom, and a few others, we said we'd *show* Dr Blake, we'd get it clean – you *see* if we don't – and I've only got another week to do."

Even when they came back as sixth formers, there were gales of laughter when they recalled that fortnight. John Paul had, in fact, risen at 4.00 am and gone down to ensure that the lavatories were clean, white, and sparkling, before the boys came down. When they did, they were formally lined up and, should a speck mar any of the china, they were ordered to wait while he carefully and ostentatiously polished it back to pristine whiteness. It was a joke and by the end of the fortnight – the joke of the school.

But at least it was over.

The next weekend, I collected him with an easier conscience. The new house had been scarcely noticed. John Paul just wanted desperately to come home. Once inside, all the furnishings, although less of them, were there, familiar and waiting. It was enough. I was therefore surprised when, even after another successful match and match tea, he was again silent.

"I'm glad you did the extra punishment, and took it so well," I told him encouragingly.

"Yes," he said, "but it wasn't enough."

The punishment had clearly misfired. The boys, instead of humiliating and shaming John Paul, had turned the situation around – as boys will. They accepted that John Paul, as the youngest pupil ever taken on by the school, had reacted well to a punishment which they considered was grossly unfair. They were prepared to help.

John Paul had therefore been taken straight into the study and faced with an ultimatum.

"Apologise for putting that cricket ball through my window and put it in writing; otherwise the punishments will continue until you do."

Resignedly, John Paul had repeated his earlier statement. He was very, *very* sorry that the cricket ball had gone through Dr Blake's window, but it was nothing to do with *him*.

His watch and clock were therefore removed from his room; he must now get up at dawn in order to get down and clean the urinals in time. Failure to do so would result in *no breakfast*.

Another fortnight passed.

He had now made some good friends at school. Also, the Head Boy oversaw the punishment now, and John Paul was kept going by their various attempts to assist him and make things easier. One had lent him an illuminated watch to hide under the bedclothes – boys have their own ways of dealing with the vagaries of adults.

Finally, that fortnight came to an end. By now, the situation was clearly becoming impractical. Dr Blake was obviously keen to find a solution. The following week when John Paul returned to school he was called to face Dr Blake in his study.

"Now, John Paul," his Housemaster said. "You have completed your punishments. Time to bring this matter to an end. I like to think I run a *democratic* ship here – the punishment fits the crime, and you have completed the punishments I set you. Now, I want your *honest* opinion – it *was* justified, wasn't it?

But Dr Blake had again reckoned without John Paul. He was always a model student; a model son – and had never been known to tell a lie. The school, one of the largest in England, was an awe-inspiring edifice – the masters and the whole ambience, were daunting to behold, and certainly to cross. To a small child it must surely have appeared overwhelming…

Not to John Paul.

The answer came straight back – between the eyes.

"The punishment," said John Paul, "was vindictive, petty and mean – and entirely in character… Sir."

"HOW DARE YOU!" roared Dr Blake.

"Sorry, Sir, but you did ask me for an *honest* opinion," said John Paul.

Another punishment followed, and then another. John Paul continued to say sorry for the fact that the cricket ball had gone through the window, but it had been nothing to do with him.

I decided that there was now no alternative but to accept the impossibility of Charterhouse. He had in fact been there over a year. He would take his GCSE's early – another three years. Somehow we would have to endure it, but once he had those results, he would have proved his scholarship status; already it was becoming clear that he had nothing at all to do with the accident, but he had conducted himself with great dignity for his age and had never once – even after an unprecedented severe beating – shed a tear or given way by an inch. He was becoming something of a hero among the boys... one who was always polite, but steadfast in his beliefs. I would have to be satisfied with that.

I had been applying, desperately, for permanent jobs. The first three I applied for, I was interviewed and accepted, over all other applicants. And after each successful interview, the Head Teacher had rung me back.

"I'm sorry," each one had said, "but we now have a new system. Our Board of Governors must now include two *parents*. I, as Head Teacher, appointed you, but these governors have pointed out that with your qualifications, you are twice as expensive – we could get two teachers straight out of college instead of you. I have, therefore, to withdraw the offer."

Finally, I had an interview with a C of E aided school. Twenty miles away; but I could now travel farther afield, and was prepared to do so. I arrived for the interview. All three of us had made sure that we arrived early, and we were settled into a small room to await our calls. We discussed the situation.

"I don't stand a chance," said one – a middle aged woman. "I got my teaching certificate, but I've never taught. Now my family are growing up, I'd like to start, but frankly, this is just *interview* experience."

"I don't stand a chance, either," said the other. "I only finished college last week; they're looking for an art specialist to do art and display throughout the school, and their music teacher has left, so they said music would be an advantage. On top of that, it's a Church school, and I don't know one end of the Bible from the other."

"What about you?" they asked.

"My specialist subjects are Divinity and Art," I said, "but I specialised in music while I was in Hong Kong and my interest in drama means that I'm used to undertaking music festivals, putting on Nativity plays, etc."

At which, the young teacher burst into tears. "I'm leaving," she said. "I'm so tired of going to interview after interview and being turned down through lack of experience! But how," she sniffed, "how am I going to get any experience unless I am given a job?"

"Don't worry," I told her. "I am just here to check out an idea I have – that I may have all the qualifications they want, and more, but they will take on the cheapest option. The fact is, they cannot afford to employ me – I'm the one who doesn't stand a chance!"

Unbelieving, the young teacher was, nevertheless, persuaded to stay.

The Headmaster came in. "As you know," he said, "the post is for an art specialist – we've just undergone an inspection and the quality of the work was deplored. We want someone who can not only take classes, but *display* work throughout the school. On top of which, our music teacher left, so there is no music... and no assembly can be held, as we have no proficient Bible student to hold it... and parents are complaining there will be no Nativity play this year unless we can find someone to undertake that also."

The young teacher was already on her feet. "I feel I am just wasting my time and yours," she said. "I can offer none of these things."

"Ah," said the Headmaster. "Perhaps you may be interviewed *first* – it's important that you stay."

We all had our interviews. Yes, I could undertake assemblies, play the piano, put on Nativity plays, arrange art displays – whatever.

The Headmaster glowed.

"How long have you been teaching?" asked one of the Parent Governors.

"Experience takes time to achieve," pointed out the Headmaster hopefully.

An hour later, we were called in to hear the decision.

"I expect you will be surprised by our decision," the Headmaster began, "but you will appreciate that, at the present moment, finance is of the utmost importance. We have therefore decided to offer the post to *you*..." he beamed at the young, new teacher.

She had already been poised for flight and was ushered, somewhat bemused, back into the interview room.

As I drove home I reflected that if I wanted work, I would clearly have to look outside and beyond Hampshire. All the money had gone into the house; I had relied on some work being available – even supply teaching. At the end of each term now, I had to find £5000 for Charterhouse fees and it simply wasn't there. I was not allowed one penny overdraft, so I either paid up or took John Paul away – to nothing.

The house was furnished and had been redecorated throughout; the garden had been overhauled and landscaped as the Exbury House gardeners had shown me. It was immaculate; I put it on the market to sell. Reluctantly, I went back to Morris Dibben – they certainly gave a good display in their window if the house was worth it. I called them in. They would be delighted to market it at £10,000 above the price I'd paid for it. The recession was easing up now and houses were beginning to sell again.

I had been assured I would never get a job in Hampshire; I now had time to apply elsewhere, but just to make sure, I applied for every single advertised job in Hampshire for which I had full qualifications. I then sent for a vacancy list from Wiltshire, Devon, West Sussex and Surrey.

In all, it cost £300. I would need to do that every month. Nothing from Hampshire; I was offered interviews, but having established lengths of teaching, the Head Teachers agreed they would not be offering posts to anyone with more than three years experience – too expensive.

Wiltshire proved the same. Devon were prepared to offer several posts; West Sussex offered interviews. Encouraged, I pointed out the distance and they were prepared to cover travel expenses for me to teach there, or suggested they helped fund accommodation in West Sussex if I were prepared to move.

Problem. There was no way I could get John Paul home at weekends. It was the only thing keeping him going at the moment. It was becoming more and more of a struggle to get him back to school after the weekend – not that he ever argued, he merely became stuck on the loo in anticipation of the following week's punishment.

There came an offer from Surrey. They were determined they could better the one from West Sussex – they would supply accommodation. They listened to my plight and were most sympathetic. They offered an excellent school for John Paul; a house would be found for me and they would assist with mortgage arrangements.

I went home. It would mean throwing up Charterhouse after all the effort of getting there. Before I decided, I sent written applications to five prep schools in London who were advertising.

The first school rang. "When can you come up to visit the school?" they asked. (Give me half an hour…)

"Any time," I offered.

The second school then rang and made an appointment, followed by the other three. By now I was inundated, and had only taken phone messages. I rang the first school back to confirm times. "I'm getting a little confused," I confessed. "I wasn't expecting to get so many replies…"

She was appalled. "You don't mean…? You are not looking at other schools?"

"Well, yes," I told her. "I am only going for interviews." (And I knew how useless that was.)

"Oh, heavens, no," she said. You are coming to *visit* – so that the children can meet their new teacher. You've already got the job, you see…"

"But I haven't had an interview," I explained.

"No. We went by your qualifications," she replied. "You're over-qualified, of course, but if you don't mind giving the Deputy Head here a hand, we would be *so* grateful."

Impressed, I put the phone down. I had a job!

The phone rang again almost immediately. It was the second school.

"I'm sorry," I said, "I have just been offered a job," and explained the misunderstanding.

"Have you accepted in writing?" she snapped.

"Well, no – I've only just put the phone down…"

"Well then, before you decide, take a taxi from waterloo and come and see us."

It made sense. I got the train up, had a look at School One. Next door to the Natural History Museum and very convenient – a five-minute bus ride from Waterloo. Then I took a taxi to School Two in

Chiswick. This was about an hour's drive – definitely too far. Still, I was welcomed and given coffee whilst I drew breath and pointed out the disadvantage of distance.

Miss Baker, a homely spinster, sat down and chatted. She wanted to know about Hong Kong, Gibraltar, and John Paul. We talked at some length.

Finally, she said, "I want you here."

"I would love to teach here," I told her.

"I'll do a deal," she said. "I'll pay from today – only half pay (it was mid-June), but I will pay from now and then you will start on full pay on a permanent contract in September."

"Done," I said.

It would mean an hour and a half's travel, daily, across London, which meant getting up at 4.30 am to catch the 5.40 train up and getting back between 8.00 and 9.00 pm. But I had a *job*; John Paul's education was *saved*.

The future looked rosy.

John Paul went back to school. I drove up at the weekend and after the match, we drove home. He fell asleep in the car, crawled out, was too tired to eat, and by 5.00 pm was sound asleep again.

"What *have* you been doing?" I asked him.

"My punishment this fortnight," he said, "is to sweep the leaves from the flat roof on top of Robinites House.

"Now?" It was November, and bitterly cold. The grove of beech trees between Robinites and the next House would be losing their leaves continuously.

"Yes," he replied. "And as soon as I clear them, more fall, of course. Unless the roof is *completely* clear of leaves when I call Dr Blake to check it, I have to do it all over again."

"But that's impossible," I protested.

"Well, it is," he agreed, "because it can be anything up to half an hour before Dr Blake comes up to check. But I am not allowed to go for supper until he has checked it, and then there's not much left. Only *this* week, Dr Blake kept saying he forgot and by the time he came up, supper was over, so I didn't get any at all. I expect that's why I was so tired," he said, "I was up there for over an hour, and then of course, I had all my prep to do."

"Now, this is just ridiculous," I said. "I'll have to write and complain. You cannot be expected to work without food. I will write again to the Principal of the Governors."

I had been somewhat dismayed to find that the Principal Governor of Charterhouse was, in fact, HM The Queen. Still, I needed to make a formal complaint to the Head of the School and it shouldn't make any difference who wore that particular hat.

I had a letter back, shortly to this effect (the original letter is still in Gibraltar):

> *Her Majesty wishes to say she is sorry to hear of John Paul's unfortunate occurrence. She has written to the Headmaster requiring a full explanation and will write again once she has been made aware of the facts.*

Well, thank goodness, I thought. Now I'll get it all sorted out. I explained to Miss Baker, my Head, that I would certainly remain for the end of my contract now. All was well.

Miss Baker, that wily old bird, merely said, "We'll see. Glad you've decided you can stay on."

Then came a second letter to the effect:

> *Her Majesty has been given to understand by Mr Attenborough, Headmaster, that since John Paul was alone at the time of the accident with no one else in the vicinity, he had no option but to allow John Paul to take full responsibility.*
> *Her Majesty very much regrets… etc, etc.*

WHAT? ALONE? What about the half dozen boys with him at the time – and in full view of the school? (Unfortunate that they had all run away).

And what about the fact that it would have been physically impossible for any ten year old to hurl a cricket ball with such velocity that it broke a reinforced window and continued to travel forty feet, nearly hitting the master at eye level?

I was devastated. I had taught at State schools, and at Private schools, but NEVER had I come across a headmaster prepared to lie through his teeth in order to protect his own reputation… and allow a child of ten to take punishment after punishment, AND THEN coerce the child into secrecy 'for the good of the school.'

Clearly, there was an eleventh commandment in force in PUBLIC schools: THOU SHALL NOT BE CAUGHT (and if, by chance thou *art* caught, blame the nearest and weakest – anyone – but NOT THYSELF!)

However, at the moment John Paul had two options: (1) Stay and take the flak and continue his education, or (2) Leave and have *no* education.

Certainly, it would be impossible for him to stay on at Charterhouse if I continued my crusade for justice.

I then received a call from Peter Attenborough, the Headmaster, suggesting a meeting. He had waved aside my demand for a police investigation. The other six boys had never been questioned. The scholarship, I was told, once rescinded could never be reinstated and, in any case, he considered his Housemaster's decision as final. Whether John Paul stayed on at the school or left was entirely my decision.

Meanwhile, John Paul had exciting news. The Ben Travers Theatre – a theatre as well equipped as any in London, and patronised by all the most illustrious actors, directors and producers – had opened their new season by setting a competition for the school. All the boys were eligible to audition; they were first to select their chosen play and the best three plays would be selected for production and then lists would go up for the boys to audition for parts.

"That's what I want to *do*," he told me.

"I don't understand," I said. "You have always been gifted in English – you are Chairman of the Debating Society, and everyone tells me you have a brilliant future as a lawyer – that is why you are in Robinites House. All the parents have to be lawyers to have their child entered there, specifically so that you have all the advantages of generations of past lawyers to help you in your career – which of necessity will be in law, like your father."

"That's what everyone has told *me* I am going to be," he answered. "But *I've* never wanted to be a lawyer, I want to be in the theatre, and now's my chance. I'll show you," he beamed, "I don't mind putting up with any punishment Dr Blake likes to give me – he knows I had nothing to do with his wretched cricket ball – but I'll do his punishments – and I'm going to do *something* in Ben Travers. I don't mind what; I've put my name down for *anything*!" And he went back to school jubilantly.

I received a courteous reply to my letter, which, I was informed, had been forwarded to the Headmaster to be dealt with.

I went up the following weekend to collect John Paul after his football match, as usual. We drove home in silence and he then went straight upstairs and threw himself on the bed with his face to the wall. He was 'not hungry'. Akita curled up at his feet.

I went up later and sat down. "What happened?" I wanted to know.

He sat up politely; there were no tears, but he was totally disconsolate. John Paul was whipped, beaten and finally, *down*.

"I've been forbidden access to the Ben Travers Theatre," he said. "I'm not even allowed to help – in fact I'm not allowed to go within a hundred yards of the theatre – it has been put completely 'out of bounds' to me."

"Is that your new punishment?" I asked.

"Oh no. I still have to sweep all the leaves off the roof every evening; I thought that *was* my punishment, but Dr Blake stopped me in the corridor and said he'd noticed my name up on all the lists in the theatre… I'd put my name on *all* the lists to make sure I could do *something*. Well, it *was*, he said, and then told me the whole of the theatre was out of bounds to me – I was not allowed to go *near* it for a *whole year*."

"That's enough," I said. "I'm going to ring the school."

"Oh, please don't," he begged. "This has only happened because Dr Blake said *you* had written to the school – *that's* why I have been punished!"

I went downstairs and cooked his favourite steak and chips with lashings of tomato ketchup, to be followed by his favourite (unpronounceable) ice cream.

"Eat up," I said, cheerfully.

"I'm not really hungry."

"You should be," I said. "This is the first day of the holidays."

John Paul stared at me. I had obviously gone out of my mind.

I smiled. "You won't be going back to school on Monday; you're leaving Charterhouse, for good."

"Honest, Mum?" he asked incredulously.

"Absolutely. You've been at the school long enough to have shown your worth. It is clear by now that you had nothing to do with the accident – and even had you done so, the punishments by now would have been considered more than sufficient. Apart from which, from the beginning it was clearly beyond the capabilities of an eleven-year-old to heave a cricket ball with such velocity that it was still travelling at five feet above ground level to pass Dr Blake's ear and then land forty feet across the other side of the room. It is obvious to me that you are going to be punished until you capitulate, and admit to something you haven't done, and I would find that quite unacceptable."

"Thanks, Mum." He picked up his knife and fork and attacked the steak and chips.

"Point is," I went on, "we've come all the way back from Gibraltar because of your gifts, which everyone has assumed you will use in order to take up and follow your father's career in law."

"I don't want to be a lawyer, Mum."

It honestly hadn't occurred to me to even think about it – or to enquire of John Paul whether or not he *wanted* to be a lawyer. Everyone had just always *assumed* that he would be.

I explained that if he left Charterhouse now, that would be the end of all education; obviously, to a twelve-year-old, a life of sheer bliss loomed.

The house had been sold immediately, for £10,000 more than I'd paid for it. The furniture would have to be sold and I would have to give up the only permanent job available and get work where, and as and when I could. Well, I obviously couldn't leave John Paul alone in the house all day. He would have to do as many other children did, and find work at sixteen without any qualifications. Only then would I be free to teach – if I could ever find work again, after such an absence.

However, we couldn't go on indefinitely with these punishments and Dr Blake, having failed in his original aim of virtually expelling John Paul, would not now be content until he had finally hounded him out of the school. May as well give up and leave now.

I rang Dr Blake. "John Paul will not be back on Sunday night," I said. "He is unwell."

"I quite understand," he replied unctuously. Of course he did. John Paul hadn't been expected back in the first place.

John Paul jumped up enthusiastically. "Can I ring Chris and Neil to play football?" he asked, his face shining.

As I drove him off to meet his friends, I saw a changed child. I had done the right thing. Now to ring my Headmistress and tell her I had to break my contract and wouldn't be back. I decided to do it later – I'd had enough for one day.

John Paul came back and settled down gleefully in front of the TV with his friends. Tearing back and forth at weekends – two hundred miles – he had never found time before. This was the life – a life all his friends at day school took for granted. His friends could now stay later, and did. I could hear their animated discussions from the other room and thought it was just as well to get it out of his system. They were going at it hammer and tongs – late to bed and much later up on Sunday morning.

He finally came down to breakfast quite solemnly, but tackled a huge, unhealthy breakfast treat of eggs, bacon and sausage, and all the trimmings, with gusto.

"Mum," he suddenly said, halfway through it, "I've decided to go back to school."

I nearly choked. "You've decided *what*?" Having been prepared to give up my career, and more or less forced into giving up John Paul's, my head was reeling.

"It just makes all the difference," he explained, "what you said… you *honestly* don't think I had anything to do with that accident and Dr Blake just *wants* me to leave. Now, I know you would accept it if I couldn't take it, but I've worked hard and done all the course work now for my GCSE's – why *should* I have to leave?"

"Absolutely," I said.

"So I've decided to go back," he said. "I mean, if *you* can get up at four-thirty am and go to work and not get back until eight or nine pm – I suppose *I* can get up early and clean his loos or stay up late and sweep his leaves!"

Well. A funny way of looking at it, but I could see where he was coming from.

"Okay," I said. "If you're sure."

So we started off early on Monday morning. I dropped him off and then drove up to school, arriving just in time to start the new week. John Paul had clearly been making his plans with his friends, and now proceeded to put them into action. Dr Blake had received him – clearly surprised at his return – and none too pleased.

John Paul's maths tutor had entered him for a competition which had been organised by a National newspaper for the 'Nationwide Maths Competition of the Year'. John Paul had been selected to represent Charterhouse. I was therefore very surprised when the phone rang and Dr Blake came on the line.

"You will remember, Mrs Donnelly," he began, "when you first came to the school with John Paul and I gave my usual introductory talk – I said if any problem arose which I felt I could solve before it became a major issue, I would ring the parent confidentially – and nine times out of ten, it could be solved without involving the pupil...?"

I did remember, and said so.

"I have to tell you, Mrs Donnelly, that John Paul's standard of work has deteriorated to such an extent and his behaviour has become so disruptive that, being aware of your financial circumstances, I hardly think it worth John Paul continuing here. He will not be achieving any results in the GCSE and, in your position, I strongly suggest you think seriously about involving yourself in any further totally unnecessary expense."

Before I could utter any comment, he went on, "I was surprised that he was returned this term, but I really cannot recommend that you spend money on further fees. He will be getting a very poor report from me this term."

"But I don't understand," I protested. "His maths tutor has entered him, on behalf of Charterhouse, for the Nationwide Maths Competition."

There was a short, sharp snort of derision from Dr Blake. "His behaviour has been totally reprehensible," he said.

Completely bewildered, I collected John Paul as usual on Saturday. He jumped in the car, bright and cheerful. As soon as we got home, I demanded an explanation.

He laughed. "When I got back to school," he explained, "Dr Blake put me back on leaf clearing – I *knew* he would."

Apparently, Dr Blake had noticed a curious queue of boys lining up by the fire escape, and went to investigate. On the roof (cleared completely of leaves) and leaning against the parapet, were about a dozen canvases. John Paul had decided to add art to his various talents. "I'll need it," he said, "if I'm going to be a film and theatre Director."

He had proved to be an adept pupil and had worked hard. He had acquired the canvases from his new (and impressed) art tutor, and completed a series of the most black, satirical caricatures imaginable, of all the tutors; they were grotesque – totally without mercy and very, very clear. I only saw sketches of his favourite tutors – what he did to Dr Blake, I cannot imagine, but certainly he had little in the way of a sense of humour, as John Paul well knew.

Tall, with a sizeable paunch, he habitually affected a huge Sanderson's flowing cape and broad brimmed hat, gaiters and plus-fours, and placed himself very deliberately on his shooting-stick to watch all outdoor activities. A pompous man, he fairly invited ridicule. Seeing the various portraits arranged, and the sniggering boys handing over coins, he exploded. Puce in the face, he had grabbed John Paul by his collar. "*Now* I've got you," he hissed. "That's expulsion; *now* you will be expelled. Taking money… that you *will* be expelled for."

Which was, apparently, a school rule.

"Oh, not so, Sir," said John Paul. "No, Sir, it says in the *Bible*, Sir (he was studying Theology and Philosophy and expected to read it at Oxford), that given one punishment, I must give myself *another* punishment, Sir, and having the gift of art, I used my gift in my *own* time and did these portraits as my *second* punishment."

"You have been taking money," roared Dr Blake. "For that alone, you can be expelled!"

"Oh no, Sir," countered John Paul. "I've been *collecting* money all during the fortnight's punishment, Sir, and I've been giving it to my Theology tutor, for *charity*… Sir."

Clearly, the other masters had been in on the joke – it had now extended beyond Robinites House and most of the staff of Charterhouse had enjoyed the joke. But it was the last straw for Dr Blake. Retribution was to be swift and savage; the gloves were off.

Meanwhile, as I had told John Paul, my decorating skills had rewarded me well. Morris Dibben had advertised the house at £10,000 more than I had paid for it, and the following day, several couples came to view. They all expressed keen interest – particularly an elderly couple who were impressed that everything had been updated and renovated to a high standard, and the garden landscaped for minimal maintenance. They immediately asked if they might make an offer. I agreed.

I rang Morris Dibben. No, I was told, I may not accept an offer – they were the agents and had already sold the house for the full asking price.

But that had been a fortnight ago; with all the hassle of John Paul at school and the fact that I was out of the county all day, I had not kept up to date.

Had they arranged a survey? No, they had not. I pointed out, here, that they had guaranteed they would not take the house off the market until it was definitely sold. Of *course* we won't, they'd said...

I drove in to see them. The photograph and particulars of the house were gone from the window. I asked the receptionist about it.

"Oh no – we no longer have the details of that house," she blithely answered. "It's been sold!"

I gave the agent an ultimatum. "Unless I have a signed contract by the end of this week," I told him, "I am withdrawing the house and putting it with another agent."

There then followed a flurry of phone calls, and finally, he rang me back. The young, unmarried couple had fallen out; they didn't, in fact, possess even the minimum suggested deposit of £2,000 and had no prospect of being granted a mortgage. I raged at him, but it was useless; if John Paul was to go back to school next term, I needed a further £5,000.

I had bought the house cheaply, having offered cash. There was therefore nothing left in the bank until it was sold; and no possibility of an overdraft, but I did go back to Lloyds bank; I would have to borrow the £5,000 from somewhere, to get him back to school.

"Absolutely not!" The bank manager was adamant.

"But you still have my last two policies," I pointed out.

"Worthless. One is worth £5,000 in 2008; the other is worth £60,000 in 2007. Until then, they are simply worthless bits of paper."

We argued. Granted, I agreed, I could hardly borrow £5,000 on a policy which, in 2008, will be worth only that amount, but the £60,000 policy – even if I failed to repay the £5,000 I borrowed, would still be to their benefit if they collected the £60,000 in 2007.

Finally, he relented. "Just this *once*," he warned.

Saved by the bell. I blessed the solicitor who had arranged that endowment when I bought my very first house.

Morris Dibben finally persuaded me to sell the house to the next buyer – for £10,000 less, but by now I was really desperate. I would either have to give up my London job and re-market the house again, or accept the lower price. The recession had slackened, but house prices were still falling and the longer I waited, the less it would be worth. There was no chance of buying another; that had taken the last of my money; it was a new term and I was another £5,000 down. Now, I could only rent, and hope John Paul could last the distance and at least get his GCSE qualifications before we ended up on the pavement.

Still, this time the house sale went through. I found a house to rent on the other side of the wood and hoped John Paul would accept it as home. What with one thing and another, his *three elements* – his home, his dog and his Mum – were looking distinctly dodgy!

However, John Paul came home full of excitement and barely noticed the fact that we were packing up to move yet again. His entry had won the National Mathematics Prize of the Year. Representatives had arrived at Charterhouse to present the enormous cheque to John Paul (who had, of course, immediately handed it over to the school) and photographs and congratulations followed; he was feted.

He had a great weekend at home and went happily back to school. However, the following weekend he came home silent and tired. He had slept in the car all the way home and when we got home, mid-afternoon, he crawled into bed and went straight to sleep.

Sunday morning came and I required an explanation.

This fortnight, his punishment had been augmented by the removal of his watch and clock. Midwinter, he was finding it difficult – he had to rise with the dawn, being unsure of the time and then, after school he had to stay up until the early hours of the morning to try and get his work done.

Having had to work extra time on the Maths project, he had got behind with his work and the masters were beginning to complain. Worse, his writing was so appalling, they were complaining that his work, as well as sparse, was illegible. I bought him a full size torch and sent him back. I was still seriously considering giving up work and removing him from Charterhouse, whether he liked it or not, but his results were so good and to leave without *any* qualifications…

During the week, Dr Blake rang again. "This is just another confidential call, Mrs Donnelly," he said, "to tell you that all the masters are now complaining about John Paul. His standard of work is *appalling*; it really cannot be tolerated and I will be giving him a very *bad* report. I have to say that John Paul is really not the sort of boy we want at Charterhouse. You really should think seriously about continuing to pay fees – in *your* situation."

Stung, I retorted, "Well, it's hardly surprising, Dr Blake – taking away his watch and clock like that – I know that after putting in all that extra work for the National Maths Competition, which he won for the school, the only way he could get his GCSE work done was with a torch under the blankets until two or three am."

"What!" he bellowed. "Working after lights out? That's it! Expulsion!" He slammed down the phone.

The next day when I went to collect John Paul, he came out of Robinites with a crowd of silent friends around him. He stomped straight over to the car and leant against it. "Mum," he said, and then the tears rolled down his face. "Mum, I can take anything this school can throw at me, but not *you – you* did this!"

Reluctantly – there was nowhere else to go – he got into the car with me. Clearly, he would not have wished to get within reach had he been able to avoid it.

"I'm very sorry," was all I could say. We drove home in miserable silence.

I rang Dr Blake. There was little point in discussion, so I came straight to the point. "Dr Blake," I said, "the conversation I had with you yesterday was entirely at your instigation and, as you pointed out, in *total* confidence. It would appear," I went on, "that there is a complete dearth of gentlemen at Charterhouse." There was an explosion at the other end, but I was already putting the phone down.

There was little to be said. There was still only one option left.

John Paul came home the following weekend. Dr Blake had ordered his light bulb to be removed every night at 10.00 pm – since "he could no longer be trusted." He must hand it over to the Head Boy at 10.00 pm and collect it the following morning which meant, of course, he had to get up and somehow dress in pitch darkness.

By this time he had made some good friends at school. One lent him a powerful torch and he continued to work beneath the bedclothes to get his extra work done, and the Head Boy trotted up and down, bearing the light bulb on a velvet cushion he'd brought from home, and turning it into a joke, but it was difficult to see the funny side of it.

Again we discussed leaving the school, but now John Paul had other plans. The end of his year's 'gating' from the Ben Travers Theatre loomed. Moreover, the results of the competition for Best Three Plays of the Year were to be judged at the end of this term. The three plays had been selected, a famous playwright from London had been invited to judge; the programmes were printed.

John Paul brought his home proudly. Play One was an excerpt from a Shakespearean play by Form 2. Play Two was by another famous playwright and was to be acted by Form 6. Play Three was written by *John Paul Donnelly* – to be acted by his friends in Form 4.

The first two plays were excellent. Then came John Paul's play. Entitled *The Big School*, it was about a boy, unused to public school life, being taunted and bullied mercilessly, first by his peers – whom he talked round – and then by his *Housemaster*. The boys had clearly enjoyed themselves. The pompous, overbearing, deeply insecure Housemaster was realistically portrayed; finally, unable to cope, he had stalked in, grabbed the unfortunate boy by the scruff of his neck for '*six of the best in my study.*' The boy turned to his room mates, "If it gives you *pleasure*, Sir," he simpered, as he was dragged away. The other boys sniggered among themselves and one of them ceremoniously ran after them as they left. "You forgot this," he said. The boy turned, collected the item – a small plant pot containing an obscenely shaped cactus – and left the stage.

The curtain came down as the boys erupted. It brought the house down. By now everyone knew of the situation – Masters and boys and it definitely appealed to the schoolboys' sense of humour.

Finally, order was restored. The famous London playwright came on stage and complimented the boys on the first two plays. "But the third," he said, "was only of eight minutes duration."

There was silence.

"But *what* an eight minutes!" he went on. "Eight minutes of pure quality." He went on to say that, whilst he appreciated John Paul came from Robinites, the famous Legal House, where all the boys were expected to follow and take up the legal profession of their parents, this particular case had to be an exception to that rule – John Paul

Donnelly would be wasted as a lawyer, and however talented he may be in various ways, he belonged to the world of theatre.

"… he has a brilliant future and I have immense pleasure in awarding him first prize!"

To rapturous applause, John Paul accepted a jeroboam of champagne and a cheque. The Headmaster appeared at my elbow. Would I care to accompany him to the Green Room? I would. Ensconced in the Green Room, a glass of wine pressed into my hand. I was thoroughly enjoying myself. "Oh yes," I was saying, "a great surprise… no, I'd no *idea* he was writing; I can't imagine how he did it with his *light bulb removed* to prevent him working, and with all these punishments – you know, getting up to *clean the loos before school* and then on the roof, *clearing leaves until dark.*"

"I *beg* your pardon?" said the famous playwright. Some reporters gathered round.

"Oh, indeed, yes," said his English, Art and Theology tutor. "He has had to work very hard."

The Headmaster again appeared at my elbow. "Er, perhaps you would like some food, Mrs Donnelly?" he suggested, thrusting a plate of canapés into my face – clearly with the intention of keeping my mouth otherwise occupied.

Oh yes, I thoroughly enjoyed that evening. Dr Blake cowered away each time I turned in his direction – which I did as often as I could. Every time I opened my mouth, someone either pushed food in it or hastily interrupted.

Then I took John Paul home in triumph. He had completed all his punishments; he had obeyed his exclusion from the theatre to the letter and had still turned the tables on his tormentor. He was a hero. I had a nasty feeling that we hadn't heard the last of Dr Blake, but I felt confident there would be no more confiscation of light bulbs or more hindrances to John Paul's studies.

We went back to the nasty little house I was now renting, but I don't think John Paul even noticed it. He was *vindicated*; he was a *success* and he was in the *theatre*!

End of term came and John Paul was feted. I collected all his end of term prizes and then the boys went back to see which room they had been allocated for the next year. He would now be on the third floor with all the other third-years, to concentrate on his GCSE exams.

He came back white-faced; stricken. "No," he said, "I can't do that – Mum, he can't do *that* to me!"

I had waited in the car for him; the beautiful silver Mercedes purring away – the only thing I had left now from my former life and which I had grimly held on to. All had been achieved, all vindicated – what could go wrong now…?

"I've been put back on the first floor – with the new boys, in the *double room*."

Obviously a humiliation. What else was new? We both knew Dr Blake was at war with John Paul.

On the way home, he explained. The going at Charterhouse was tough; his beloved Head Boy, who had cared for him so assiduously, handing him back his light bulb so ceremoniously and making a joke out of it, seeing to it that somehow, he could get on with his work… he had despaired, and so affected by circumstance was he, that he jumped from the fourth floor window in the middle of the night. He had somehow survived – fortunately he had landed just beyond the concrete path, but he had broken his jaw, his hip and his right leg… he would never play football again. But, he was no longer there to help John Paul. His father, the Dean of Guildford Cathedral and his wife, a practising lawyer, refused to comment; it was important that their son complete his education at Charterhouse.

John Paul explained the situation tersely. One of the boys in Old School – the traditional part of Charterhouse, which still kept the boys in dormitories and where there were the traditional old desks and lockers that their fathers had used – one of the boys, under the stress and strain of the workload, had run amok with a knife. He had stabbed at least one boy – now in hospital – and awaited obvious expulsion. His parents had been advised to remove him. However, Dr Blake had proposed a solution; he had offered the boy private accommodation in Robinites. That would obviate all homicidal tendencies and the boy may complete his studies. The parents were, naturally, delighted.

"But why should that concern you?" I asked John Paul.

We spent a strained, tense vacation. John Paul was white-faced, difficult, enclosed with his good friends – all now attending as day boys at excellent public or secondary schools in Southampton, and all too soon, back for the new term.

John Paul left the car and raced in to see where he had been placed. On the first floor, he'd said – the only floor with a double room – an isolation room where a nurse or parent could sleep with a child, if necessary.

Dr Blake had put him in to share with the boy who had stated his intention of knifing any boy during the night if he was to be kept at school. Everything had gone so well. John Paul had been acclaimed as the Success of the Year – his achievements had been superb in spite of all the difficulties – but John Paul had proved his worth.

"Whatever else," I said, "Dr Blake couldn't put you in a *dangerous* situation."

John Paul just looked at me, disregarding my concerns. "I told Dr Blake I am staying," he said. "I am staying."

I continued to collect him at weekends. I was now finding the going hard. The horrid house I was renting could not be a permanent arrangement. Rented as 'unfurnished', so that I would at least have a home for what furniture I had left, the owner had moved all his unwanted furniture in at the last minute; mine had now to be housed in the garage. I was desperately looking for a new home.

All the money had gone – once John Paul had completed his GCSE's, and the final fees paid, all I could look forward to was B&B in a hostel. At least he would have qualifications. Up at 4.30, walk Akita, train to London, back at 9.00 pm – the routine began again.

11.00 pm; the phone rang. "I'm *here*," said a desperate voice.

Oh no. Not another *accident* at school...?

'I'm in the Hall," said John Paul. "And I am just leaving."

"You can't," I replied, anxiously. "You'll be *expelled*!"

Anyone caught outside of their room after lights out faced immediate expulsion. Dr Blake would not hesitate to apply his option.

"Oh no," said John Paul. "I won't be *expelled*. I am going to get out of here – walk across the park and knock on Mr Attenborough's door and tell him I am leaving his school! I will then walk out, through the gates and..." here, his voice broke for the first time, but recovering quickly, he went on, "...and if you don't want me at home, I will *keep on walking...*"

"But what happened?"

John Paul spoke calmly now. "He went for me with a knife. He said he would get me while I was sleeping – that way he would get out of this school. I've got my brown judo belt now, and I've kept awake at night – ready for him. But," he said sadly, "I was so tired, I finally fell asleep, and he attacked me. So I am leaving here."

"I'll be right there," I told him. "*Don't* start walking! You know," I said desperately, "it will take me an hour and a half to get there, but I'll *be* there. Go to the Headmaster's house and wait there for me. I promise I will have you out of there, right now – exams or not – you leave right now, but *don't start walking!*"

"Okay, I'll be there," he said.

The phone went dead.

I rushed upstairs, dressed, and dashed down again. Think. *Think...*

I rang the Headmaster. "Just to tell you – I'm collecting John Paul," I said.

"John Paul is here," he replied. "There is no question of expulsion – he will be staying at Charterhouse."

"I think we have both just about had enough of Charterhouse," I told him. "I promised I would collect him and I intend to do so. This is just a courtesy call. I'd appreciate it if you would keep him there until I collect him…"

"Stay where you are," said Mr Attenborough. "John Paul is staying here. You have to appreciate, Mrs Donnelly, that John Paul is not only our top scholar, but the *best* top scholar that has ever passed through the portals of this school. He cannot leave – whatever it takes, I will *do* it."

"Too late," I told him. "I promised John Paul I would be there to collect him and I will, but it will take me an hour and a half."

"Give me half an hour," said Peter Attenborough, urgently, "and John Paul will ring you back himself – are you prepared to give me half an hour?"

"I will wait exactly thirty minutes and then I start off."

I suppose that was the longest half hour of my life.

At 11.45, prompt to the minute, the phone rang. "It's *me*," said John Paul joyously, "and I'm *staying!*"

"I have my keys in my hand," I told him. "I am about to drive up and collect you. I'm glad you haven't been expelled, but enough is enough and I'm on my way – you are leaving Charterhouse."

"I can't *tell* you, Mum," he explained, "it's confidential – it's between me and Mr Attenborough… it's for the good of the school, so

I can't tell you, but I *want* to stay. I've done all the work, Mum, I *need* to stay."

"Your decision," I told him.

"I'll stay now, Mum."

Peter Attenborough came on the line. "You *will* allow *me* to settle this, Mrs Donnelly? I *am* the Headmaster of this school. John Paul *must* stay and take his examinations and from now on, *anything* that stands in his way will be removed."

I really couldn't argue any more. I would see John Paul at the weekend and, if necessary, take him home for good. "Very well." I wearily put the phone down; it was now past midnight and I had to be up at 4.30 am.

On Saturday, I drove up, prepared to take him home, with all his belongings. He greeted me, surrounded by a crowd of boys, hugging and cheering him. I assumed they had won a match. He got into the car, nonchalantly. "Can I get a video?" he asked.

We stopped at the bottom of the road, collected a video and then drove to the horrid little house. Akita fell into his lap and both enjoyed the entirely unwholesome huge fillet steak, chips, ketchup and unpronounceable ice cream I had prepared.

We had a wonderful holiday; John Paul played cricket and football and had endless barbecues with his friends. They sat for hours on the verandah, discussing, laughing, talking. I didn't tell him I'd had to bury poor beautiful-but-dim Sam in the garden, just close to where they were eating and drinking.

Poor Sam; we were now back in Bassett, but on the wrong side of the main road to London. The wood was between us and Batemans. One night he'd escaped and tried to get back to his (and my) beloved home. He hadn't made it. The lorry driver had kindly placed him on the pavement where he lay, still beautiful, eyes glazed over; but he'd made his last try for home. However, we had Akita, the furniture was at least in the garage, and John Paul was still at Charterhouse.

That September, I drove back warily, prepared to take John Paul home at the drop of a hat. I had warned my Headmistress; the job was excellent and so far I had achieved one hundred percent success getting every pupil in my class through the tough selection examination to St Paul's and Westminster schools. I was also looking forward to completing my final year there with Miss Baker, the Headmistress. We would both then retire.

So we drove up; I was ready to confront Dr Blake and do battle.

"Welcome, welcome!" cried a voice. A young man, followed by his wife and sturdy small son, hurried up to us.

"Meet my new Housemaster," said John Paul, grinning broadly. "Mum, this is Mr Gammell."

Mr Gammell held out his hand. "Welcome to Robinites," he said – and I felt that I was.

From that day, John Paul flourished as the green bay tree. He baby sat for the Gammells, and excelled in sport and academia; nothing was too much trouble or effort – life at Charterhouse was a dream: he excelled in everything.

Finally, I found time to look round and survey my own empire. It was not good. All the money from the house had gone; there was nothing left. Provided I kept working in London, I could pay the £600 rent, but when that finished, certainly I would be out on the pavement with all my goods and chattels; but at least it now looked as if John Paul *would* get his qualifications and show his worth.

I found another house. It was so neglected it was 'going for a song'. There was no money left to buy, but there was a possibility that I could rent it, renovate it, and then perhaps buy it. It required a deposit of £6,000, but at the end of my contract I would get a £14,000 lump sum payment, which would secure a mortgage.

So all I needed now was £6,000. I went back to my solicitor. My bank manager had long ago foreclosed on my accounts; he had no more faith than I in Desmond's maintenance payments. However, I pointed out that his son was now doing brilliantly at Charterhouse. Top scholar – indeed the most impressive top scholar to ever have passed through their portals – one last chance to get at least one payment out of him?

Word came back. Desmond is dying of cancer, I was told, and could hardly be asked for payment *now*.

"He was dying of cancer twelve years ago," I pointed out. "To date, he still owes £68,000 and hasn't paid one penny." Dying of cancer, what had he been living on for the past twelve years?

"I could *enforce* payment," my solicitor said, "but of course, if he doesn't pay, it would mean disbarment and a prison sentence – you wouldn't of course want *that*."

"No," I agreed. I wouldn't want that; Desmond had finally come back to argue that John Paul *must* be baptised in the Catholic faith, and then gone straight back. And, as the Dean of the Church had explained, to Desmond, an old Irish Catholic, his Catholicism was like his left arm – he didn't really need it and could do without it, but it was there and he was *stuck* with it. No matter where he went, it went with him; his penance awaited him and the Triads had moved in – they provided servants and even Desmond had been cowed. Their servant had moved in and he was directly in touch with them.

Edward Heath had been out three times to see him; the Attorney General had interviewed him; the Governor of Hong Kong had interviewed him. Desmond didn't care. Desmond was above the law. Oh, he could practise – he could lay down the law to everyone else – as a leading Queen's Counsel he could and did, regularly sentence men to death. When asked 'how can you sleep at night?' he said, "They can always come back to me on Appeal – I just charge twice as much."

Now I was begging. I needed just £6,000 to secure the house. The Court was told no, Desmond could not supply bank statements. No, he hadn't paid; no he had no intention of doing *any* paying. He was still 'dying of cancer' and couldn't be held accountable.

On leaving Gibraltar, aeons ago, waiting in the departure lounge, a fellow had come rushing up to me. "Mrs Donnelly!" he gasped.

"Yes?" I said.

John Paul had looked at him curiously.

"*The* Mrs Donnelly – the one who left *Desmond*?" he asked incredulously.

"Left him? *I* didn't leave *him*; I was *left* – in hospital having John Paul!"

He was astounded. Word had gone round Hong Kong that I had left Desmond – totally disconsolate (but willing to be consoled); but no one was aware of the imminent arrival of John Paul and the total abandonment of his father.

I introduced John Paul to him and boarded my flight to the UK.

So that was the story that Desmond had plied in Hong Kong...

Later, I heard, everyone plied *him* with beautiful women to distract and distil his sorrow, all of which he had thoroughly enjoyed. However, the problem was now immediate. His son, having overcome all obstacles, was now on the way to a brilliant future. His academic results were a foregone conclusion – Oxford was now in touch with offers. *Now* would he send at least *one months* payment? The answer came back: *None.*

"You could," said the QC, "enforce payment."

"What use?" I asked bitterly. "London High Court has enforced payment. Hong Kong High Court has enforced payment. And what happened? *Nothing.* Everyone else has to pay a Court Order – but not *Desmond. Desmond is above the law!*"

The lawyer retired – he knew when he was beaten.

Desmond was right; he was totally outside the law. Yes, he *could* and frequently *did* condemn men to death, but he was considered (and rightly, apparently) totally above the law.

No help there.

In any case, used as I was to rising at 4.30 am, during the summer vacation I had risen early, cut down the overgrown hedge that swamped the property, bagged and tied it, and deposited at the local 'tip'.

A neighbour from the opposite side of the road accosted me. "My," he said, "I have to admire you; one day in and you have transformed the property... you do realise it's rented?"

Well, of course I did. "Yes," I replied. "But I have to live in it – and, apparently, it's for sale."

If I could find £6,000...

However, John Paul was now thriving at Robinites. The toast of Charterhouse, having overcome all opposition; the toast of his class; the toast of his House; the toast, of course, of the Principal Governors of the school, who came to present the prizes. He was on top of the world and, as long as I could provide the fees, it would continue thus, and lead to an illustrious future.

John Paul had become firmly embedded in religion; it was not to leave him for the rest of his life. Obviously, his father had totally failed him; his mother was apparently equally useless against the full-on opposition provided by such a school as Charterhouse. He was on his own and, at fourteen, obviously felt he could cope.

Rising at 4.30 am and working until I returned at 9.00 pm, I finally had no alternative but to admit defeat. "To keep my job," I said, "I am going to have to stay in bed at weekends."

John Paul, on a high, didn't give a damn. "Fine," he shouted, turning the radio up even louder. "Fine! I'll go home with Jez – he lives in Godalming; always inviting me there!"

Feted wherever he went.

I merely had to drive and collect him now at the beginning and end of each term; I continued to rise at 4.30 and reach home at 9.00, resting at weekends.

The future was rosy.

Eight

Driving back to Charterhouse was sheer bliss; no more desperate, prolonged trips to the loo, or running back to the house for a last hug for a surprised Akita, and no more staring desperately back home as we drove off. He looked forward to school now.

Dr Blake had *gone*. I had no idea where and, frankly, couldn't have cared less. John Paul's new Housemaster, Mr Gammell, greeted us with his charming wife. John Paul had immediately been reinstated to his own room on the third floor, with the other third-years. They had given him a rapturous ovation – 'up from the dungeons,' as they put it.

Now he came into his own. Encouraged and praised by Mr Gammell, he was back on form – top of the class. Brilliant at languages, I was told he must take both German and French for GCSE's... he was a gifted linguist. Of course, this would entail *at least* a month in France, to perfect their accents, and then the same in Germany – in their own Schloss. Captain of the cricket team (special uniform), as well as football (complete kit as goalkeeper – ditto for hockey, all from Gieves Outfitters).

"Please Mum, can I have my own face guard?"

"Don't the school provide *anything*?"

"Yes, but I really need my *own*, Mum!"

Well, really! "No," I said, for once. "I really think if the school provides them, you'll have to use theirs."

I went to the first of the season's hockey matches to watch him lead his team out and take up his position as goalkeeper. Out he came... and I was horrified. The smallest child on the field – he was always going to be a head shorter than his year, having gone to the school under age. He strode out and confidently took up his position in the centre of the goal. I had bought the entire goal-keeping outfit, except the face guard. The one he wore consisted of a little piece of chicken wire attached to a plastic balaclava-type helmet. I quickly checked out the opposition goalkeeper; twice the size of John Paul, he was wearing protection that would have put a 1930's deep sea diving helmet to shame. A strong, motorcycle-type helmet with a face visor, it was a terrifying sight.

The game began. John Paul was the obvious weak link. With all the advantages at their disposal – Charterhouse played to win. The teams consisted of hulking great eighteen-year-olds, most of whom were athletic six-footers… and tiny John Paul was defending goal with a small piece of chicken wire for protection!

They went straight for him.

John Paul's sporting practice stood him in good stead. He dashed forward, hockey stick parrying blow after shattering blow. At times he was surrounded by half a dozen of the opposing team, all clearly going for the weakest point – his head. Obviously, the first blow to get past his guard would knock him senseless – if it didn't kill him outright!

I approached the Games Master, who was engrossed in the match. "You will have to stop the match," I told him anxiously. "That's my son in goal – that isn't a hockey match – they are out to *kill* him!"

He, too, was concerned. "I may have to," he agreed. "I'd no idea John Paul had no face guard – we only provide emergency practice ones and, outside a match, they're not supposed to attack the *head*." He hurried over to the opposition's Games Master, exchanged a few words and returned to my side. "He refuses to stop the match," he said. "It was up to John Paul to make sure he was properly kitted out – and he *assured* me he was."

However, by this time, John Paul had demolished all the opposition; the rest of his team, realising his problem, had gathered round him. Now it was up to him to deflect all genuinely aimed shots, which he skilfully did.

I went back to my place.

"Brilliant goalkeeping," said one of a bunch of spectating fathers.

"Absolutely," the others agreed. "Can't understand him being sent out kitted up like *that*, though!"

Conversation ensued; of course, everyone agreed, uniforms *were* expensive – and sports gear was the worst, especially *this* goalkeeper's kit, which of course would have to be renewed each year as he outgrew it. But really, was the consensus of opinion, it was such an honour to have a son come out like that, at his age, and fearlessly show his ability.

"Hm, can't understand any father sending his son out without proper protection…" "… a disgrace…" "… shouldn't be allowed…"

The comments continued; luckily, John Paul's sheer ability had saved him. Triumphantly, he led his victorious team off the field to a storm of applause.

He stopped as he came abreast of me. "Coming to the match tea, Mum?"

"Oh, yes," I replied, faintly. "And… of course, you must have your own helmet in future."

"Are you sure, Mum? They are over seventy pounds, you know."

"In future," I assured him, "you will order whatever you need from the School Games Shop. If you are going to play in the team, you *must* have the right gear – especially as *Captain*."

"Thanks, Mum," he beamed. "See you at tea."

After that, I just paid the bills as they poured in. No more arguments. In any case, the little house had finally been sold. It had, at least, cleared my debts – and John Paul's expenses – but my account was now totally cleared out. I was living, literally, hand to mouth. But the three elements were still intact – the dog, the house and me. Poor Akita now had to be left on her own all day – something she accepted with her usual goodwill.

Since there was nothing left with which to put down a deposit on another house, I had found one I could rent – with a possibility of purchasing later. Again, it was similar to Batemans and, in fact, almost directly opposite, on the other side of the main road. It meant paying rent of £600 a month, but as long as I could keep earning – and I now had a permanent contract – I could manage it.

My teaching contract ended at exactly the same time as John's GCSE year, so I could see no future University place, or even the opportunity to stay on for A levels, but since Desmond had again been ordered to pay by both the London and Hong Kong High Courts, my Counsel assured me it *must* be paid eventually. Desmond had now been officially in Contempt of Court for several years. Obviously, it was impossible for him to continue to practise as a Queen's Counsellor if he refused to accept the spirit and the letter of the law when it came to himself. And, as my Counsel pointed out, it would be a most unnatural father who disowned his only son and prevented him from following a brilliant career.

The trick, obviously, was for John Paul to continue his education at Charterhouse and prove his brilliance when it came to exam time. As part of his course, he had also taken the usual instruction in Philosophy and Theology. Suddenly, he decided this was for him – may he be confirmed at Charterhouse?

I was delighted; he had gone, with his friends to a local modern-type church – a tin hut in the wood – where everyone did as they pleased, and mostly went on to enjoy their own boy-band type of music and then to a local boy who had the benefit of a swimming pool in his back garden.

But now John Paul became immersed in the subject. To be honest, I think he felt that if ever he was going to get any help in life, it would have to come from the Almighty – there was no one else in sight.

All his tutors now foresaw a brilliant Oxford career. He would, of course, *definitely* go to Oxford, which would bring further accolades to Charterhouse. John Paul himself came to a decision; yes, he would go to Oxford, but *only* if he could read Theology and Philosophy. He would like to go into the Church. In vain, his tutors protested; he was brilliant at English; brilliant at Maths; brilliant at Languages, and pretty good at Games, too. He could *not* give it all up to go into the Church. He was a member of Robinites House – a House devoted exclusively to the promotion of the Law – most of the nation's famous judges and Attorney Generals were educated at Robinites of Charterhouse, and now John Paul was their top scholar (albeit without the benefit of the assured scholarship); he *must* take Law at Oxford.

But John Paul, having rigidly put his foot down in the matter of not owning up to an accident he'd had no part of, now stated firmly that he had been put to Charterhouse against the wishes of both of us, but he had put his heart and soul into everything they had asked of him, including taking every unjustified punishment they had been able to throw at him, but he was now *fully committed* to his religion. All arguments failed; that was his *final* decision.

And, finally, I accepted it. I discussed it with the Masters, and with the Headmaster. I pointed out that having had his scholarship taken away for no good reason, he had a perfect right to choose his own future. He had the right to, and would, reject Law totally.

"Ah, yes," stalled Peter Attenborough. "But, you see, there *was* the accident and his Housemaster *insisted* on the retraction of his scholarship; there was nothing we could do."

"You *could*," I said, "have interviewed the other six boys who were with him at the time. You could have done as I requested – since it was a serious enough *alleged* offence for John Paul to be virtually expelled by a Housemaster – you *could* have called the police in for a full investigation, but you *refused*."

Driven on by indignation, I continued: "I have the doctor's report on the savage beating he took, and he also confirmed that, in his opinion, any eleven-year-old would have been physically incapable of launching a cricket ball with sufficient velocity to smash it through a strengthened plate glass window from a standing position, and unnoticed by his companions. However, as you pointed out, without the benefit of Desmond's legal expertise, I was just a simple school teacher, with no ability to argue against a House of legal experts, and I was *forced* to accept your decision. But *now*, I am paying full fees and the decision is entirely *mine*."

John Paul came home in despair, but grimly determined. He was surprised and delighted to find that, whilst I privately agreed with the school that he would be wasting his gifts in the Church, the final decision was his and I would back him to the hilt. By now he was heavily involved in the Ben Travers Theatre and had written further acclaimed plays. I merely said his future was entirely in his own hands.

"In any case," I had told Peter Attenborough, "without the Scholarship, I can only afford, as far as I can see, to pay fees up to the year before he takes GCSE's; it's a moot point whether there will be any funds for A levels, or University. So far, I have failed to get one penny out of Desmond."

There was consternation; the matter would have to go before the Board of Governors. He could not be allowed to leave. They must have the glory of a brilliant Oxford Scholar attributed to Charterhouse.

It went before the Board of Governors.

I was called in. The Board of Governors had decided it was vital that John Paul stayed at Charterhouse. They had contacted Lord McAlpine, who had subsequently come forward to make up a bursary; whatever was sufficient to keep John Paul at the School would be found. He would pay £1,000 a year to boost finances – and more, if and when necessary.

At the moment, I could cope. I received a disability pension of £6,000 a year for my back injury, and I was allowed to work as and when I felt able, provided there was no physical exercise involved. Now that I had my London job, although it certainly was not recommended, I spent five hours a day travelling to and across London, plus eight hours teaching in between. My Headmistress had told me proudly that I was there to get a class of bright pupils through their selection exams to Westminster and St Paul's Public Schools and, provided I continued to achieve a one hundred percent success rate, she had no intention of asking me to do anything else. In any case, she employed a specialist male teacher to undertake all physical activities and a professional musician to take music. All that was required of me was to get academic results.

With my salary of £24,000, therefore, whilst I continued to teach, I could afford to pay Charterhouse fees. Unfortunately, I then discovered that I was required to pay an annual rent of £7,500, plus fares to London of £2,500, plus £2,000 for car parking, plus expenses for travelling to and from Godalming which amounted to another £1,500, as well as all the extra equipment as John Paul outgrew uniforms and sports gear… and fees of £15,000 a year. It left very little for items such as gas, electricity and dog food – incidentals as far as Charterhouse was concerned, but essential nevertheless.

But still, John Paul was the 'golden boy' of the school and, it seemed, would be 'going places'. Accolades followed; Lord McAlpine took a keen interest now in John Paul and his career.

Lord Wakeham's sons, deposited early at Charterhouse, required a guardian – their mother having been tragically killed in the Brighton bombing, and their father obviously with his vital duties in London. There was only one possible choice; John Paul took over immediate guardianship of the two boys. As Mr Gammell later told me, he had left a great deal of responsibility with John Paul.

"Many a night," he confided, "I would hear footsteps creeping upstairs long after 'lights out' as the two young boys crept up to the third floor and John Paul's room for discussion, coffee or Coca Cola and much TLC." It was much appreciated, he assured me.

John Paul continued to excel; he was put in charge of Robinites bar, since he could be relied upon not only to drink sparingly himself, but also with sufficient authority to regulate even the worldly sixth-formers, who were keen to over-indulge. As well as studying for his exams, he would ride his bike (which had to go in the back of the car every week) around Godalming until 2.00 or 3.00 am, searching out all the sixth-formers who had escaped and were rollicking in the local bars. He would also 'do the rounds' before Mr Gammell, checking rooms for 'funny smells'. As Mr Gammell said, John Paul would merely suggest that the 'fuming' cigarettes were disposed of before the Housemaster did his official rounds.

"The boys accepted it," Mr Gammell told me. "It avoided expulsion on several occasions; no one was expelled at all while John Paul was there," he added proudly.

Since it was a time-consuming occupation and, obviously as their 'guardian', his two wards were the most time-consuming of all and regularly in need of counselling and assistance, I felt Mr Gammell had asked (and received) a great deal from John Paul, since Lord Wakeham as an ex-Carthusian, and prominent member of the Board of Governors had obviously been aware of the difficulties that had arisen through the reneging of John Paul's own scholarship.

All my investments had to go through Lloyds Bank to be scrutinised and then sold. All excellent investments, they had done well and had kept us going so far – except two. These were useless, I was told. I could keep them. They were the two endowment policies my aged but responsible solicitor had insisted I take out when I first purchased Batemans many years ago.

"They will ensure that you never have to sell Batemans," he'd assured me. He had never met Desmond!

I wished to God I hadn't.

Still; they were there. One, worth £5,000 would mature in 2008; the other, worth £60,000 would mature in 2007. Finally, I took them to Lloyds Bank. Mr Moon and Mr Johnson saw me. I explained that I now had prospects; I held an excellent post in London and was now earning £30,000 per annum. John Paul had a brilliant future, now guaranteed, at Charterhouse. As the educational psychologist had said, he merely had to choose which of his gifts he should follow, and his future was assured. Lord McAlpine had jumped in to offer assistance and, if nothing else, I would collect £65,000 by 2008.

I explained that my estate agent had found me a suitable property to rent, with an option to purchase for £60,000, so I could rent it and eventually buy it. The only problem was that my own money and salary would run out before John Paul could take his A-levels – so no Oxford.

Messrs Moon and Johnson surveyed the two policies disparagingly.

"I have *got* to find £5,000 per term," I told them, "for Charterhouse. I need it now, to get him back there next term; with no overdraft facility, he simply will not make it – I need to borrow it; I can pay it back from my salary, but I need it *now!*"

They both laughed. "You cannot *seriously* expect us to lend you £5,000 now, in the *hope* that you will collect £5,000 in 2008... *ten years' time!*" exclaimed Mr Moon.

"No," I had to agree. "But I am *desperate*. As far as I am aware, I collect *sixty* thousand – albeit in ten years time. I need to borrow £5,000 *now*. You will keep both policies in your safe deposit and if I don't manage to repay the £5,000, then you stand to collect £60,000. As I see it, you can therefore afford to let me have an interim overdraft facility of £5,000."

"Mrs Donnelly..." Mr Johnson spoke now. "These are two *worthless* pieces of paper!"

"But you stand to collect £65,000 in ten years' time," I insisted.

We argued for about half an hour. Finally, and with great reluctance, they agreed. I left the two policies with them and an agreed overdraft of £5,000. I then wrote out a cheque for £5,000 for the forthcoming term and rang Mr Attenborough to tell him *probably* John Paul would be allowed to stay on.

Next, I rang Denfords, the estate agents. May I view the property he had found?

"I'll drive you there," he said.

I soon saw why.

He collected me. "It's the right size," he said. "A manse. Been rented for fifteen years, but the Church Elder has done little to it in that time and, the church being sold, he moved out two years ago. So it is to be rented, and probably sold." We drove up. "That's it," he said.

"Drive *on*," I said. It was like the witch's house in fairy tales. The wall was crumbling; an erstwhile Forsythia overhung the house and pavement, whilst an ancient Buddleia had reached the roof, obscuring the bathroom window. In the tiny front garden a Privet hedge straggled up to the front window – tendrils escaping at intervals to meet the Forsythia. And dirty curtains hung lopsidedly at the windows. Speechless, I was driven home.

"I know it's been unoccupied for two years," said the estate agent, "and unkempt for fifteen before that, but it's going on sale for £60,000, and it *is* quite a large, substantial property. I will look out for something else, but you must see that the recession is now, finally, over and prices are rising fast."

At home, I thought about what he had said. Clearly it was that – or nothing. With no reserves, I was out of options and time was running out. When my contract ended, all I could look forward to was being shunted out onto the pavement – with my rosewood furniture – and presumably, into B&B.

And nothing for John Paul.

I rang Denfords. "I'll take a look at it," I said.

"Right. I know it's neglected, but it *would* only take £6,000 deposit and you could buy it. Redecorate, and you have a very nice house... an opportunity."

I was sold. We arranged to see it the following day. *A home again!*

We went back to view.

"Oh, my God!" It was even worse than I had thought. "I couldn't live in *that*."

We fought our way to the front door, almost needing a machete to hack our way through. But... *if* the Forsythia were cut right back – and I knew how quickly it recovered – and the privet, which took up at least six feet in width...

The door wheezed open; it reminded me of a Boris Karloff film. Inside, it was filthy; wallpaper hung off the walls, the carpets were just heaps of rotting fluff and torn curtains dangled sorrowfully among thick cobwebs around the window-frames.

But 16′ x 14′ into a bay window, with original Adam fireplace and Victorian ceiling rose – it *could* be a pleasant room. Through a spacious, if dark and dirty, hallway, into an equally dingy dining room. Look again – a spacious, elegant room, into... surprise, a modern, clean oak kitchen; 16′ x 10′, the agent pointed out, and fully fitted with modern oak cupboards, finished with marbled worktops.

Upstairs, and into bedroom one, with ghastly ochre roses adorning the walls, but, again spacious, with a bay window and a 16′ fitted wardrobe with cupboard space above. Bedroom two – this time painted out in bright salmon pink.

"As I said, you will want to redecorate," said the agent, helpfully.

Another pleasant, spacious room, though. One yellow ochre; one bright pink… dare I see a third, I asked? He insisted. Unbelievable: bright baby blue – but equally sizeable.

"The bathroom?" I enquired, hopefully.

"Ah."

He showed me the bathroom last. Just as well – originally, a vile yellow bathroom suite had been installed. The bath itself was stained dirty brown from about halfway down. The plughole, probably once chromed, was now rusted brown, which extended over the enamel and was met by similar staining from the rusted-in taps. The lavatory defied description, and the basin wasn't much better. It was surrounded by a level of cracked, once-white, now dirty-yellow tiles – the whole finished in soiled beige paint.

I looked from one eyesore to the next. "I think I'm going to take it," I heard myself saying.

"You *are*?"

"If it had an old-fashioned, but *clean* bathroom," I told him, "I would have felt bound to keep out; as it is – all you can do with the *whole* house, is gut it and start again. As you said, it's an *opportunity*."

The agent had been exceptionally honest; he hadn't *sold* it to me – it was *exactly* as he'd said – an opportunity. The price was within my reach – the same £600 per month that it cost to rent. Stripped, it would be up to me to make it work, and I had checked – there was just nothing else, this size, for the price. Besides, the house, though old, was sound and everything put in over the last tenant's occupation of fifteen years was quality – oak fitted cupboards and wardrobes, new boiler, new electrics and central heating.

"I'd need a garden," I said.

His face dropped. "It needs some work," he admitted, "but we *have* kept the lawn cut."

We went back downstairs and out through the dining room French windows.

Disaster!

In front, to one side, was a bank of honeysuckle. It had grown out at least eight feet from the fence. What flowers there were, hung over the other side of the fence, where it had clearly been clipped back. It hung – gnarled and twisted, leafless and flowerless. A knotted grey mass of lifeless destruction.

I stood speechless. A forest of brambles, ivy and nameless creepers stretched endlessly before me. Not a flower or a tree could be seen. Directly in front was a lawn, no more than eight feet square, which had certainly been recently mown. To the left, rose a laurel hedge. I was used to laurel hedges, but this one towered sixty feet above, with brambles and briars climbing up to meet it.

"The last tenant just let it go," said the agent, quite unnecessarily.

I really *hadn't* needed him to tell me *that*.

But the initial shock passed and, again, I saw the opportunity. Look again at what it *really* was… stand back and *think*…

Stripped of all vegetation, the back garden consisted of a pleasant and spacious tiled patio area, outside the French windows. Cleared of the encroaching vegetation, it ran the length of the house – about sixty feet. Beyond that, steps ran down to a lower lawn and, looking beyond that, a garden of about half an acre. Admittedly, buried under eight feet of tangled undergrowth, but it was there.

And it could be mine…

"Yes. I'll take it."

The agent was delighted. I wasn't surprised. But I had a future.

I rang the Teachers' Association: I would be retiring in a few years – could I have an assessment? Before, I had to admit, I hadn't dared ask.

"Oh yes," I was told. "Of course, you are receiving £6,000 per annum disability pay, due to your car injury, but – off the cuff – you should still receive a lump sum of £14,000. We'll have to work it out; we'll let you know."

£14,000! A *fortune*. It would make up the difference. It would cover a £6,000 deposit – the house was mine. *Mine*! It would cover John Paul's stay at Charterhouse and he could take his GCSE's. With the bit between my teeth, I now contacted King Edward VI Public School. It was literally at the end of the road – no more than three minutes walk. An excellent Grammar School, it was where I had originally intended John Paul should be educated, on a scholarship, of course, and he had looked forward to it.

They would be delighted to have John Paul back. They were so sorry I had turned down their offer in favour of Charterhouse, but they would welcome him back – on a fee-paying basis. Could I perhaps pop in for coffee and a chat?

I thought I recognised the voice...?

"Oh yes," he replied. "I taught you – a long time ago. You took over a Deputy Headship and went off to Hong Kong – I'm now Deputy Head of King Edward's!"

So, round I popped. I was shown round the school and proudly introduced to all the new amenities – tawdry, of course, compared to Charterhouse.

"Of course," said the Deputy Head, "no comparison to Charterhouse, I know."

"No," I agreed. "There isn't; but neither is there one in *price.* Your Headmaster quoted me £3,000 per annum – I am currently paying *£15,000*; there *is* no comparison!"

"My God!" was his reaction. "But, you know – as a teacher yourself – how would John Paul feel about coming here from all the advantages he has at Charterhouse?"

"He'd be delighted," I said. "And so would I. It's where I always intended him to be. At home. Walking to school every day. With friends. He's done all the work already," I told him, "to provide excellent GCSE results. He is putting on another play as well, at their Ben Travers Theatre – so that must be completed, obviously, but after that, we leave Charterhouse for *good.* John Paul will come here and take his A-levels, and then there will be sufficient funds for him to go to Oxford. Where he will study whatever he chooses."

I was introduced to all the staff, most of whom I remembered.

"I must point out, Mrs Donnelly," said the Head, "our last A-level results *equalled* Winchester and were *better* than Charterhouse!"

"I know," I smiled. "I checked."

We parted on excellent terms. The future now *did* look rosy.

So we moved; rescued all our furniture from the garage and this time, the removal van drove up to an *empty* house. Having supervised the loading up, I drove ahead, and parked almost outside the house to await the van.

Before I could get out of the car, an irate housewife accosted me. This is *my* car parking space," she shrilled, "and *you're* in it!"

I was completely taken aback. I had not been introduced to the niceties of off-road parking. "I am moving in next door," I explained. "The van is arriving at any minute."

"Not my problem," she snapped. "You're in *my* space; move out!"

Not an auspicious start. But a neighbour… I had better keep calm and make my peace. "I am really sorry," I told her, "but I have only a limited time to move in – and then I have to drive up to Godalming this evening to collect my son from school."

"Godalming?" she asked. "What school is that, at *Godalming*?"

"Charterhouse," I replied, "and I have to be there by seven this evening for a parent-teacher meeting (and tell them he's leaving). If I may borrow this space," I pleaded, "just for two hours, and allow the removal people to at least unpack, I would be most grateful. I had no idea what was involved in off-road parking, and hadn't realised the driveway was too narrow to park in."

"Well," she replied, eyeing my Mercedes 280 Estate – the now ancient banger that I'd driven for fifteen years, "it *wouldn't* be…"

She suddenly smiled. "But of course – take it for as long as you want – no problem, I can easily park outside next door, as they're away. You *will* come in for a coffee tomorrow, won't you? I'll introduce you to my two daughters. What did you say your son's name was?" (I hadn't.)

"John Paul…"

"What a charming name; my daughters are Elizabeth and Annabelle. I'll see you tomorrow, then. Anything you want – just pop round."

Then, an afterthought. "Oh, in any case," she said now, "you'll be *exhausted* after moving and then driving to *Charterhouse* and back, so *I'll* come and see *you* tomorrow."

She waved, and I went. The furniture had arrived; there followed a hectic couple of hours. As soon as they left I drove up to Charterhouse for the parent-teacher meeting.

After that, my new next-door-but-one neighbour, Doreen, rang every day to invite me for coffee. I went when I could, but I was *very* busy. I was pleased with the new house. An ugly, squat, little property, it was surprisingly spacious inside and all the main features were modern and of good quality. The agents and original owners had certainly spared no expense; it had merely been neglected.

At the back was a patch of patio, and eight feet circle of lawn which poor Akita could just about turn round in, and then a sea of vegetation. It spread as far as I could see – six to eight feet in height of tangled undergrowth. The only answer was to do the same as I'd done to the front. Armed with a scythe, I attacked the patio first. It soon became apparent that it had once been a honeysuckle hedge. It totally covered the dining room French windows and continued far beyond.

I fetched bin liners and began hacking. To my surprise, it cleared easily and by the end of the day I had cleared the patio. The dining room windows were clear and I had exposed the beginning of a curved lawn and eight-foot border. Beneath the honeysuckle, now stripped back to a good six-foot fence, were several rose bushes, lavender and various shrubs. The patio was now ten feet wide and extended for about forty feet.

At 5.00 pm, I took the bin liners to the tip and then sat down on the patio to survey the rest. In fact, the lawn, when cleared, extended to about forty feet across and sixty feet in length, with excellent broad borders all round. The shrubs very quickly revived, and began to show signs of new life.

My neighbour, impressed, told me the original owners had been keen gardeners. "I *think* there used to be a line of apple trees down there," she said, waving vaguely.

Well, *that* I *didn't* believe; you could not *possibly* bury a line of apple trees!

The lawn had appeared; its edges were trimmed back to professionally sharp lines and, once cut, it was immaculate. The far border was cleared – and then I met with a massive obstruction. Buried underneath were five apple trees! Clearing them, I saw how it had been – it was a kitchen garden. As I strimmed through tangled remains of netting and canes, there appeared the bramble, raspberry and loganberry bushes in a wonderful riot; they had levelled out at about six feet and completely smothered the whole area.

It was at that point that I chickened out and began work inside the house, but finally I faced it again and discovered, beneath the strangling ivy, a small orchard of cherry, plum and walnut trees.

Eventually, John Paul and I laid it all down to lawn and as I finally began work on the far side (which was hedged in by several sixty-foot trees, obviously requiring professional treatment), I discovered not one, but *two* excellent garden sheds. When I creaked open their doors – for the first time in fifteen years – there were rows and rows of garden tools, all meticulously cleaned and ready for use.

In all, the garden was almost half an acre of professionally laid out lawns, trees and orchard, and I was well pleased with my new property. If only I could afford to buy it now... I was paying £600 per month in rent and £5,000 per term to Charterhouse.

Each term, I would approach Lloyds Bank and make an appointment with Mr Moon and Mr Johnson. There was no money available for next term. Each time we argued, and I pleaded; 2007 was getting closer, I pointed out and then I could collect on my £60,000 policy... seven years yet, they snarled... but the £5,000 policy would be due in 2008... eight years to wait for that, was the sardonic reply. But each time, after a good half-hour's haranguing – which I dared not lose – I was grudgingly offered a further £5,000 overdraft.

Back to work I could go, and teach for the term. Now it was winter, so the holiday was spent stripping each room in turn, scrubbing it out, and decorating. And then back for next term... another £5,000 to borrow before John Paul could go back again.

I picked him up from Charterhouse at the end of another successful year. He'd shown me his name up in gold on every board there was in the school – as Top Scholar and Head of House, he was invincible.

I saw the end, finally, of the interminable £5,000 per term fees. The fees at King Edward's were £3,000 per *annum* and, at sixteen, John Paul would now have to become accustomed to being a 'latchkey' boy. I could complete my teaching career in London – and retire.

So, all we had to do was clear the trees – half a dozen laurels that, over the last fifteen years or so, had grown to a height of over sixty feet. I arranged a skip; it was provided for two days at £70.

John Paul set to with a will, and cleared the pathway. His activity training at Charterhouse proved useful. "Leave this to me," he'd said, taking a saw from the shed.

"Fine," I said, more than happy to do so. "I'll go to Sainsbury's and stock up with food for the workers."

The previous weekend, I'd had the builders in. Could they dig a bore hole to check the drains? Fine, I'd said. I locked Akita in the house. So far, she had left a complete set of teeth marks in five workmen.

Each had begged for her to be forgiven. The first (at Batemans) had, on inspection of the central heating, lunged across me without warning and snatched the coping wood from the pipe work. "Rotten!" he rasped. "See?" He pushed the six foot spar in my face as evidence... wrong move...

There was a blur of silver as Akita swept across the room, pinioned his shoulders against the wall and turned to look at me: *Please may I take his jugular out, Mum?*

"Akita," I managed to say. At once she was at my heel.

"Your own fault," accused the workman's mate. "Can't blame the dog, Fred; you shouldn't have crossed the room like that and took down that rod of wood."

After a mug of strong tea and half a pound of chocolate biscuits, Fred agreed. "Some dog, that," he said admiringly, as Akita accepted a chocolate biscuit (her one failing) as a reward. But after that, her word was law.

Before I left, the house was repainted. One workman, Bill, came. It was summertime and the weather was good. The phone rang; could I do some supply teaching? Could I? Try me...

I went out to Bill. "I'm sorry," I said. "I've been called out to teach. I'm afraid you'll have to come back another time – I can't leave you here with Akita."

"Why not?" asked Bill. "Akita and me is *friends* – and I need the money – you promised me two days work."

"Well," I began, doubtfully – certainly Akita was dozing on the top lawn, guarding the goldfish. "You promise you won't *touch* anything of mine?"

"Course not," said Bill. "'Ere, what you take me for?" he asked belligerently.

I said the dog was ordered to be put down for one more misdemeanour.

"I'll look arter Akita," he assured me. "No way will she be put down; no way."

"You won't go into the house?" I insisted. "You won't *touch* anything?"

"Leave it to me," said Bill confidently. "I've just to finish painting downstairs."

I drove off. The school was the other side of the forest. I drove back at 4.30, through the two sets of wrought-iron gates up the drive – and was suddenly transfixed. Bill was kneeling, in an unnatural attitude, clutching a ladder. At his feet was Akita, sitting, I thought, very comfortably. Stopping the car, I got out. Automatically, I called Akita. She came at once and sat, obediently, 'at heel'. "What happened?" I asked.

"I finished early," Bill replied. "Didn't want to waste an hour – thought I'd make a start upstairs, only me ladder weren't long enough, so without thinking, I took yours from the garage – I knew you wouldn't mind, like. As I took it down, Akita come and sunk her teeth into me ankle." He wriggled round, hoisting up his trouser leg. "Look," he said proudly. "A complete set of teeth marks!"

He was as proud of Akita as if she had been his own. "Some dog," he said.

I made an attempt to apologise, but Bill would have none of it. "No, no. You did warn me – I just thought me and the dog was friends, like… but, arter all you *did* say *not* to touch anything, and I did, so…"

I came back from Sainsbury's, armed to the teeth with groceries. I suddenly realised I could now get in the back way. Normally it was kept locked – anyone approaching would be stopped by Akita. But Akita was now locked up inside the house!

I lifted the latch to open the back door – and fell six feet into a void. Somehow, I had hung on to the latch; my mistake! I crawled out and shouted to John Paul for help. There was no response – only a whisper had come out. I remembered from the car accident… "the amount of damage depends on the length of paralysis." I could feel nothing.

The trick was to get upstairs and into bed before the pain set in. I called John Paul again. This time, the voice worked and he came running. Upstairs I went while the feet still worked, and stayed there.

John Paul somehow managed to cut down six sixty-foot trees, sawing them into manageable pieces and laying them, in perfect order, in the skip for collection.

It was the end of the summer vacation and there was no way I could get back to school. I rang Dr Simmonds. A hospital job, he said – damaged sciatic nerve, torn spinal muscles and ligaments and a cracked disc.

"No," I protested. "No. It's John Paul's last summer – I *can't* go into hospital; someone has to be *here*."

"Well…" he said doubtfully, "… as long as you can get to the loo?"

But, either way, there was no feeling from the waist down…

Could I make it? I did, just.

"I'll come back in a week," he said. "You should go into hospital… going to be a long job, anyway."

A week later, I could just get down the stairs on my bottom – but at least I could get downstairs. I rang my school in London to say I wouldn't be back for 3rd September.

Louise had been installed for her first Headship at the Falcons – the most expensive pre-prep in London. Her inauguration had not been impressive. On arrival, she had sacked six of the younger staff; they were Montessouri trained and she would only have *state* trained staff. On the last day of term the sports/open day was held and the PE master (also sacked) had knocked out the microphone, making all the events defunct. The parents were being harangued by a local QC parent – "We *can* sack this appalling woman… and we *will*," – and I, as senior teacher, felt it was up to me to reinstate the status quo, so I strode out to accompany Louise as she attempted to regain order. The crowd around the QC broke up, everyone came back and the races were resumed – the microphone having undergone a miraculous repair and order was restored.

Louise ushered me into her car afterwards and we drove back to the school. "You will be my Deputy Head," she enthused in her study. "We will soon sort this lot out!"

I had to tell her that, as a professional teacher, I had felt honour bound to support her, but I disagreed totally with her treatment of the staff. All the young teachers had been sacked without any provision – or even references to help them get future employment. In such circumstances, no, I could not accept her offer; I would merely complete my final year of teaching.

Her fury had then known no bounds and so, when I rang to say I would be unable to get back on 3rd September, she was delighted. "I've *got* you," she screamed down the phone. "I've *got* you!"

She had apparently overheard a conversation I'd had concerning teachers' pensions. Since I had recovered sufficiently to enable me to return to full time teaching, (with no money from Desmond, there had been little choice) I was now eligible for a full pension – of £10,000 per annum. All Louise had to do was report that I had hurt my back and I would then go back to a disablement pension of £5,000 per annum. Since I was paying £600 per month to rent the house in Bourne Avenue, I would be a dead duck – and so, of course, would John Paul.

If I rang the doctor, I would be confined to at least six months sick leave – either in hospital or, at best, strict bed rest. On my bottom, I could get downstairs; next step – *walking* down.

John Paul, having worked like a Trojan in the holidays, got a lift back to school. Then came a phone call from King Edward's. They had requested reports from Charterhouse, who had come back, all guns blazing. *No way* could John Paul leave Charterhouse; not only was he their Top Scholar, but also the *Best* Top Scholar who had 'ever passed through their portals.' No way could he leave Charterhouse.

Lord McAlpine was called in; he would make up the balance, whatever it might be, but John Paul was *not leaving Charterhouse*. I therefore had no choice but to continue paying £5,000 per term... but *only* if I completed my last year teaching.

I had managed to get downstairs; could I get to London? I could barely walk, but I could get a taxi.

September 3rd came, and with a taxi, which deposited me at the station. So far, so good. I tottered out at Waterloo, managed to stagger to Platform 17 for Richmond – and tottered out at the other end. The rest was just a nightmare...

I remember crawling up to the nearest tree and clasping it firmly to my bosom – before staggering on to the next one. Fortunately, the road from the station to the school was an avenue, and I lurched from one tree to the next, hugging each one until I was in full view of the school, when I managed to walk fairly steadily up to the front door.

I'd made it! At least I could be assured of a month's pay; all I had to do was maintain my record of one hundred percent success in getting the children through their Scholarship exams. The problem was – the reason for the last Head Teacher's early resignation – the summer exams had now been brought forward to January. Could I get the results that had taken me a year to achieve, in just three months?

I staggered, limping, into school each day, and we finally arrived at Christmas – and vacation. There were no Christmas festivities, just – thankfully – complete bed rest. John Paul entertained himself as best he could, and all his friends rallied round.

Then came the new year, and another term. In January I had to make the journey to London again. I was heartened and relieved that all the children had passed their selection exams – but, with no warning, I suddenly collapsed in a heap. Now, it was total agony just to get downstairs. Heaven knew what damage I had done to my spine – as my doctor had warned me – a broken spine can be mended if you go *straight* into hospital. In my case, it hadn't been just the teaching, but the four hour journey *before* I reached school – I had been asking for trouble. Still, the children had all got through their exams, and now I was prepared to go into hospital and sort myself out. Not that simple…

Louise phoned. "If you are not back here *immediately*, your pay will be stopped!"

"No," I argued. "You can't do that; this is a serious injury and I am *entitled* to go into hospital." But no; I checked my bank account. My salary had been stopped. There was nothing there now to pay for John Paul's last term at Charterhouse; and he *must* take his GCSE's.

Well, my back had gone for good; I could barely walk. As far as I was concerned, I may as well keep going and at least see that John Paul continued. I went back to work, and the parents greeted me happily. As Louise had said, my leaving would have been the last straw – the one that broke the camel's back (not to worry about mine). Either I went back, or all the children would leave, and since it was a private school, there would be no fees and the school would close.

However, on my return to Falcon's, I was shattered to find myself classed as an *assistant* teacher… at the beck and call of all the newly-qualified teachers; to earn my pay I was now required to hump furniture, paper walls – whatever menial tasks could be found for me. Louise certainly lived up to her nick-name of Poison Ivy – God help anyone who fell foul of her. And I certainly had.

Meanwhile, the house in Bourne Avenue was now up for sale. Doreen, my next-door-but-one neighbour, had invited me round for coffee (a daily ritual).

Would I accompany her to a Midnight Mass at the local Church?

I would be delighted…

I *must* bring John Paul.

He would be delighted…

I was disappointed in Annabelle, Doreen's daughter. Although, at fourteen, most things could be overlooked or forgiven, her behaviour left much to be desired. Over-effusive, she exuded such enthusiasm for any and all males she could find; it was left to the boys to treat her like a snake to a rabbit and the teenage girls to ignore her.

Finally, Doreen came back to me. "The Church," she explained, "have ostracised Annabelle. Please could John Paul take her to *his* Church?"

"Of course," I agreed.

John Paul and his friend, Neil, duly took Annabelle to church with them.

Next Sunday I was met by a thunderous Doreen. "How *dare* they?" she stormed. "They were supposed to take Annabelle to Church – where *are* they?"

"I'm sorry," I explained, "but John Paul and Neil are Servers of the Church – they have to be there half an hour early. If you want Annabelle to go to Church you have to drive her there – as everyone else has to do."

She fumed, but there was nothing else to be done about it; I myself went to a very traditional, old-fashioned church. However, after that, I gathered that Annabelle duly attended without further problems.

Annabelle wanted to take Drama for GCSE's; would John Paul please help her?

John Paul was busy; however, if it's English and Drama, maybe I could help her?

"Good God, no!" was the reaction to *my* offer of assistance…

Annabelle was passionately fond of dogs; may she walk Akita (and see John Paul at the same time)?

"I'm afraid not; I have a problem with Akita, although she is a lamb when it comes to children or old people."

"But please may she *try*?" Doreen had pleaded.

Certainly it would be helpful… when teaching, I had to leave the patio doors open, I could hardly leave her in the house for eighteen hours…

So I went with Akita and Annabelle every day, down to the park, a two-minute walk away – and Akita was trained; all Annabelle had to do was let her out of the house and then put her back in. Finally the day came when I ordered Akita to walk on without me. She barked, and refused, but then went the short walk to the park with Annabelle – and without me. After that, she accepted that if Annabelle came to the door, she would walk to the park with her.

Fine. It meant at least I could work and leave Akita to Annabelle. But then, to my surprise, Doreen demanded eight pounds a week for dog-walking! Bruce, my ex-neighbour, as a trained dog handler working for Kenya Police, had only asked for six pounds… still, it meant that Akita did get some exercise while I was working.

Later, when John Paul was at home on vacation… would he come to see his favourite video on Annabelle's TV?

No. He was busy. However, Neil would. Neil's mother helped run the local church – they were dedicated churchgoers.

To my surprise, Doreen turned up on *my* doorstep. "*Neil* is coming round," she announced, all smiles, "to see the video. Please may I stay for a while?"

"Of course." Surprised, I let her in… it was company.

"Is there somewhere I can *stay*?" she asked. "I may have to stay *all night*."

I suddenly had a nasty feeling. Neil's parents were both teachers – I had taught alongside his mother, and his father taught at King Edward's. Still, Neil was not my responsibility…

At 10.30, my phone rang. Doreen rudely rushed out and answered it. "It's Annabelle," she said, "and Neil's *gone*!"

"Well," I replied, "the video only lasts about an hour and a half, and it's ten-thirty, so Neil *would* leave."

"Oh my God," groaned Doreen. "You people went out with the Dodo!" and she slammed out.

Next, we were invited out, but John Paul *had* to come. We went. To Mottisfont Abbey Festival. I had suffered a broken ankle, so John Paul arranged our two chairs at the end of a row for convenience. After the obligatory picnic, we returned to our seats to find that mine was at the end of the row – on its own. John Paul's had been placed a hundred yards away, next to Doreen and Annabelle. Without a word, John Paul merely replaced the chair in its original setting, next to mine.

The half-time interval came, and I hobbled across to enquire whether Doreen and Annabelle would care to view the celebrated rose garden with us?

No, she snapped; she would not. It was left to Margaret, her immediate neighbour, to drive us home.

On John Paul's birthday, I took him into town to buy a cravat, since he was not into formal wear. Off we went, to the tie shop, but the only cravats they had were mustard coloured.

"Oh my God," he lamented. "I'd rather do without *anything* than wear *that* awful colour!"

I bought him a proper bow tie, instead. He spent hours learning how to tie it and finally appeared before me with a perfectly tied bow tie.

Again we were invited out by Doreen and Annabelle. John Paul was forced to sit in the back of the car with Annabelle. "I've got you a birthday present," she breathed at him.

"That was *two days* ago," he said, unmoved.

"I know," she pouted, "but I've bought you a *present*, anyway."

John Paul opened it up, and there it was – the mustard coloured cravat, with black spots. I had innocently mentioned to Doreen that I was looking for a cravat…

Nothing if not honest, John Paul said, "Saw that in the tie shop; Mum offered to buy it for me, but I couldn't face that *awful* colour. Still, nice thought; thanks." He opened a second, smaller package. A *plastic* bow tie…

"What are you doing on Saturday?" Annabelle asked him. "I *know* you've got a spare evening suit here – your Mum said so, and now you've got a *bow tie*. It's our High School Ball on Saturday – will you take me?"

John Paul packed up the presents. "Thank you for these," he said politely. "No, I can't take you to the Ball."

"But you haven't any plans for Saturday, have you?" wailed Annabelle.

"I haven't made *any* plans yet," John Paul told her. "But certainly the last thing I would *ever* want to do is take *you* to a High School Ball!"

Oh Hell! Doreen's hands gripped ever tighter on the steering wheel until her knuckles showed white. I can't remember *where* we went, or *how* we got home…

The following week, Doreen greeted me with enthusiasm. "Annabelle has got a *boyfriend*," she beamed.

Thank God.

"That's nice," I said, pleasantly.

"Yes. He's thirty-two. A builder. Of course, he has a ponytail and wears a gold earring… but he's a boyfriend. Annabelle has been invited round to his flat to cook dinner."

"A first date?" I asked. "Wouldn't it be a good idea to invite him to *your* home and let Annabelle cook dinner?"

"Oh my God," she said, rolling her eyes skyward. "You are just not of this world!" She stomped off impatiently.

The next day she came round, beaming happily. She had apparently filled Annabelle's handbag with condoms and practically thrown her out. "Annabelle fell in at 4.00 am – totally *paralytic*!" she boasted. "Threw up all *over* the place, but she's got a *boyfriend*."

So Annabelle was written off. Next in line was the elder daughter, thirty-two year old Liz. "Can't get a boyfriend," Doreen kept complaining – then, finally, "We've got one!"

On a flight back from Paris, a fellow had accepted her offer of dinner. Doreen hurried round. "I have the menu," she said. "Home-made lobster soup, followed by roast lamb and my own profiteroles."

"How did the meal go?" I enquired next day.

"It didn't!" she snapped.

Apparently, she had left the two of them in the house and when she returned, the fellow had brushed past her coming downstairs, doing up his trousers, on his way out. "He didn't even bother to mention his name!" she said, bitterly.

Finally, *finally*, the year came to an end. I was *retired*!!! No more alarm clocks at 4.30 am; no more 5.45 train to London. I had earned my retirement – albeit with a broken back and no home, but at least it was finished with.

I rang Nationwide to check my mortgage offer. My retirement lump sum of £14,000 was just enough to get John Paul through university and pay £6,000 deposit on the house. With the work I'd done on it, the house was now worth £85,000.

"Sorry," they said. "Did we hear right? You are retiring?"

"Yes," I replied happily. "Everything is now sorted and I can afford to buy the property; I have a retirement lump sum of…"

"Sorry, no," they replied, without hearing my explanation. "We can't offer a mortgage on a *pension*."

"But you have *already* offered me a mortgage," I pointed out.

"Sorry, not on a pension. Goodbye."

I rang back. "The offer," I said, "was on the basis of three and a half times my income. My income (pension) qualifies me for that."

"Ah. Yes… your mortgage offer is being processed through our Bristol office. You will need to deal with them."

I rang the Bristol office. "Ah. Yes…" they said, "your paperwork is being processed by our office in Southampton. It will take about three weeks."

There were several similar telephone conversations, the last one with Nationwide's Southampton office, who finally admitted to having the papers.

"You mean you have them there right now?" I asked.

"Oh yes, I have your offer in front of me now," said the clerk, "to be processed – it will take about another three weeks."

Fine. I put the phone down and took a taxi to their Southampton office. "I'd like my mortgage papers back," I said.

"Sorry," I was told, "your mortgage is being dealt with by Bristol Head Office. It will take another three weeks."

"I have just put the phone down," I informed her. "The person I spoke to said, 'I have your papers in front of me right now.' Obviously there is no mortgage offer, so I would like the papers back *right now*, or I call the police and *demand* them."

There was a pause before she left briefly, came back, and then ushered me into the Manager's office. There, on the table, were the papers as I had first left them at least two months ago – untouched.

"I would like them back," I said. "*Right now.*"

"They *have* been up to Bristol," she said defensively.

But, clearly, they had been nowhere. So, in fact, I had sold the house in Bourne Avenue, but without buying it first! Fortunately, the couple who had bought it, a police inspector and his wife, were delighted with it, and so determined, they rushed me out to a solicitor to sign there and then.

First things first... I *must* get a mortgage. I sat down and went through Yellow Pages.

The first one I managed to speak to accepted. Yes, he could deal with the mortgage... yes, on a *pension*. He would require a fee of £280. No problem... well, just *one* problem – he only worked from home and everything would have to be done by post. By this time, I was on such a high dose of morphine – Dr Simmons had warned me that even when I stopped travelling, I would be 'hooked' on it. Still, if that was what it took, then that was the only option.

Later, the phone rang; it was a return call from one of my earlier enquiries.

"You were enquiring about mortgages?" asked the voice.

"Yes," I said. "I've already got one, though."

"Ah," replied the voice. "Ah, but I offer a specialist service – I am prepared to come to your house and deal with *everything* – you do not need to leave your armchair."

"You would come to my house and deal with all the paperwork?" I asked him.

"Certainly. Just let me make a note of your address and I can be there in ten minutes to deal with it. My name is Brooks," he said. "Albert Brooks."

Nine

Within ten minutes, there was a knock on my door, and Mr Brooks did indeed arrive. I greeted him quite coolly.

"I have said that I have already got the mortgage arranged," I reminded him. "I have paid Mr Revere £280; he has all the paperwork. I really don't know whether he has started work on it already – if he has, then of course that has to be considered as final."

"Oh, but you see," gabbled Mr Brooks, "I would offer you a personal service. You said you had suffered a personal injury – that is what I specialise in. I go mainly to the elderly and infirm who cannot get out, but who need a mortgage arranged."

"Well, that *is* me," I agreed ruefully. "I've got the mortgage in hand. The problem is, there's a limited time factor. I have tried *everywhere* this past year and *nowhere* can I get a mortgage on pension – only on a salary."

Mr Brooks made a few notes as he listened.

"I retire officially on 30th August," I continued. "I will collect my salary and a lump sum of £14,000 on 30th July. During that period, I *must* complete the mortgage and the purchase of this house. If not, at the end of August I will no longer be able to afford to rent the property and I and my belongings will be out on the pavement – homeless by September. In other words, it is crunch time."

He had a look at the grounds – now half an acre of landscaped gardens – and the ground floor of the house. "Rest of the house – upstairs – decorated to the same standard?" he enquired.

"Except for the bathroom, yes. The tilers are working on it now," I told him. "They will complete it tomorrow."

He sat down with all the figures. "Well, that's fine," he said at length. "Yes, definitely, I can guarantee to complete the mortgage in three weeks; it's now mid-June, so, yes... no problem."

"And by coming to the house when necessary, for me to complete the forms?" I asked. "Without even having to walk up to the post box?"

"Absolutely. As far as the mortgage is concerned, I guarantee you will not have to leave your armchair." He stood up, to shake hands on it.

With difficulty, I too, struggled to my feet. The relief was so great that, for a moment, I stood with my hands covering my face. Suddenly, there was the most appalling stench that overwhelmed me, and I recoiled. Simultaneously, Mr Brooks leapt backwards with an anguished howl, clutching his behind.

Seeing my distress – in fact, my relief – he had attempted to put his arms round me. As long as he'd kept his arms to his sides, his personal hygiene problem had not been apparent. That aside, seeing his arms outstretched towards me, Akita had merely leapt up from her normal, watchful position and firmly bitten his buttocks. (That was the last set of teeth marks she left on anyone's flesh).

There was a shout from above and then John Paul came clumping down the stairs in his football boots. "What's up, Mum?"

The look on Mr Brooks' face told me that he had thought I was alone in the house. He recovered quickly, and spoke hurriedly. "I've just told your mother yes I can do the mortgage, she was a little upset and the dog…"

John Paul surveyed the room doubtfully. Mr Brooks clutching his behind, Akita smirking at my feet, and my face a mask of dismay. (My God, in *two* seconds I'd lost the mortgage!)

"She bit Mr Brooks," I told John Paul. He immediately realised the position.

"Oh, but she's only a *puppy*," he said to Mr Brooks. (A three-year old puppy?) "Does that to all my friends; it's a game she plays. Didn't hurt you at all, I hope?"

"She really doesn't *mean* to, Mr Brooks," I added.

"No, no," he replied, as white as a sheet and backing away.

"So you *can* still do the mortgage?" I gasped.

"Oh, er… yes," he said doubtfully, "I can still do *that*."

I offered him tea, coffee, sympathy, but he declined, and retreated backwards until he reached the front door, which I closed, thankfully, behind him. I had a mortgage; he could do it well within the time, whether I was on my feet or not. True, I had to pay him an extra £175 to do it, and when I rang Mr Revere he was apologetic, but no, his fee was not refundable. I didn't care; I'd got the mortgage problem settled.

Two days later he returned; Mr Revere had reluctantly handed over the papers, which were in order – we could now proceed with the mortgage. He was prepared to do everything from my house, he reiterated; I would not even need to walk to the post box. However, he *would* need to check *all* my documents... my last year's pay checks?

"Upstairs," I explained. "I'll get them." It seemed too ignominious to go upstairs in my normal fashion – backwards, on my bottom. So, clutching the banisters tightly, I slowly and carefully made my way up – looking longingly at my bed on the way – but collected the papers, and tottered down again.

"Ah, good. And the year *before*?" Mr Brooks murmured.

"I'll get them," I gasped. I got them, then collapsed back into my chair and settled the hot water bottle firmly against my back.

"Tax returns for last year?" asked Mr Brooks, sweetly.

"You don't need them," I said firmly. "Mr Revere had everything in hand; he is ready to arrange the mortgage *now*, *and* I have already paid for it. Can you, or can you not do it? If not, I go straight back to Mr Revere – *now*."

"Of course, of course. Oh yes, I can do the mortgage," he replied hastily. "It's just that I am used to dealing with incapacitated ladies – and you are clearly in that category. I like to check *all* documents, you see, while I'm at it – call me over-efficient if you will, but I *am* a financial adviser, and I like to make sure that everything is in order." He smiled knowingly. "Why don't I go up and collect the *folder*, and then I can check *all* the documents for you?"

I didn't think so. "Another time," I said. With luck I might just get him out of the house before I collapsed completely.

He was back again in another two days. Everything was fine; all was in hand, nothing to worry about. He seemed to have nothing else to do but spend his evenings checking papers with his clients. "Now," he said, "I'd better go through the rest of those papers..."

"But you don't need to," I insisted. "The mortgage is going through."

"Ah, Nationwide are a little unhappy," he said. "The figures *do* work out, but only just – it leaves you little to live on, you see. They are not sure whether you will be able to keep up the payments."

Wearily, I explained the situation to him.

If I could get to London and make it through until the end of term, I would then collect my £14,000 lump sum. That would pay the £6,000 deposit on the house and £5,000 for John Paul's last term at Charterhouse, in order to take his GCSE's. He would then be taking his A-levels at King Edward's school opposite. I would then sell the house – I already had a buyer to provide me with £25,000 profit. As security I had two policies totalling £65,000 which matured in 2007/2008. The trick was, I pointed out, lasting out until 2007. Here we were in 1996, and although the bank allowed me to borrow on the £65,000 in order to keep John Paul at Charterhouse, the policies were worthless pieces of paper until that date.

"Well, I've nothing better to do," sighed Mr Brooks, "and it's been a long drive – I've had to drive down from Northampton to check all this out…"

I hastily offered coffee.

"Thank you. While I'm drinking it, let's have a look at these policies, and then I can reassure Nationwide."

I staggered off upstairs to fetch them. As I came back into the room, Mr Brooks was just removing his jacket prior to getting down to business. As he leant back, somewhat heavily, against my settee, that same, foul, odour wafted across the room. Even Akita stiffened.

Beads of sweat were now rolling down his face. He took out a large handkerchief and began mopping with it. "May I have a drink of water?" he asked.

Taking a pill box from his pocket, he took out two white tablets and swallowed them with two gulps of water. *Then* he went through the file. Suddenly, he sat up. He'd picked up the £60,000 policy. After going carefully through it, he looked up, his piggy little eyes glittering. He was obviously excited. "May I take this with me?" he asked.

"Of course."

"I'll just need to show it to Nationwide," he said, "and that will clinch your mortgage."

I didn't understand; he looked exactly like the small, greedy child, who turns up at every child's party, spots the cream cake amongst the buns and is prepared to snatch it. He clearly thought he'd struck gold. But *now*? Yes, the policy was worth £60,000, but not for another *twelve years*; until then – as Messrs Moon and Johnson at the bank frequently impressed upon me – it was just a useless piece of paper!

Mr Brooks was Action Man now. He threw down the file, pulled his coat on and headed out, barely managing to say goodbye, and was gone. I looked aghast at where he had been sitting – on my pale yellow velvet Edwardian chaise longue. There was a great dark imprint where he had leaned back; it was sopping wet and stank of sweat. I'd certainly got the mortgage, but Mr Brooks had got a problem…

I dug out a cotton throw and draped it casually over the back of the chaise longue against his next visit.

It was sooner than I expected. I had reached home at 9.00 pm as usual, and was just preparing for bath and bed when the door bell rang. He was in a livid temper; gone was the ingratiating smile and the deferential approach. He stormed in and threw himself down in a chair without invitation and thrust the policy at me. "It's a COPY!" he roared, his little eyes blinking rapidly in fury.

"Well of course it's a copy!" I retorted. "It will, eventually, be worth a great deal of money. The original is held in a safe deposit box at Lloyds Bank – as security. As I have told you – repeatedly – I may borrow on it, but until 2007 it is just a worthless piece of paper!"

Mr Brooks sat there staring at me; his eyes and mouth popping. Then he pulled himself together. "Of course, of course," he parroted. "Yes, now I understand… but the original *is* in the bank?"

"Nationwide may check with Mr Moon and Mr Johnson if they are in *any* doubt," I told him.

"I, er… I didn't realise you had given me a *copy*," he said.

"Well, I'd hardly have handed over the *original*, now would I?" I laughed. "That would be pretty foolish." He gave me such a startled look, I then said hastily, "Not that I don't *trust* a financial adviser, you understand, but – obviously – the safest place for it is in the bank."

"Of course, of course," he said smoothly. "I quite understand. In that case, everything is in order, and I'll be in touch." He put his arm casually round my shoulders. I was beginning to get used to the stale cabbage smell by now. Akita merely raised herself, equally casually knocking his arm down again. I smiled and carefully moved out of reach. "Such a *playful* puppy," I murmured as I showed him out. Then as I shut the door I remembered – he hadn't given me the copy back. But at least the mortgage was in the bag. John Paul could now stay on at school for A-levels – provided I could still make it until the end of term.

I was fast running out of pills; Dr Simmons pointed out I was using up my four-week allowance in three weeks, and had finally refused to prescribe more. I had taken my limit of morphine. I had gone to other doctors on the panel and explained that "...Dr Simmons would have given them to me, but he's not on tonight..." and they had helpfully given me extra 'just this once.' But I had done it once too often and now, the receptionist told me, Dr Simmons had given strict instructions that *no one* was to give me more pills.

Finally, I went back to him and explained that John Paul *must* take his GCSE's; everything depended on it. He had unjustly lost his scholarship award, but it was essential that he excelled when the exams came up, which would clearly expose the fact that he had been more than worthy of it.

"I cannot keep supplying you with morphine," Dr Simmons insisted. "You *must* go into hospital – you've had no x-rays, and I've no idea what damage you have done, or are still doing."

"Just four more weeks?" I begged. "I *have* to be there at the end of term."

"But I can give you a *certificate* to cover you," he replied.

I'd tried that; I had staggered into school in January, got the children successfully through their selection examinations – and collapsed in a heap at home. But Louise had immediately phoned. She had listened in on my conversation with the Teachers' Pensions people. If I taught full time, I could retire on a full pension; any sign of illness, and I would be returned to 'disabled' status and have my pension halved. My pay had stopped from that day – with or without a doctor's certificate. As far as I knew, that was illegal, but I couldn't afford to argue at this late stage – I'd gone back to work. The damage was done; too late to alter it now.

I tried more pleading. "Just four more weeks," I wheedled. "Then, I *promise* I'll never come back for more pills again."

"Oh, but you will," Dr Simmons said. "That's the problem; you are now on such a high dose of morphine just to keep you going – you wouldn't be able to stop taking them even if you wanted to."

I was horrified. "Give me the pills now, Dr Simmons, and I will personally guarantee that I won't be back for more once the term has finished."

He smiled at me doubtfully, but handed the pills over.

With three weeks to go, it did look as if I was going to make it; but it had been *such* a close thing. Financially, every penny had been used.

As I'd explained to Mr Brooks, *either* I collected the lump sum and the £25,000 profit on the house at the end of the month *or* the house would revert back to the original owners – the Church – who were waiting to sell. The house had to go, one way or another, at the end of August; if not to me, it would be sold to elsewhere at the increased value and the Church would collect the £25,000 profit. I had personally increased the value of the house – and I would be the one left sitting on the pavement with my furniture!

But, I had to admit, thanks to Mr Brooks, the mortgage *was* going through. I *would* collect the profit and John Paul *would* stay on for his A-levels.

I paid off all the last minute bills to clear the house – milkman, baker, electricity, etc. None of them over £10 – but all done. My penultimate salary would be credited on the 26th, so I arranged all the bills to be paid that day, knowing the money would be there.

I was devastated to open my bank statement and find that all seven bills had been 'bounced'. Not only that, at a charge of £25 per bounced cheque, I had amassed another £175 on an 'unauthorised overdraft'. Immediately, I rang Lloyds. "This cannot be so," I insisted. "The bills couldn't have gone out until the 26th and my salary automatically gets paid in on the 26th."

"Ah, yes," they said, "but our computer *debits* the money at *six* am, whereas your salary is *credited* at *nine* am."

Unbelievable.

"The point is," I said, "I have arranged with a removal firm to move my furniture out and I need to pay them a cheque for £250... you will honour it?"

"Oh no." I was told. "It will bounce."

"But, at twelve o'clock, I need to give them a cheque to move me *out*," I attempted to explain. "And at one o'clock I receive £85,000 for the house, which will provide me with a cheque for £25,000 to pay into my account."

No joy.

"Very well," I said tersely. "I will make arrangements somehow, but be assured of this: as soon as I receive the cheque for £25,000, I will be opening an account at another bank with it. After forty years with Lloyds... I will be changing banks!"

"As you wish," they said.

As soon as the term finished, I told myself, I will clear my account from Lloyds once and for all – rid myself of Mr Moon and Mr Johnson and their constant 'worthless piece of paper' and put my two policies into another bank.

Roll on 2007!

Every other evening now, the doorbell would ring – Albert Brooks – 'just passing.'

"Any news yet?" I would enquire, more and more desperately. "Is the mortgage through yet?" Ten days to go and I would be on the pavement with my furniture and John Paul on the streets.

"Not yet. Just got back from a long drive."

He certainly seemed to travel long distances – Northampton, Chester – looking for mortgages. Each time, he asked for water with which to take his pills. He explained that he had to take them so many times a day; he'd break his journey, take them, and then go home. I had to admit he worked hard – and late, and did seem to be a sick man.

He noticed the cotton throw over the chaise longue. "My wife does that to all the chairs at home," he confessed. "Diabetes. Makes me sweat so. And put on weight… this job is killing me," he would end up with.

Each time, he gazed at the mirrors. They had come from one of the big houses in the forest. Two huge Venetian mirrors with heavy scrolled gilt surrounds, and two smaller mirrors to match. Strategically placed to reflect back on each other in the sitting room and dining room made the rooms look enormous.

"They're what sold the house," I said. "People don't realise I'll take them with me when I go; but at least they sold the house… and that will take John Paul to University."

"I'd kill for those mirrors," he murmured dreamily.

After that, he seemed to get into the habit of popping in to gawp at the mirrors. One day, I thought hopefully, he'll tell me he's come to finalise the mortgage. Each time, before he left, a clammy hand would be placed on my shoulder in a friendly fashion, and each time, Akita eyed him as I quickly negotiated him to the door, making sure his hand slipped away before Akita helped him on his way in her customary 'puppy-like' manner.

It was becoming increasingly difficult to get rid of him. "Nothing but *water*," he sneered as he took his pills. "I could do with a gin and tonic!"

I got some in. Not that I thought it would do much good – he'd had to 'up the dose', he told me dispiritedly. "This bloody job is killing me – I *mean* it," he said moodily as he set off for home. "But I *want* those mirrors!"

Each time he called, he'd travelled to secure a mortgage, but it had always fallen through. He certainly seemed to be going through a bad patch.

Then he turned up one Saturday afternoon. John Paul was out playing football; Annabelle turned up, breathless. Too late – she'd missed him – oh well, she'd take Akita for her run in the park.

Mr Brooks stomped into the sitting room. I had collapsed into my chair, surreptitiously cradling a hot water bottle at my back, hoping I could get rid of him and have half an hour in bed before John Paul came in for a meal.

"One day," he began, dramatically stomping up and down, "…one day, I shall make wild, passionate love to you – on that golden chaise longue – beneath those Venetian gold mirrors!"

I shuddered involuntarily. Do that, I thought, and my back will break in half. The thought of seventeen stones of white lard stinking of stale cabbage landing on me was too much. I bared my teeth, politely. "Ha ha," I managed, weakly. "Yes, they are a bit over the top, but as I say – they helped to sell the house."

"I mean it," he said.

I thought the conversation had gone far enough and staggered up out of my chair. Akita had gone out, I remembered. "You will excuse me, Mr Brooks," I said hastily. "I have to take some strong painkillers – as you know, I damaged my spine, which is why I needed help getting the mortgage." I escaped to the kitchen.

Then the phone rang. Hoping it was John Paul, I answered it.

Joy of joys! It was a Headmistress from a school nearby. Could I teach for three days?

Could I? Try me! For next term? Even better – I'd have six weeks holiday to recover, and then *work*.

"It could be longer," she said. "The teacher has to go into hospital. We don't know for how long – but three days initially."

Saved by the bell! I'd have the summer holiday to recuperate – and with a longer spell of teaching, I could get a good reference... I could be back teaching in Southampton.

Suddenly, I was aware of an overpowering stench of rotting cabbage, and an arm crept round my waist... then clutched higher. I had a mug of hot coffee in one hand, and the phone in the other. I carefully spilt the coffee; there was a gasp and the hand was retrieved.

"How many in class?" I asked. "What age?" As she began to explain, my dress was suddenly unzipped at the back and it fell to the floor as hands seized the back of my bra.

"Are you alright, Mrs Donnelly?" said a concerned voice at the other end of the phone.

"Yes, fine," I gasped, bending down to rescue my dress and giving a vicious kick to Brooks' shins. But detestable, clammy hands were now round my waist.

"Are you *sure* you're alright?" the voice repeated.

"*No*, I am *not!*" I roared down the phone, before throwing it down. The pain in my back had been growing steadily worse and the pills had not yet kicked in. I picked up my dress with as much dignity as I could muster.

"How *dare* you?" I hissed at Brooks. "*How dare you*? You have just cost me my job! You are *here*," I roared, "to arrange a *mortgage*; that does not involve coming here to *slobber* over my mirrors and *soak* my furniture. I appreciate it's nothing *personal*," I went on. "You'd attack a dead *sheep* if you found it lying in the middle of the road! I will give you credit – I *think* you'd check it was a *female* sheep first, but I'm not *entirely* sure about that. However, one thing I *am* sure about is that I am in considerable pain. I have a damaged spine and do *not* welcome seventeen stone of smelly, wet blubber descending on me. Understand *this*," I continued, furiously wagging an index finger, "the *only* reason you have been allowed in this house is because I have permanent spinal damage and need a mortgage arranged."

There was more; out it all came: "If it gives you any satisfaction, you do not need to attack me from *behind* – a mere poke from a *finger* at the moment, even a *feather*, would knock me flat on my back and render me *entirely* at anyone's mercy. So if that gives you satisfaction, that's all you have to do – as I've said – *entirely* at your mercy. As would a dead sheep..."

I suddenly realised I had been jabbing my finger at him on each point, in true Deputy Head fashion.

"Sorry… sorry… sorry," he spluttered as he backed up the hallway to the front door. "Only I…"

"Out!" I snarled.

"But I need…"

"*Out*!" I hissed.

"… the mortgage…"

"*OUT*!"

He went. Indeed, he couldn't get out fast enough. I leaned back against the door and cursed fluently and fast.

If only I'd taken the pills earlier… if only I'd managed to keep my temper… if only the wretched Headmistress had rung before Akita left…

If only…

Clearly, the mortgage was blown. In ten days time the house went back to the church and they would collect the £25,000 profit on all the hard work I'd put into it. What to tell John Paul when he happily rolled in with his friends after football to enjoy a barbecue on the patio? Oh, John Paul, by the way – no university, no mortgage, no home; Mum lost her temper and shrieked like a Billingsgate fishwife, and threw Mr Brooks out of the house…

Akita and Annabelle returned, and I ignored Annabelle's effusive greeting and attempts to join in the barbecue. The boys also managed to avoid her, and she left, discomfited. I usually encouraged her to stay for the barbecue, however reluctant the boys were to accept the inevitable, but today they crashed out onto the patio, full of end of term plans and hilarity – which university – and their all important exam results.

I would have to ring Brooks and apologise – eat humble pie – anything. Of course, I had been in *such* pain, I had *entirely* misunderstood his intentions (I hadn't). *Anything*. But I *must* have the mortgage; that was clear. Still, I couldn't trust myself to keep a civil tongue in my head at the moment… I'd ring later… when I'd got John Paul back to school. But I'd get that mortgage somehow.

I saw my QC; John Paul had done brilliantly at Charterhouse, and everything now depended on his being there at the end of term to take his exams. My mortgage offer had fallen through; I needed £6,000 to secure the house (and pick up £25,000 profit and ensure completion of

John Paul's education). *Surely* he could persuade Desmond, with High Court Judgements against him in London and Hong Kong, to pay £6,000 now; forget the £80,000 plus what he owed me – I needed £6,000 *now*.

He was apologetic. Yes, Desmond owed the money; yes, he was in contempt of court for non-payment, but after a highly successful career in Hong Kong and Singapore of many years' duration, he is now preparing to retire. As a self-employed QC, and *no* check on his income – I would get *nothing*. In reality, of course, he should be disbarred for being in contempt of court – indeed a prison sentence had already been passed, with no effect. But whatever the outcome, there would still be *no money*. Apart from which, should John Paul ever decide to take up law – as was first intended, to have a disbarred father would mean total disgrace before he even began.

"And another thing," he said. "Desmond has contacted me to say he is now living with his son in Los Angeles – so God knows how we would contact him, anyway."

"But he doesn't *have* a son in Los Angeles," I told him (though *nothing* about Desmond surprised me any more). He had left his wife and three daughters twenty years ago. Even then, he had refused to pay maintenance and his wife – to his fury – had been awarded their house in London in lieu.

"To be honest, Mrs Donnelly," my Counsel replied, "I'd believe *anything* of Desmond after the times I've tried to get him to Court… God knows how many sons he might have – all over the place; we don't even know where *Desmond* is!"

A dead end.

I went home. No way out. But I *had* to have that mortgage, no matter what it took. I braced myself to ring Brooks and eat humble pie, and the next day I dosed myself up with morphine so that I was pain-free and decided to take the bull by the horns. I picked up the phone, just as the doorbell rang. Putting off the evil moment with relief, I opened the door. "Mr Brooks," I said. For a moment, I could have hugged him, but then a rush of bad cabbage mixed with a strange metallic, pear-drops tang felled me, and I recoiled involuntarily. But he was used to that.

"I've got your mortgage settled," he said, pleasantly enough. "I came straight over – thought you would like to know."

Gleefully, I showed him into the sitting room.

"I just need to check the house again," he said. "You have personally added a considerable amount to its value? I need to get back to Nationwide… may I check the garden? I believe it is now quite extensive?"

"Oh, *quite* extensive," I said. "Let me show you." I led him out to the huge patio, now cleared, with colourful planted urns dotted about. The wide borders were filled to overflowing with hollyhocks and yellow broom standing proud behind the masses of roses and aubretia. Then the manicured lawn, looking like an eighty-foot billiard table, ran down to a line of espaliered apple trees which screened a further lawn and small orchard of plum, pear and walnut trees.

Immaculate.

However, he stomped out, looked, and then stomped back in without a word. "Bathroom was a bit of a mess, as I recall…"

"All done," I said, obsequiously. *I'll show him.* Upstairs, I threw the door open proudly. A rose carpet stretched before us. The walls gleamed with off-white, top-of-the-range tiles with randomly placed rose-pink fleur-de-lys, and gilded so that the sun caught the reflected gold. The far wall was finished with pale bronze mirror tiles, giving the room a palatial look and showing off the snowy five piece suite with, of course, gold taps and fittings, bath rail and shower. Snowy, fluffy, silk-embroidered white towels hung from golden rings. It looked, in keeping with the rest of the house, like a cross between the Palace of Versailles and a Turkish bordello. Either way, it had been effective – it had sold within twenty-four hours.

"And all the bedrooms up to standard now?" he enquired.

"Of course," I beamed. "Fourth bedroom." I showed him into what was obviously a child's room, decorated in soft pastels with full-length co-ordinated Sanderson curtains and duvet, matching the Sanderson wallpaper. Third bedroom – navy Sanderson wallpaper and Wilton carpet with co-ordinated curtains and bed linen; second bedroom – rose pink, co-ordinated, full length, swagged curtains, etc, and the Master Bedroom (my triumph) with white, full length drapes trailing the white Wilton and king-size white satin duvet, with matching pillows, swathed with huge borders of Nottingham lace.

"Everything completed," I said proudly, and looking at him expectantly; he had been silent so far.

He merely put out one stubby forefinger and poked me, none too gently, in my chest. Surprised, I took a step backwards. The bed was directly behind me and I simply tipped over onto it, like a beached flounder, unable to move.

"Now I've got you *close*," he crowed, and his little, piggy eyes lit up delightedly. He then threw off his tie and ripped open his shirt; then, taking a look at my face – a mixture of horror, terror and panic – he laughed aloud. This obviously added a frisson of pleasure to the proceedings.

He hadn't seen what I'd seen...

Akita, as always, had padded dutifully and silently behind. On reaching the thresholds of the rooms, she was forced to stop – she knew she was not allowed in the bedrooms. She therefore waited patiently in the doorway. She had watched while Mr Brooks had prodded me in the chest and she had seen me fall.

There was a blurred streak of silver, which was what caused my terror and panic – certainly not the objectionable Albert Brooks, with whom I felt adequately able to deal... but, oh my God, not with *Akita*.

In one bound, she crossed the room, leapt upwards and landed with all four feet astride me. Her huge, silver mane was an aureole around her head as her hackles rose; her lips curled back revealing a gleaming set of white, deadly incisors and her gaze was irrevocably locked on his jugular. I suddenly had a mental picture of Brooks' blood, gushing, bright red all over my nice white satin duvet – it would be *ruined*. And poor Akita would have to be put down... no reprieve this time... and the *mortgage* would be lost forever.

I tried desperately to pull myself together. "Akita, DOWN!" I roared. But it came out as a feeble croak. *Nothing*. As I watched, her hind legs relaxed slightly backwards before she stiffened again.

She was preparing her final spring.

Albert Brooks simply stood transfixed.

"Akita, DOWN!" This time, it came out. She flicked a glance at me, then straight back to the throat.

"AKITA! *DOWN!*" This time it came out as a forceful command which reached her consciousness. She turned and glanced at me, then suddenly realised where she was. In my *bedroom. Forbidden*. Even worse, she was *on my bed. Forbidden*. She had *done wrong*. Her great mane quivered and then began to slowly subside as she shook her hackles. With one last sheepish glance in my direction, she slid gracefully to the floor.

Unrepentant and as determined as ever, she landed in front of Albert Brooks. He took a step back; she took a step forward, her eyes never leaving his throat.

Painfully and with difficulty, I struggled to my feet. "Oh, my goodness, Mr Brooks," I began, trying to smile cheerfully, "when you pointed out of the window, you accidentally poked me! Of course," I gabbled, "with my severe back injury – as I told you – I have no balance whatever. Dear me…"

Mr Brooks found his voice. "That dog," he said faintly. "That *dog*…"

"Akita?" I said brightly.

"She's dangerous," he said in a whisper.

"Oh, nonsense," I replied dismissively. "Just a playful *puppy*. We often have *romps* on the bed, don't we, Akita?"

Akita took her eyes off his jugular for two seconds to give me a baleful glare. She had never, ever, stepped into my bedroom before.

"Now," I said. "I think that's *all* the house (more than enough, for Mr Brooks). Is there anything else you'd like to see?"

"No, no," he replied hastily as he warily left the room, walking backwards. Akita carefully paced him, step by step, and as he reached the stairs, he fairly fell down them, wrenching open the front door the instant he reached the bottom.

"Oh, Mr Brooks, the mortgage papers! The mortgage papers you brought," I reminded him. "I haven't signed them yet."

"Didn't bring them," he mumbled.

That much had been painfully obvious.

"Next time, then," I called out happily as he fell through the front door and ran to his car. "Next time!"

Closing the front door, I collapsed against it. The pills were beginning to wear off; straight to bed with a hot water bottle and up again at 4.30 am. But not before I'd gone to the kitchen and fetched Akita's dog-chocs. I tipped half a boxful into her bowl. It wouldn't do her any good, I knew, but it would certainly make us both feel a very great deal better.

But I had made a bad enemy in Albert Brooks.

Two days later, the doorbell rang as I was preparing for bed. "Mr Brooks!" I said in dismay. "It's ten o'clock!"

"I came at eight, and again at nine," he said shortly.

"You've got the mortgage papers for me to sign?" I said with relief. At last.

"That's done," he grunted, stomping up and down the living room. "I need a drink."

I knew he was pill-popping; he called in every other day, demanding a drink and tossing back pills. He was driving as far as Nottingham and Chester, getting back as far as Southampton and calling in, demanding a drink, before completing the trip home to Winchester. His wife refused to let him drink alcohol – on strict medical advice. He would totter in with his '…this job is killing me…' and collapse on the chaise longue (on which a thick cotton cover was now permanently placed) and proceed to exude gallons of fluid, before gulping down pills and returning home, as he said, without ever completing any business. His partner, he mourned, after demanding a stiff gin and tonic, wanted him *out*. It was clear that he was becoming pretty useless.

I fetched him a glass of water.

"*Water*," he growled. "I don't need *water*!"

I fetched a gin and tonic. He took the gin from me and poured himself a more generous measure. "The mortgage is done," he said. "All you need to do is sign."

Relief flooded through me; it had all been worthwhile.

"I need a cheque *now* for £1,000 he said."

"Wha... wha… what for?" I finally gasped, in disbelief.

"Expenses."

I pulled myself together. "I paid you £175 to arrange the mortgage," I protested. "You know I had already paid Mr Revere £280 – you offered to do it all *in situ*."

"I've come here two or three times a week," he argued. "Well after office hours."

"Yes, but mostly only to tell me you hadn't got the mortgage arranged," I objected.

"Either way," he said, gulping down the gin and pouring himself another, "I need a cheque for a thousand *now*, or you get someone else to do your mortgage."

"But I don't *have* a thousand pounds!"

"You *will* have – I *know* you're making £25,000 on the sale of this house. You *have* got it."

"Not until I sell the house," I reminded him. But he knew very well I had an overdraft facility of £5,000 on my £60,000 policy. There was no way out. I wrote him a cheque for £1,000 without a word, and handed it to him. Without a word, he took it and, pointedly, I showed him the door. Akita, aware of a tension in the atmosphere that could be cut with a knife, followed his every move, hackles up. He carefully circumnavigated her, and left.

Still, I thought, I've got the mortgage; with a week to go. Wearily I climbed upstairs. Next week I had two parent/teacher meetings, interviewing the parents. Fortunately, their sons had been successful, so I was merely required to sit there and accept their thanks. Even so, I wouldn't get home until after midnight. It would be a dash across London to get the last train at 10.05 pm, arriving back in Southampton just before midnight – and up again at 4.30 am.

One evening the following week I was home early; just made the 5.15 from Waterloo and got in at 7.30. Incredible. Bath and bed; too tired to eat. The bell rang.

Albert Brooks! "Need a drink," he said.

I sleepwalked over to the cabinet and poured him a gin and tonic. "Have you got the mortgage completed yet?" I asked.

"On my desk. All complete."

In that case, I didn't mind staying on my feet; neither did I object when he fetched the gin bottle and poured himself a generous second drink, downing a handful of pills with it. As long as I signed the mortgage first, he was welcome to kill himself.

He performed his usual stomping up and down the room. "Need another cheque," he said.

"Absolutely not!" I was furious. "Even if I wrote it – which I wouldn't dream of doing – it would *bounce*. We have gone through all my finances, and until I move house, there is *no money!*"

But he had obviously come prepared. "I'll take the mirrors in lieu," he said.

"The mirrors," I gasped, "are worth a good deal more than a thousand pounds, as you well know. One hundred and seventy-five pounds, you told me, to take the mortgage arrangements away from Mr Revere and let you handle it. Even the solicitor you recommended as part of the service has not yet contacted me – after *guaranteeing* he could complete in three weeks, I haven't even been able to contact him yet!"

"All in hand," I was assured. "It'll all be done in time. I'll bring the papers for you to sign tomorrow and then it's done. But I'll take the mirrors when you move."

Somehow, I *had* to get to bed. So far that week, I had been without sleep for thirty-six hours and had another parent/teacher session tomorrow after school. "Oh, take them," I said. "But bring the mortgage papers on Friday for me to sign. No good bringing them tomorrow, I won't be back until midnight."

"Will do." He left, under the ever watchful eye of Akita.

By Friday, I was practically on my knees, but I got back by 7.30 again.

Brooks arrived shortly afterwards. "I need that cheque for a thousand," he said.

"But, look here," I reminded him, "you've got the mirrors instead."

He shook his head. "Business is bad… I've *got* to have the cheque."

My turn to shake *my* head. "No way."

"Then get yourself another mortgage," he replied, and walked out.

I suddenly realised I was days away now from finishing at school – and being homeless. I was exhausted. Everything else had been completed, and the new owners were desperate to move in. There was a £25,000 profit to collect; John Paul could go to university; I could retire; no more teaching.

I called after him. "I'll pay you one more thousand pounds."

He looked back, grinning triumphantly.

"But this is simply and solely to get *rid* of you – once and for all," I told him. "Clearly, I am over a barrel at the moment; I've no alternative – I desperately need that mortgage, and you *know* it. In the circumstances, it's worth it to get rid of you." I fetched my cheque book and wrote it out in front of him. He almost snatched it from hand.

"Now," I said, "where are the mortgage papers?"

"In the office. I'll bring them first thing in the morning, and then the house is yours."

Nothing I could do about it; too late to insist he collected the papers now. Still, it was clear that he needed the mortgage completed as much as I did.

"One more thing," he said. "Can I come back tonight? Anytime… anytime at all…?"

I stared at him, aghast. "My God," I said. "I don't know whether I'll ever be able to *walk* again… could you not find a *dead sheep* somewhere?"

"I've got the mortgage done," he said excitedly. "Now let me come back tonight and I'll bring the mortgage over first thing."

"Oh, come anytime you like," I sighed, weary with it all. "But either you bring the mortgage over tomorrow and I sign it, or I have to ring the church and tell them the deal's off."

"Fine," he said. "Fine." He jumped up and scurried off, seeing himself out.

Next morning he was back. "Where were you?" he demanded. "I came back at eight pm, as I said I would, and then nine, and ten…"

"Well, I did explain about having to take strong medication," I parried, "and after coming home well after midnight for two successive nights – I just went out like a light! Have you got the mortgage papers?"

"I'll come back tonight, then," he said.

"Come back when you like," I told him, "once the papers are signed and the house is sold and I am in my new one."

"Really?" With a delighted smile, he drew the papers out of his briefcase. *Finally!*

I signed them… the house was *mine*. John Paul could go to university – he could even have the luxury of a gap year. I could put a deposit down on the next house. I had paid Mr Brooks two thousand pounds to get out of the house – but it was worth it. Now I could scrape all the crooks off my feet once and for all.

I had finished with teaching – three days to go, and then *no more alarm clocks at four in the morning*… Wheeeeeeee!

I'd even had a job offer in a most prestigious pre-prep in Hampshire. They needed a music specialist. I had done a year in Hong Kong as a music specialist, I'd told the Head Teacher, but of course that was one of the gifts I'd had to forego when I sold my beautiful Steinway Grand. Still, I could now get a little keyboard for some practice.

The last three days at Falcons were, by comparison, bliss. I picked up my £14,000 lump sum at the end of it, and *Poison Ivy* – the dreaded Louise – had finally failed in her determined effort to see me reduced to *disabled* status, thereby reducing my pension to half. No; I had done everything asked of me, even though it *was* illegal, immoral and downright vindictive of them. I had been reduced to the status of Assistant – in my own classroom! A first-year student had taken over and I had been reduced, in front of all the staff, to a common servant – fetching and carrying at the whims of teachers and pupils, stripping wallpaper, re-papering – even taking the boys out for rugger practice…

Still, I'd done it – my back had certainly paid the price and, clearly, I had suffered permanent spinal damage. *But I'd done it.*

Time for a fresh start now.

Albert Brooks turned up. It obviously annoyed him to see me on Cloud Nine. He was still unable to get any more work. I was happily playing on my new toy – a small keyboard.

"I could play that," he said.

"Practically *anyone* could play that," I replied. "It's automatic!"

"I want it," he bleated. "And don't forget you still have to hand over that £60,000 policy to Nationwide – they can still cancel the mortgage!"

"Oh, take the bloody thing." I threw it at him in disgust. "I'll get the policy from Lloyds and drop it in to Nationwide; then I'm rid of the lot of you."

I went to Lloyds Bank and politely asked for the policy. Their reaction was one of fury. I told them that it had amused them greatly to bounce my last five small cheques because my salary had arrived *after* (a full three hours) they were presented, which left me with an unauthorised overdraft of £250 – *and* I'd had to beg the removal men to accept a post-dated cheque. Now it amused *me* to remove my policies from their safekeeping as well as my £25,000, and place it with Nationwide – after forty years with Lloyds.

They spitefully kept me waiting nearly an hour, but finally handed them over and I got a taxi home. I was surprised, not to say irritated to find Brooks on my doorstep.

"Have you got the policy?" he greeted me. "If Nationwide don't have it by midday, then your mortgage is cancelled."

"I'll ring them," I suggested. It was twenty-five minutes to twelve. The taxi had gone. "I'll take it in on Monday."

"Too late, too late... it has to be there *now*! Give it to me, I'll deliver it for you – just got time."

I looked at it (and him) doubtfully. No one in their right mind would trust this man any further than they could throw him, but as Messrs. Moon and Johnson had been at pains to tell me – frequently – at the moment, it was not worth the paper it was written on. In eight years time it would be worth £60,000; who was likely to steal it and then wait eight years to collect the proceeds? In any case, I had eight years to deal with it.

"Okay," I agreed. "Let me have the copy I gave you."

He opened his jacket, releasing stale cabbage, then slapped his pocket. "Damn! Left it at the office," he said unconvincingly. "My secretary will send it to you first thing Monday morning."

"You are not having the original," I told him firmly, "until you give me back the copy."

"My God!" he howled. "It's twenty to twelve – do you want this mortgage or don't you?" He got into his car. "Well, I can do no more," he said. "Do you want me to drop it off for you, or not? If you don't trust me – fine; it's *your* mortgage. It's in the bag... or *was*. I can do no more for you."

"Oh, very well," I reluctantly agreed, and handed it over. "But I will be ringing Nationwide first thing on Monday," I said, "for confirmation."

"Make sure you do," he shouted, as he drove off with it.

On Monday, I rang Nationwide from a school payphone. It cost me five pounds in small change to have three brief and absurd conversations. Having explained my reasons for calling, the Receptionist assured me I would need to speak to the Mortgage Manager... she put me through and he listened as I parroted the story to him. Oh no, nothing at all to do with the Mortgage Manager, I would need to speak to the Finance Manager... again I was put through and again I explained the situation. Oh no, nothing to do with the Finance Manager... most *definitely* the Mortgage Manager...

Having run out of change and patience, I had now to wait until the end of term, and then ring from home.

End of term came. Very successful, with expensive presents and effusive thanks. It had almost been worthwhile. The end of my teaching career; I had finally retired – and on a full pension. I made the final journey home; no more pills; no more 4.30 alarm.

Next morning I rang Nationwide. I was again batted backwards and forwards. "If you gave the policy to Mr Brooks and he left it here," I was told, "then it will certainly be here *somewhere*, but we don't normally hold policies. Anyway, there is no one here to discuss it with." *So* reassuring.

Eventually, I wrote, saying that I was *assuming* they were holding a £60,000 policy as security on my mortgage, and if they did not have it in safekeeping, perhaps they would kindly let me know.

As there was no reply, I assumed it was, therefore, now in their safekeeping. But in any case, there were yet more problems when I finally managed to get through to the conveyancing solicitors – an old friend of Mr Brooks was dealing with it, I had been told. When I was eventually put through to the Senior Partner, she told me that he had left, last week. "I've checked his work," she informed me, "and your mortgage papers are on his desk – *untouched*."

"What do I do now, then?" I asked. "He guaranteed to get it done in three weeks, and I have to move out tomorrow."

"I'll see what I can do," she offered, helpfully. "If I stay here all day, I can get the paperwork done, but you will have to come to my office to sign it."

"Impossible," I insisted. "I have damaged my spine and can barely stand, apart from which, the removal men will be here tomorrow, expecting me to have everything packed up and ready to move out at midday…" Oh, hell, *now* what was I to do? "I will have to ring you back," I replied anxiously.

As I replaced the receiver, the phone began to ring. It was the estate agent. There was, he said, a problem. I had specifically bought a house with vacant possession; now, he told me, the vendors had moved back in. He had no key…

I rang the removals firm. Too late to store the furniture, but they were very sympathetic. "Leave it to us," they said. "We will collect the furniture and park the van round the corner for a week until the house is vacant – it will cost you a grand for the time, and storage, etc."

A familiar cry – but what's another thousand in the circumstances? "I'll pay it," I agreed.

A knock came on the door. If it is Albert Brooks again, I decided, picking up the carving knife to pack with the other cutlery, I shall simply plunge it straight in between his ribs. No problem…

It was the purchaser – the wife of the police officer. She was even more hysterical than I was. "The solicitor…" she gasped. "Are you going to sign the papers? *Please* don't let us down *now*!"

I explained the position.

She rang her husband. "Leave it to me," he told her. He nipped out the twenty or so miles to Stockbridge and collected the papers and then drove out to his solicitor and deposited them. He then came back for me. "All you have to do now," he said, kindly, "is get in my car and I will drive you to my solicitor to sign the papers."

I left the removal men packing while he chauffered me to his solicitors, where I signed the papers, and then came back to supervise the rest of the packing. I then booked into a hotel for a week, rang for a taxi to take me there, was peeled out at the other end by a very helpful driver, and finally collapsed in a heap at the hotel.

I was confined to my room for that week, with strict orders of bed rest until I could manage to stand unaided. Then all I had to do was attend John Paul's fantastically successful end of term, making sure I had enough plastic bags to hold all his trophies and accept all the congratulatory eulogies – and then… *the end of schools and education*!

What a prospect; John Paul's gap year – affordable now, and my *permanent* retirement and *holiday*. The sun was shining, the sky was blue – not a cloud in sight.

I'd been lying flat on my back for a whole week – on a mattress on the floor. The removal men had been obliged to manhandle everything through an upstairs window, the doorway and hall being too narrow to get any of the furniture through, but they'd thrown a mattress on the floor, which was sufficient. It had hurt like hell, of course, but no more morphine. Ordinary painkillers would do now – *and* I was driving again. The old Mercedes was automatic and power-steered – a remnant from more affluent days.

I was on the road to collect John Paul. Carrier bags were in the back at the ready, along with the hamper. Smoked salmon (obligatory), barbecued chicken, chilled white wine, etc.

It was the Charterhouse version of Glyndebourne, except there was a cricket match – Carthusians v Old Boys. It was a match to the death, with no quarter asked or given. The fathers were all determined to prove that their paunches, wrinkles and receding hairlines concealed a latent Ted Dexter; they would beat the boys to a pulp. The boys, at eighteen, were confident they could teach their parents a lesson they would never forget.

I drove in to the main driveway on Cloud Nine. I had achieved my wildest dreams. John Paul totally vindicated – the hero of the hour. Top Scholar; every prize board throughout the school boasted his name at the bottom in gold. Top results in A-levels, top of the class for the year. All subject prizes and, most importantly, not only the Integrity Prize, but also the most respected Head of House that his Housemaster could possibly have wished for – I had been told. In short, a blissful culmination to his stay at Charterhouse. We could now wipe the misery of the first two years from our minds for ever.

I parked the Mercedes in the bay in front of Robinites House and walked round the side to the green. A goldfish pool bounded one side, then a path ran beside the House – the fateful path where the cricket ball had flown over John Paul's head and smashed through the patio windows. Beyond the green where we were to foregather before making our way down to the huge grounds for the picnic and cricket match, was a narrow road which separated Robinites from the next House, with a small copse of beech trees between them.

I reached the lawn in front of the patio windows and stopped short. A group of about twenty boys were gathered, all awaiting collection during the afternoon by their parents. But they were all shrieking hysterically, some doubled up, and with tears streaming down their empurpled faces – some with their parents standing helplessly by. From the faint grins on the parents' faces, I assumed the boys were not ill or injured.

"What happened?" I asked.

No one answered. The boys continued to writhe in agony on the ground. One of the senior boys, who had been making use of the wall to hold himself upright, pointed to the Housemaster's study. "Cricket ball through the patio window!" he gasped, tears streaming down his face.

Oh, my! Oh *help*! *A cricket ball through the patio window… again*?

"Where is John Paul?" I asked.

Again, no one answered. No one appeared to be capable of answering.

Finally, the same boy looked at me as I stood there, stricken, ashen-faced. "Oh, it's all right, Mrs Donnelly," he said. "John is inside with Mr Gammell, dealing with it. He *is* Head of House now, you know."

One of the parents stood forward. "Not a problem," he said, condescendingly. "It's *tradition*, you know. Used to happen every year when I was here," he reminisced. "Dr Blake always was unpopular with the boys... stopped, though, when one of the youngsters got blamed and almost expelled, but it's started up again now that he's left..."

The man's wife elbowed him viciously in the ribs. "That was *John Paul*, you fool!" she hissed.

"Oh. *Oh*!" he gasped, and turned puce with embarrassment. "Oh, hell... well, yes," he muttered. "Bad show; bad show, yes."

"*Very* bad show," offered another father, against a background now of general murmuring. The boys were beginning to sit up, their mirth contained as parents hastily collected them, and, one by one, they disappeared.

I was left standing there. Speechless.

Tradition. *Tradition?*

It had been a *tradition*; every year, someone had aimed a cricket ball at the Housemaster's window. The cricket team were proud of the prowess of their bowlers. The most capable one, I gathered, stood in the grove of beech trees and aimed the two hundred yards to see if he could get a bull's eye on the Housemaster's window.

For a joke.

A sixth form joke.

So everyone had known from the start that it was nothing to do with John Paul. As he had pointed out at the time, '...you don't have to *believe* me even, Mum. Just *think*, I couldn't possibly throw any ball that far or that hard...' *and* from a standing position directly outside the window – with half a dozen of his peers as witnesses.

Of course the Headmaster had heatedly refused any question of a police investigation. *Of course* there would be no interrogation of the six boys. Dr Blake had simply rushed out of his room in a filthy temper – understandably – the ball could have killed him, grabbed the first and only child available as the others had run away, and given him a severe beating just to vent his spleen. Having done so, he would clearly be seen to be in the wrong so, ridiculous as it may be, John Paul must apologise and admit guilt, or Dr Blake would have to own up to a straightforward assault. Unacceptable, even with Charterhouse standards.

It explained the two years of unremitting punishment; the unrelenting fortnightly summons to his study to 'apologise' and 'own up'. At the end of which, when John Paul finally broke, after the knife attack, and walked across the park to tell Mr Attenborough he was leaving, I had been phoned back.

"I am dealing with this," Mr Attenborough had said. He could not afford to have me collect John Paul, leave the school and go to the media with the story. It explained why he had been closeted with John Paul for half an hour, and it explained John Paul's self-satisfied call – "I want to *stay* now; I can't *tell* you – it's *confidential*; it's for the good of the *school*."

None of this, of course, had occurred to me at the time. I could not believe that a Headmaster of Charterhouse School could swear a twelve-year-old to secrecy for the good of the school. He was prepared to hide behind a disabled, single teacher and a twelve year old boy, to save his own skin – and that of the school, of course. And after that – when Dr Blake's ultimatum had come into force; "… a scholarship, Mrs Donnelly? Oh no, I have revoked that – because of the misdemeanour, Mrs Donnelly; a cricket ball through my window, Mrs Donnelly… unheard of; he must be punished, Mrs Donnelly!"

And he had been… and so had I! No scholarship.

"Sell the house, Mrs Donnelly; in a recession – you only get half price? Too bad, Mrs Donnelly; bite the bullet Mrs Donnelly; stiff upper lip, John Paul; take the beatings like a man, John Paul…"

And the nightmare continued, inexorably; sell your investments, Mrs Donnelly; we'll have all your savings Mrs Donnelly; come out of disabled retirement and go back to work Mrs Donnelly; nothing in Hampshire? Try London, Mrs Donnelly; yes, commute, play the game, Mrs Donnelly; oh, you've broken your back, Mrs Donnelly? Never mind, keep going… only a few more terms, Mrs Donnelly.

It's a *joke*, Mrs Donnelly – a *sixth form joke*. Only, it's important no one finds out, Mrs Donnelly; but we've covered that. The Headmaster has sworn John Paul to secrecy, and we *know* John Paul – if he gives his word, he will *never* tell. So we are safe, Mrs Donnelly – as long as you keep paying the bills, no one will ever know.

And they hadn't. John Paul had certainly kept his promise – he had never breathed a word. I had lost my home, my savings, my career and my health – but the *school* was fine. I was stunned.

I was due to collect John Paul and join the cricket match, but instead I went and sat in the car. All the Rolls Royce cars were now turning up, younger sons emerging with crates of champagne and ice-coolers, as groups spread out on the lawn with their food and drink hampers.

I sat in the car and poured myself some wine. What to do?

I had lost the house for nothing – indeed, I had lost *everything* for nothing. I knew I should insist on a full investigation and demand that the money be repaid. Lord McAlpine, who had stepped in to ensure that John Paul stayed on, must also be repaid.

Was I prepared to take on the fight? Was I up to it? I felt totally shattered and certainly didn't feel I could take on such a confrontation at the moment – I would need time to recuperate.

But John Paul was leaving now. Did I really *want* the money back? Would that solve anything? How much was it worth?

After a second glass of wine, I calmed down. At the end of the day, what had actually happened? Whilst terribly wronged, I had paid for my own son's education. Granted, I hadn't wanted John Paul to go there; granted, John Paul himself hadn't wanted to go there, but he'd certainly had an excellent education, and he had achieved the potential I'd been promised. He'd had all the advantages of the Ben Travers Theatre, despite Dr Blake's efforts at prevention, and he'd enjoyed all the expertise of his tutors and their enthusiastic encouragement – in short, he had achieved absolutely every iota of his potential. Not a single facet had failed – he'd had the opportunities and excelled at everything.

John Paul had actually put the school to shame; he had accepted every punishment and completed every task, however humiliating. He had excelled academically and his integrity had shone throughout. No. I would not now demean all his efforts by asking for my money back. Frankly, I wouldn't want it, anyway; I would consider it tainted. And John Paul would certainly not want it. *He* had given *his* word he would cover up for the sake of the school, and it was not my place to tell. We would not descend to Charterhouse level and end up bickering over money.

Better to forget it.

Now I could wipe out Desmond as totally unworthy; neither of us owed him a thing. And now we could wipe the mud of Charterhouse off our shoes once and for all – we owed them nothing either.

Somewhat unsteadily, after the cricket match, I lurched back to the prize giving (there wasn't much left of the bottle of wine for John Paul) and happily collected all his final trophies and presentations. Accepting his Housemaster's eulogies with dignity and with carrier bags overflowing, we finally drove away from Charterhouse; with a sense of triumph, I steered a course to the new and even more ghastly house.

We had achieved great things, with *no* help from anyone else – we had done it all ourselves… now a new start was indicated.

At home, the new house needed renovating throughout. Every room would have to be stripped and decorated – the courtyard was just a sea of mud.

John Paul was able to enjoy a gap year before university, and after long arguments he had won through and turned down three offers from Oxford to read Theology, Philosophy and English. He'd had enough of being pressurised. It was getting late and I feared he may miss out on university altogether, but at the last minute, Leeds placed him.

All his Charterhouse friends enjoyed privileged gap years; some were in Peru doing charity work – others backpacked across Australia. Not John Paul. He spent the year working in a Threshers wine bar, but at least it was not academic, and it was his first experience of *life*.

My spine had recovered as much as it ever would. There was considerable paralysis now down both sides, and the sciatic nerve would give trouble for some time to come, I was told. There would be no more horse-riding, tennis or golf – or indeed, any of the things I had looked forward to in my retirement. But I was still able to decorate; with no sense of balance I now had to make sure I had a steady platform and a rail to hold on to, but even so, the new house was beginning to take shape.

I began to look forward to the future – and cashing in my two policies when they matured. It was now 1996 and I began to plan what to do with the money.

Suddenly a news item flashed up on the television. We were being advised to cash in endowment policies; there would be shortfalls on maturity; people should not expect them to clear their mortgages.

It was like an explosion. Suddenly, everything fell into place. Mr Brooks' insistence on grubbing through all my financial documents; his glee on finding the £60,000 policy – his fury on discovering that it was just a copy. And I'd handed it over! Almost certainly, if it were possible, he would have cashed it in.

I still didn't panic; that would be theft, and the police would investigate. Lloyds Bank had held the policies for two years and I had regularly borrowed against them. They would have all the details in their Securities Department; I knew they retained their records for many years.

I rang Shirley police station for advice and explained the position.

I was put through to PC Clarke from the Fraud Squad. "Hampshire Police do not investigate fraud," she informed me.

"No, no." I told her. "You don't understand. This broker, Mr Brooks, has stolen a policy worth a considerable sum of money. I had thought it to be worth £60,000, but having spoken to Scottish Widows, they have explained that it should mature at £300,000 to £350,000 in 2007. I need the fraud police to investigate."

"This *is* the fraud police," replied PC Clarke, "and we don't investigate *fraud*."

Silence. I would have to work that one out. After a while I managed, "You are Fraud Squad, but you don't investigate fraud? What *do* you do, then?"

"Oh, we investigate corporate fraud," I was told, "but only if it's worth at least a million. We don't investigate *private* fraud."

That did shake me. "Who does then?" I enquired.

"I can only suggest you consult a solicitor," she replied.

I rang my solicitor I'd known in London. He had successfully dealt with two accidents I'd had. Southampton solicitors had given up, but he had taken over both times and won compensation.

No, he said. He only dealt with personal injury.

Desperately, I tried his other branch, and finally Mr Andrews of Stone Rowe Brewer accepted the case. First of all he went through the events. It was clear the man was a crook – the two payments of £1,000, the mirrors, etc. were all totally unacceptable for a bona fide businessman.

The immediate problem was, how much money did I have available? John Paul must now go to university – I had promised money would be available. Mr Andrews said he would see what he could do. First, he wrote to Lloyds Bank. No reply. He wrote again; no reply. The third time, they did reply – no, they had never had a customer of my name.

"What?" I exploded. "I have been a customer of Lloyds Bank for the past *forty years*!"

It took about a dozen letters before Lloyds finally agreed that I *had* been a customer of theirs – but I had left, and taken the policies with me.

"But they must have a record of them," I said. "In any case, my frequent visits to Mr Moon and Mr Johnson would certainly be remembered. They had checked the policy each time they allowed me to borrow on it."

"I'd have thought so," agreed Mr Andrews.

Frequent letters followed. Could Mr Moon and Mr Johnson be contacted, since they were the ones who had dealt with the policies?

No reply was forthcoming.

After a year, Mr Andrews had spent the £1,000 I had allowed. I paid him another £1,000, but he had no satisfaction.

Further announcements on television news gave details of a takeover of Scottish Widows policies; there would be a *minimum* payment of £5,000 on any 'with profits' policy. Just as I was digesting this information, the doorbell rang.

Albert Brooks danced into the room. "There had been a takeover offer for Scottish Widows," he crowed. "You will get at least five hundred pounds."

I said nothing and showed him out. Then I rang Mr Andrews. "Brooks is about to grab the £5,000 bonus from Scottish Widows," I gasped.

"I don't see how he can do that," he said. "On the other hand, I am not entirely sure what he has been up to."

There was certainly no question – the bonus would be worth at least £5,000.

A few days later, Brooks returned. "There will definitely be a pay out now," he gabbled happily, obviously relieved that I hadn't questioned his earlier statement. "I've checked with Scottish Widows for you," he stated confidently (how, I wondered...?) "and you'll definitely collect a payment – five, er... two hundred pounds."

Again, I said nothing and showed him out. I rang Mr Andrews again.

"Hm," he said. "This is taking a good deal longer than I imagined – and after two thousand pounds, I've got nowhere."

Clearly, I had either to drop the case and let Brooks get away with it, or find more money. I would have to cash in the second policy. The 'worthless' £5,000 policy would in fact realise £30,000 at maturity in 2008, but I needed the money now. If I were to cash it in now, I would collect £10,000 plus the bonus; gone were my hopes of riches in 2007/8.

"Trouble is," said Mr Andrews, "there's no proof. If you are going to spend *more* money, we need *proof*."

I rang Shirley Police again and explained the position to PC Clarke. Could they just visit Mr Brooks? If he were to be questioned 'out of the blue' by two police officers, they might be able to 'surprise' an admission from him...?

"We do not investigate fraud," I was told firmly.

"There must be a specialist firm that could trace the details of the policy," I said. "Lloyds Bank have the details, obviously, but their principle of total confidentiality prevents them from giving me details."

"Look in Yellow Pages," she said. "You might find a private investigator that would undertake it for you."

And that was all I could get out of her.

The next day, the doorbell rang. Mr Brooks again. The police were not prepared to help; clearly, if anyone were going to surprise him with a sudden attack, it would have to be me.

"What did you do with my £60,000 policy?" I asked him.

He was obviously – and understandably – taken aback.

"What policy?"

I pointed out that I had paid him, in total, £2,175 plus £1,000 worth of mirrors and I expected him to be aware of any policies I may have had.

"Have you the name and number of this policy?"

I said no, I hadn't, since he had taken both original and copy and failed to deliver a receipt.

He nearly danced around the room with glee, so apparent was his relief. "You have neither the name, nor the number? Nothing you can do!"

"On the contrary," I said. There is a great deal I can do. Lloyds Securities certainly have a record of it, and I will now contact the Fraud Squad."

At this, he collapsed into the nearest chair. His face turned waxy white and the sweat poured off him. His eyes became glazed; I became quite concerned... "My God," I thought. "I've killed him."

Then, in a whisper, "Oh, my God..." I could barely hear him. "...all I wanted was a nice retirement."

So, at least I knew now. He *had* taken the policy; it had never been delivered to Nationwide. The trick now was to find out whether he'd cashed it.

I fetched a glass of water and pushed it into his hand. He fumbled in his pockets and produced his pills. He took some, and gradually began to come round.

"Mr Brooks," I began. "I *know* you took the policy; I just need to know... you *did* deliver it to Nationwide, didn't you? Only, you see, I haven't been able to get in touch with them... but of course, as my financial adviser, I just need you to tell me it's quite safe with them, and then I can forget about it."

I had to repeat it all about three times, before it finally sank in.

"Oh, yes. Yes," he muttered, as he struggled to his feet. "The policy's quite safe; leave it to me... yes, it *is* with Nationwide." He suddenly recovered. "Of *course* it is!" he snapped, then made for the front door and made a quick exit.

I rang Mr Andrews. Brooks had certainly taken the policy, but was still desperate for more money, and clearly had not cashed it in yet. But it was equally clear that he fully intended claiming the Scottish Widows bonus which had just been declared at £20,000.

"I still don't see how he intends getting hold of it, though," Mr Andrews said. "I've gone about as far as I can with it; I still haven't had a reply from either Mr Moon or Mr Johnson. You really need a specialist in fraud – which I am not – and preferably someone local. Either way, to continue is going to take a considerable amount of money."

Which I did not have. As Brooks very well knew. There was no way I could take it further. Except... I still had the other policy, for £5,000. This would mature in 2008 at £30,000, but it was more important to have the money now. I knew there was a cut-off date for personal injury claims; if the same applied to fraud, I would lose all claim to the money by then, anyway.

Next, I rang Scottish Widows. When would the pay-out for the takeover arrive? I had signed the paper in October – it should have been paid in November, it was now December.

Possibly in January, I was told. In October the policy had a cash value in excess of £10,000. In the new year, I would be entering the fourth year – and in danger of running out of time. It was essential that I have the money *now*.

I rang them again.

"It should be paid in April." I was told. "But we have encountered so many problems trying to calculate each individual claim, it might be even later."

I was waiting for the bonus to be paid out, I said. Would it affect the bonus if I cashed the policy in now? The bonus should have been paid out in November.

"No, no. The bonus is based on the length of time you have held the policy, i.e. twelve years – and the monthly payments over that time. It's based on what you have paid in – so nothing can alter that."

I could wait no longer. At least I would collect the £20,000 bonus when it was finally calculated. I cashed it in and was delighted to receive a cheque for £10,600.

Mr Andrews, however, was not, and tackled Scottish Widows. "In February," he insisted, "the policy was worth £10,400. Mrs Donnelly has received a cheque for £10,600; should not the £20,000 bonus be paid with it?"

Scottish Widows replied that a £3,000 bonus had been included.

"What," we asked, "did that relate to?"

"A five hundred pounds policy was included," they said. "Your policy was considered as a 'dead policy'."

"I hadn't even known it was *ill*," I told Mr Andrews.

We were totally confused. He wrote, requesting a detailed explanation, but there was no reply.

"Mr Brooks is psychic," I told him. "He told me I would get a £200 bonus, and that's exactly what I got. What happened to the £20,000 I *should* have had?"

Mr Andrews had no explanation. "But, I think it just as well you cashed the policy in, before Mr Brooks got his hands on *that* one as well."

Still, I now had £10,600; John Paul could go to university. I went to the Citizens Advice Bureau – there was an excellent solicitor in Southampton who specialised in such cases. I contacted him. He was apparently the best in Southampton, but only undertook clients with whom he could deal personally. I had just managed to obtain a music post in a pre-prep school in Fareham – a mere twenty miles daily drive, but even so there was no way I could be back by 4.00 pm – the latest time he would see clients. *No*, he did *not* deal with clients by phone.

Having cashed in the policy – and lost £20,000 by doing so – I was not prepared to give up the case. Again I rang the police. Could they at least recommend a private firm who would investigate? No. They could only repeat their advice to try Yellow Pages.

"There is only one firm listed that appears to deal with fraud," I said.

"Then try them," said PC Clarke dismissively.

I rang them. Nationwide Investigations Group. They seemed very efficient. Mr David Waight arrived within minutes. He was, he told me, an ex-Fraud Squad officer, now working in a private capacity with his colleague, also an ex-police officer. Yes, any policy could be traced; certainly it was possible to research and find the missing policy. He would need £2,000 in advance. I wrote the cheque out, relieved that something could be done. He would be in touch within forty-eight hours, I was told, with information.

A week later, I rang them. And rang. And rang. After a couple of days I rang Trading Standards. "The firm went into liquidation *months* ago," I was told. "You didn't give them any money?"

"Two thousand pounds, in advance," I replied.

"I'm afraid there's no chance of getting it back; there is a queue of creditors a mile long – all claiming. Waste of time trying; sorry."

I rang Shirley Police again. "But they insisted they were from the Fraud Squad," I pleaded, "albeit retired. If they are ex-Fraud Squad, is there nothing you can do?"

"Only thing you can do," sighed PC Clarke, clearly not interested, "is to go there yourself and try and get the money back."

"And how do I do that? They would recognise me; no, I need an officer to go on my behalf."

"Well, you would need to alter your appearance," she said, "so they don't recognise you. Perhaps you could get in through an upstairs window – I doubt they'd be locked."

She *was* joking, wasn't she? Me, disabled with a spinal injury, put on a raincoat, moustache and trilby hat, shin up a drainpipe, break a window and face a couple of hefty ex-policemen turned crooks?

"Well," she said, "if you *want* the money back…"

I wrote several times and went to their offices, but they had been closed down for months and there was never any answer. I had merely thrown away another two thousand pounds. Eventually, I approached the Law Society. Could they recommend a reliable solicitor in Southampton who at least had some experience of dealing with fraud cases?

A Mr Gibbons was recommended; he was happy to undertake the case and confident he could locate the endowment policy. He would require an advance. I agreed, and explained that negotiations would have to be conducted by phone – as a supply teacher, I dare not take time off.

That was out of the question; he did not leave his office.

I explained I was still suffering from a severe and long term back injury and I desperately needed to hold down this temporary post, and I dared not take time off.

He was adamant. *He did not leave his office.* "I am willing to undertake the case," he told me, "but you will not find any solicitor who will visit you personally. If you want me to take the case, I'm sorry, but you will *have* to get yourself to my office."

I had no alternative; I took a day off and visited him at his office. He looked through Mr Andrews' papers and then questioned me. "But the man's a *crook*!" he exploded.

"I know that," I said, uncomfortably. "But he is clearly a very experienced crook. He deals exclusively with elderly and infirm clients, insists on going through every bit of financial information, obviously looking for policies to steal and cash in. At the moment," I said, "I am hoping I have allayed his suspicions, but if you accept the case, it has to be kept *absolutely* confidential. At the moment, I am pretty sure he has not yet cashed the policy in, but either way, it must all be done in the strictest confidence – should it turn out that he was simply incompetent and carelessly dropped... lost, both the policy and the copy, he could sue me for defamation of character."

"Of course," replied Mr Gibbons.

"I mean, of course, confidential as in... well, you know, the confessional, or a doctor's surgery. Apart from anything else, I am nervous of Mr Brooks. Thwarted, I feel he could be a very unpleasant man to deal with and I live entirely on my own."

"But of course, Mrs Donnelly." He was clearly offended by my request. "All cases are treated in confidence. That will be £800 in advance, if you please."

A fortnight later, I had a letter from Mr Gibbons. Hopefully, I scanned its contents: "... I have visited Mr Brooks at his new office at his request... we have discussed the matter... I am no longer prepared to take the case..."

I did not understand; my solicitor could not visit me – his client, with a spinal injury – but felt able to travel twenty miles out to Totton to visit the man I had accused of stealing from me, for a personal discussion. And after I had been at pains to explain the need for total confidentiality.

The letter was followed by the return of my file. The only paper in which Mr Brooks had once mentioned handling the policy, was missing – the only concrete evidence I had that I had actually handed the policy over to him. Instead were three other letters I had never seen before – in each, Mr Brooks was apparently begging me not to cash in the policy – in case I lost the bonus.

Considering the letters were dated during the period when Mr Andrews had advised that the matter be kept confidential until proven – for fear of reprisal – this was, indeed, odd. Throughout that period, our only concern had been the *lost* policy. As far as Mr Andrews and I were concerned, there had been no notification of a £20,000 bonus. Mr Brooks was, indeed, psychic.

Well, there certainly seemed no point in continuing my association with Mr Gibbons if he was now taking instructions from Mr Brooks as well.

Ten

The last time Mr Brooks visited, he had driven up in a brand new scarlet Audi.

"What happened to your old black Ford?" I asked him.

"Gave it to my wife. We now have *two* cars," he told me. "Can't stop. I've become a member of the Winchester Masons, and I'm just off to another function," he said grandly. "And then I have to supervise the move to my new office premises."

He had, until then, been working from a tumbledown bungalow; now he was moving in to grand commercial premises in prime position in the High Street.

I got in touch with Mr Andrews. "Mr Brooks has quite clearly cashed in the policy," I told him. "New car, new office, oh... and he explained his new tan – he'd taken the whole extended family, three sons, their wives, and grandchildren, for a three week vacation in the Algarve!"

"Been too busy to drop in before," he'd sneered; "just checking to make sure you are keeping up the payments with Clerical and Medical – your cheques keep bouncing."

"I'll make sure they don't in future," I'd said; anything to ensure he had no further excuse for visiting. I was just about back on my feet and able to drive now, and accepting work from anywhere in Hampshire – indeed, even a couple of schools in Wiltshire – *anything, anywhere*, to make sure that extra £225 per month was covered.

"But you need *proof*," stressed Mr Andrews. "You must get him talking – sooner or later, he will make a mistake."

Okay; let him come bombasting in once a week. I forced myself not to mind as he swaggered through the door in full evening dress and leaned back in my chairs negligently. (All the chairs were covered with throws now, in case he sat in any of them.)

"I'll have a gin and tonic... my God, call *that* a gin and tonic? For God's sake, top it up... that's better. I'm on my way to another Masonic function. Of course, I'm Chairman now – after just a year! Of course, I am organising the latest Charity Ball – two grand, and that's just for the band!"

"You have to organise it yourself?" I asked humbly.

"Of course!" he snapped and then, remembering I was still in the human race and had at least one grain of intelligence, spoke calmly. "Of course... but naturally, I get it all back. It's not my *personal* money, of course," he finished with an oily smile.

And then, finally, when he strode in, unable to keep his good news to himself. "Just got the mortgage settled on my youngest son's new house! Was worried about him – just divorced, two kids to maintain, and in that police house..." he shook his head. "No," he said expansively, "I've put the deposit down now – a house in the next block – the wife can keep her eye on the kids. All sorted now."

Really? How interesting...

I relayed the latest information to Mr Andrews.

"You need to continue with the case," he urged me.

The only way to do that was to cash in the second Scottish Widows policy. Back to the drawing board – I had now lost too much money over this fraud case to draw back. I wrote again to the Law Society. Could they recommend a reliable solicitor to undertake my fraud case? I was given a list. Heading it was a firm called Berrymans Lace Mawer. I rang and made an appointment with their Mr Tye-Reeve.

Mr Tye-Reeve was charming and most helpful. I explained that by this time I was practically penniless; I *had* managed to put down a deposit on my present house and, to date, I had kept John Paul for his gap year and paid for his university lodgings, but without the lost policy, I could see no future and I needed an experienced solicitor to deal with a very clever fraudster. The Law Society had recommended his firm...

"I've handled a couple of fraud cases," he put in.

I assumed he was being modest.

"The problem is," I said, "as I understand it, fraud cases have to be brought within six years. Is that a strict cut-off date, as with Personal Injury claims?

"We are within that limit at the moment," he decided.

If that was so – this was 24th December 2000 – the six years could be up at the end of the year. "Either way," I said, "I must be able to accuse Mr Brooks of fraud within the time limit."

Mr Tye-Reeve consulted his diary. "I'll have it ready for you by Boxing Day," he said.

I was most impressed.

"No. On second thoughts," he reflected, "I will have it in writing on my desk for you to come in and peruse by the thirty-first. It will mean working over the weekend, but I will do it."

I was so grateful.

"I will need a cheque for five hundred pounds as a retaining fee."

I wrote the cheque out gladly and left, feeling that I was getting somewhere at last.

I heard nothing on the thirty-first. Still, it *was* Christmas. I assumed he had everything in satisfactory order by now. A fortnight later, I was really concerned. There was no reply to my telephone calls – Mr Tye-Reeve was out; he was busy; at lunch; at home. Finally, I received a letter from him informing me that he 'no longer wished to continue with the case.'

I was shattered; now what did I do? He still had Mr Andrews' file and all the relevant data. I rang the Law Society. Miss Warner was most helpful; she would 'find out.'

The following day, I received a letter of apology for the misunderstanding – Mr Tye-Reeve was, in fact, happy to continue with the case.

He rang on 2nd February, suggesting a course of action, for which he would require a further £300. I forwarded a cheque, but I was now becoming concerned. John Paul would soon be nearing his final term at university and I was in financial difficulty. I had no idea this case was going to drag on for so long.

A phone call the next day informed me that he had now changed the plan; he would get Lloyds Bank to forward details of all direct debits and would give me 'a buzz' when he received them.

I never heard from him again. Eventually I wrote and asked if he would kindly return my file if he no longer wished to continue the case. No reply. Three weeks later I wrote again. No reply. And rang. He was 'still at lunch'... 'out with a client'... 'not in the office today.'

Finally, I asked for an appointment. He was on holiday, his receptionist informed me.

"This is important," I told her. "May I speak to the senior partner?"

"He's on holiday, too."

At the time, I was still trying to complete my teaching contract at Fareham. Eventually, I rushed home from school early and hired a taxi, at a cost of ten pounds, to Berrymans Lace Mawer to collect my file. The assistant returned empty-handed. I demanded an explanation.

Mr Tye-Reeve was away, I was told.

"But it is nothing to do with Mr Tye-Reeve," I protested. "It is *my* file – or at least, Mr Andrews' file. All Mr Tye-Reeve has done so far is *read* it – if, indeed, he has even done *that*! I have paid for the file; it is *my* property and I need it urgently. He has now had it for *four* months. During that time I have contacted the Financial Ombudsman and he has agreed to a full, *free* investigation, but there is a two month time limit which starts from the beginning of next month."

"Sorry. Can't help you."

The Financial Ombudsman wrote again. Yes, they would throw all their resources into a full, free investigation – for two months only. But they *must* have Mr Andrews' file. Various phone calls and letters from them followed, but without the file they could do nothing.

At the end of two months I wrote pointing out that they were now experiencing *my* dilemma – I could not continue without the file. There was no reply. I wrote again. The two months have now expired and I have had no reply to my letter; does that mean you have now given up the investigation? If so, you appear to be playing directly into Mr Brooks' hands.

Still there was no reply. I contacted the Law Society. "Mr Tye-Reeve has now had my file for ten months," I told them. "I had arranged for a full investigation by the Financial Ombudsman; *that* has now run out of time. The dice certainly seems to be weighted against me."

They would look into it.

They rang me back. "Ah!" they said. "We have discovered the reason why Mr Tye-Reeve has kept your file for ten months and refused all contact. The reason is that your cheque bounced."

"It most certainly did not," I argued. "And, even if it had, are you seriously telling me he couldn't lift up the phone, or expend a second-class stamp in order to *tell* me so?"

"Of course," she replied, "if you're *sure* it didn't bounce, *that* would make a difference..."

Another month went by while I collected copies of statements. Nationwide offered a full photograph of the cheque in question – more expenses, and it would take up to three weeks to arrange, but it would be legal proof. I agreed.

In the meantime, would I care to send Berrymans *another* cheque for £500, which would release my file. Then send it to her, and, if I was correct, she would see that my original cheque was returned.

Wearily, I drove to Berrymans, handed over *another* cheque for £500, and collected my file. Back home. I rang the Law Society, but told them that, frankly, having got my file back, I was not prepared to let it out of my sight again. Copies of any papers would, of course, be available.

It did not go down well at all.

But I had wasted almost a whole year; it had cost nearly £900 and, as far as I knew, Mr Tye-Reeve had not even read the file.

I never heard from him again. (Almost two years later, I received a cheque for £500 from Berrymans for 'overpayment'. There was no apology.)

It was, by now, well over the six year limit – seven in fact. And I had completely run out of money. I could see no way of getting John Paul through his final term at university. He had, of course, done brilliantly, and was about to take his final exams. He would, no doubt, get a Double First. There was no way I could pay his rent. Others in similar situations had dropped out of university just before finals through lack of funds – three years just wasted!

Finally, I wrote to Lord Wakeham. After all, he was still a Senior Governor at Charterhouse. He had known full well that John Paul's scholarship had been falsely revoked. He had been a student at Robinites himself; his sons had been under the careful guardianship of John Paul during their term there, and John Paul had been personally commended for his careful and sympathetic pastoral care of them, particularly after their mother's death.

In his capacity as a Senior Queen's Counsel, therefore, could he *persuade* Desmond Donnelly to contribute *some* of the money he was in Contempt of Court for not paying? After all, the High Courts in London *and* Hong Kong had insisted Desmond *must by law* either pay maintenance or face disbarment and a custodial sentence.

He wrote, but there was no reply from Desmond.

Back to the drawing board.

By now, as far as Mr Tye-Reeve and the other lawyers were concerned, Mrs Donnelly had, at last, been satisfactorily run out of both time and money – they had each checked my bank statements to reassure themselves of this. Perhaps Mrs Donnelly would now (God help us!) give up and give us all some peace.

She did.

At least the little house was nearing completion. It had been stripped from top to bottom, repainted, repapered, recarpeted and redecorated throughout as a Neo-Georgian residence, and ready to market.

The Dockland area had, as anticipated, gone up-market. Southampton now had a new and highly expensive Ocean Marina of international renown, and the surrounding area, being busy and over-populated, was much in demand and property was at a premium. My tiny property was now worth almost three times the amount I had paid for it – albeit practically in a state of dereliction six years ago. So, in spite of the solicitors writing me off as 'finished at last' I was still in there – and fighting.

At any rate, the following day, John Paul came home. He travelled, as usual, overnight by coach, to get the cheapest possible fare. He was homesick, and travel-weary, but triumphant, after incredible success at university – and his play had won Best Writer, Best Actor and Best Director awards at the prestigious Edinburgh Festival; the first time anyone had achieved all three awards. And, yes, a Double First at University.

So, finally, all our efforts had been vindicated. But at *what* cost!

Still, we had:

Finally got rid of Brooks.

Finally got rid of Desmond.

Finally got rid of Charterhouse.

And *finally* got rid of the *law* and all its weird manifestations.

Accept it.

However…

The election was near. Campaigning was reaching fever pitch. My local MP advertised on TV, and in a roving van with speakers. He was holding consultations; any *wrongs* would be *righted.* He could be *relied* upon…

With nothing to lose, I made an appointment to consult.

Could he help?

Could he? My goodness, of *course* he could! Leave this to *him.* Most certainly the police should have investigated; now he would personally see to it that it would be investigated, at least to the level of the Director of Public Prosecutions. I must understand, however, that if the DPP investigated and decided there was not enough evidence to secure a conviction, then the investigation would cease. But at least they would be able to establish whether there was fraud. Or not. That was quite acceptable; Mr Whitehead would take over.

A letter from Hampshire Fraud Squad followed. There would now be an immediate investigation; two senior officers would be in touch shortly.

I waited. With trepidation.

The election was held; Mr Whitehead was still my MP, fortunately. A fortnight later, I received another letter from the Fraud Squad. There would be 'an investigation' by 'two officers' in the near future 'at a local level'.

A fortnight later, I received the final letter. There would be no investigation.

It appeared Mr Brooks had won. He *was* right; his son *was* a Detective Inspector with Hampshire Police. Mr Brooks, now with money (mine), was a leading member of the influential Winchester Masonic Lodge, and, as he had said, there was *nothing* I could do.

End of case.

End of story?

Time to go shopping at Tesco's. I drove out to the supermarket, collected some earthenware pots, on offer, from outside the store and proceeded to the food aisles.

Mistake.

I slipped in a puddle of oil – my foot shot forward, there was a sharp, double crack as I fell. Then, hauling myself up and using the trolley as a support, I navigated to the frozen peas and sat amongst them, waiting for assistance. It was, for Tesco's, a quiet half hour. But it was twenty minutes before an assistant hove into view.

I finally managed to secure her attention. She was less than eager. "Perhaps you suffer from Arthritis?" she suggested, looking at the frozen peas surrounding my ankle. "Perhaps the swelling will go down?"

After half an hour – when I had refused, forcefully, all attempts to dislodge me into my car – '…drive home, it will be better in the morning…' an ambulance was called. My ankle was wrapped in gauze and bandages and I was pushed, in a trolley to the exit.

"Please may I be taken to a cashpoint?" I asked.

"Too dangerous," I was told. "You must not move that foot an inch!"

I had to pay for my pots with cash from my pocket; they could not use my credit card – too far away, I was told – in the frozen pea department.

"How do I get home?"

"Not our problem," said Tesco.

The ambulance delivered me to hospital at 11.00 am. By 4.00 pm I had been bandaged, put in a wheelchair and deposited on my doorstep with two crutches. I explained that, due to my existing disability, I was unable to use crutches; may I have a walking stick? I was given one.

Tomorrow, I was told, I would be put in plaster; my ankle, now swollen to more than twice its normal size, would be reduced sufficiently.

"How will I get a taxi to the hospital? Tesco's have taken all my cash for the pots…"

The ambulance men didn't know. But at least they had brought me home; they were doing their best. I hobbled in. They left.

I surveyed the room. I had recovered sufficiently from the previous fall into the bore-hole; the spinal cord was, of course, permanently damaged now, through being forced to work with it and teach in London for my final year. But after a few months, I had decided I still had sufficient use to do limited work.

But not with a broken ankle.

The old Georgian house, neglected for more than twenty years, had responded to TLC and was now resplendent with (admittedly Victorian) cut glass chandeliers in every room, full length velvet curtains throughout, and Wilton carpeting. It was *almost* complete. But not quite.

And I was immobile.

The doorbell rang. Oh, thank God. Someone had realised I was totally alone – my ankle shattered. I had managed to get upstairs and was now in my nightdress. I was used by now to getting up and down stairs on my bottom. *But how to get a cup of tea*? That had been too much; I'd had nothing to drink since 8.00 am. It was now 9.00 pm. Obviously, the hospital had finally realised my predicament, and responded.

Clasping my stick, I carefully negotiated the passageway to the front door. And opened it.

Oh! My God... Albert Brooks!

"No!" I shouted. "I've paid Clerical and Medical – I've paid! I've paid!" I tried to close the door on him.

"So you have," he said, and pushed past. I retreated to the sitting room.

And no Akita. After twelve years faithful service, she had finally succumbed to cancer.

I fell thankfully back into an armchair.

He stood in front of me, little piggy eyes a-glitter. "Now I have you!"

My God. Some mountain bred rustic ram must have said that same thing to the last spindle-legged ewe on the planet.

But there he was – his tie ripped off and shirt buttons undone. His trousers fell to the floor as he lunged towards me. I do not *know* what happened next. (I should insert a row of *asterixes* here!) I like to *think* that, as he lunged at me, I put my hands out towards him to protect myself.

I *like* to think I did that – I'm sure I did...

Whatever, as he came toward me, his unattached trousers drifted floorwards, revealing all – to anyone interested. I leapt out of harm's way, in an instinctive attempt to evade the seventeen stones of lard hurtling towards me – and obviously intending no goodwill. I promptly landed on my right foot – which was no longer there.

There was a moment of hysterical glee as I witnessed his denouement... Albert Brooks, now naked from the waist down, sporting a little pink string in front of him – which might have done credit to the nether end of a tiny, pink pig.

Oh God – so *that* was what I'd been so scared of!! *That* was what I had hidden in the hall from, hoping he would grow tired of ringing the doorbell and go away. This hysterical joy lasted but one brief moment. I had leapt from my armchair to my right, and landed on my right ankle, which was no longer there, but underneath me now.

A single bolt of white hot agony seared through me as I made the leap. I am sure I only meant to hold onto him for support when my ankle gave way. He retreated, seeing only scarlet talons aimed straight at his eyes.

I sank back into the armchair; he circled it, warily. "Sorry, sorry, sorry," he kept muttering. "I've been taking pills – I thought they would help... I'm *impotent*!"

Now he tells me!

He fairly ran from the room. Somehow, I hobbled up to bed. I never did get that cup of tea.

Totally shattered now. Down and out... or was I? I reviewed my situation. And then rang Mr Andrews' partner, Mr McNutt.

"Give me details," he said tersely.

I had already checked with three solicitors in Southampton. It was *impossible* to sue Tesco's. They had, apparently, taken out an injunction two years ago – no one had been able to sue them since. They were totally immune from paying out compensation.

Mr McNutt sent for the relevant paperwork. "Read the small print..."

They are totally exempt from compensation, provided an assistant checks every aisle every five minutes...

"Regard that," he said, sternly. "Every *five* minutes, not six minutes; not five and a half minutes, but *five* minutes."

I shook my head. "Not necessary. I was sitting amongst the frozen peas for at least twenty minutes – as my bottom will testify," I said ruefully. "And then another quarter of an hour before the ambulance finally arrived. There was *no* assistant checking aisles – indeed, for at least twenty minutes, there was no assistant *at all*."

Data was provided from all in-store cameras, times were checked – no assistant had patrolled the aisles. Taken to court, Tesco's had no option but to pay damages. £10,000. Now I had funds... if *only* I could get proof of fraud, I could continue with my case.

But I had none.

My house was almost ready to market. By now, total disillusionment had set in. I recalled longingly my pre-marriage days. Two holidays a year, abroad. A beautiful house; great social life…

Suddenly, I'd had enough. The house, when sold, would make at least £70,000 profit from the hard work I had put into it. Forget Hampshire. Forget the police. Forget Brooks. *Get away.*

Gibraltar sprang into my mind. Days spent lazing on the Wisteria Terrace at the Rock Hotel. Sailing from Marina Bay. Swimming at Catalan Beach, and tea on the verandah afterwards at the Caleta Hotel…

Set against the rat-ridden, maggot-infested Park Road, it certainly had advantages. I'd sell up and *go*!

Finally, a lick of paint on the outside, to impress buyers. A bit wobbly on my recently de-plastered ankle, I set my step-ladder up defiantly and repainted the front door.

"Hello," said a voice.

I turned round, and all but fell off the ladder.

Brooks.

He enjoyed my consternation. "Painting the house are we?" he asked conversationally.

"*We* are not. *I* am." I said coldly. Wasted on him – like sticking a pin in a rhino. He neatly dodged the ladder and pushed past into the house. Still, as I had seen with my own eyes – there was no reason to fear him. I followed him.

We passed the hall table. "Good Lord," he exclaimed, goggling at the psychedelic purple key on the table.

"John Paul's spare key," I said, automatically.

He pushed into the living room. "See you've done it all up now," he observed.

"I have. And now you're here, I have to make it clear I want no more financial advice, and as for the Clerical and Medical endowment I was forced to take out (having had the other one *stolen*), I no longer need it and can no longer afford it; so I no longer need financial advice – or a *financial adviser*!"

"Oh, very well," he said, amicably. "In that case, I'll get in touch and have it stopped for you. No problem. In fact," he murmured generously, "I might even be able to get a couple of hundred *back* for you!"

"A couple of hundred *back* for me?" I repeated. "How?"

"They are personal friends of mine," he said. "They will do it as a favour."

I ushered him out and rang Clerical and Medical.

"Well of course you can cash it in," they said. "Any time you wish. If you cash it in now, it is worth £7,600."

Hm. A bit more than your two hundred, Mr Brooks. Time I left the UK for good. However, without that one policy, I could not get another mortgage.

Brooks had been checking up. Yes, I told him, before he left; I would be paying the compensation into my account. In fact, it had gone in that day – meaning I couldn't draw on it for *three days*. "After which, Mr Brooks, I am solvent again!"

Then I counted the days... one, two, three – and, sure enough, there he was again, on the doorstep. He was so sure of himself now, he didn't even bother to think up an excuse. He came straight in and demanded £200 for expenses.

I said I certainly didn't have it, and in any case, I certainly didn't owe it, but he said he knew how much I'd got from Tesco's and I *could* afford to pay. His attitude was threatening and I was suddenly aware that, having been humiliated in front of me, he wanted revenge; with a damaged back and a wobbly ankle, I was uncomfortably aware of my vulnerability. Frankly, I was scared – for the first time. Still, I decided, it may well be worth enhancing it.

"B-but I haven't got my cheque book," I quavered, "and... and in any case I don't even *owe* it." Then, in a more desperate manner, with the little old lady touch, "I-I don't know whe-where my handbag is."

As always, the slightest sign of fear provoked Brooks' bullying tactics. He stomped into the hall, snatched up my handbag and came and threw it on the table in front of me. I scrabbled around in it pathetically, finally coming up with my cheque book.

He picked up a pen and handed it to me. "Sign it!" he snarled. "Two hundred pounds."

"Two hundred pounds?" I gasped.

"Huh," he grunted. "May as well make it *five* hundred."

"May as well," I said, sweetly. Two hundred or five hundred, it made no difference to me.

I made it out for five hundred. He snatched it from me and left. The moment the door closed on him I rang Nationwide and stopped the cheque. I then rang Hampshire Police and explained what had happened. I pointed out that, living alone and, temporarily at least, very disabled, this incident had worried me considerably. It certainly had – I was *genuinely* shaking.

"We don't investigate fraud."

"This is demanding money with menaces," I retorted. "Or don't you investigate that, either?"

Even I was surprised when he returned ten days later to complain that the cheque had been stopped. I told him that the compensation money had merely cleared my debts.

"I'll accept that – *this* time," he said meaningfully.

However, I now felt that at least I had proved he was no bona fide financial adviser. And he had made the journey at some risk; shortly after taking possession of his new scarlet Audi, he had immediately been 'done' for speeding and drink-driving and banned for a year. At least he wouldn't be back.

Wrong.

By now I was able to walk quite well. Every lunchtime I walked a little further up the road until eventually I was able to reach the coffee shop, collapse, have a coffee and then walk back. I returned home and walked into the sitting room – and saw a *shape* in the far armchair. Against the window, it was quite scary… then I realised. Brooks.

"How did…?"

"Picked up John Paul's psychedelic key," he grinned. "Now I have *access*."

"I need that key," I protested. "It's John Paul's…"

"I'll leave it for you," he replied cheerfully. "Better than forever standing on the pavement ringing the bell when I know you're in, but you don't answer."

"Too right, I don't."

"Just to say," he went on, "I've checked, and Medical & Clerical's cheque hasn't bounced – *so far*."

A fortnight later, I came back from town – driving now; I'd bought some Chinese water colour paints – I'd take up my Chinese painting again. Popped the £100 from the cash point under a paperweight on the coffee table for safety, and took my usual walk up to the coffee shop. I felt I was well on the road to recovery, but this was the only physiotherapy available to me now.

On my return, I went to collect the £100 pounds to put in my bag ready for tomorrow's shopping. It had gone. I searched; had I made a mistake? No, of course not – there were the Chinese water colours where I'd left them, but no £100.

I sat down. A burglary? No – everything was in its place – the silver, the small jade ornaments, easily pocketed. All there.

Of course – the key; Brooks had still got John Paul's key! But surely, even he couldn't… yes, he could. Nasty little sneak thief – that's *exactly* what he was. But at least I now had enough to make a formal complaint. I rang the police and did just that.

They heard me out politely and I put the phone down.

Nothing.

I had just about had enough of Southampton; indeed, I'd had enough of the UK. I booked a flight to Gibraltar. Almost certainly I was viewing it through rose coloured spectacles after my jaundiced view of Southampton; but I would go.

But first – one last go at Albert Brooks. With the value of my property now, I could afford to borrow. I rang the Law Society again. Was it not at all possible, I enquired, to have a list of firms who *could* trace a missing policy? Could they, by any chance, give me a list?

Yes, they could.

I sat down next morning at 9.30, as soon as the solicitors' offices opened and went through the list systematically. By one o'clock, I was on my thirteenth. All twelve so far contacted had listened to the information patiently, and at great length, before politely declining to help.

However, number thirteen showed an interest. Mr Lloyd was a sole practitioner, he told me, and dealt almost exclusively with fraud. This looked distinctly promising; at least he was experienced.

"However," he then said, "I deal only with corporate fraud; the fraud I investigate is pretty massive and, of course, very expensive. But certainly it is possible to trace *any* policy and find out what has happened to it. I haven't actually undertaken a private case before, but I *could* do so."

It would cost me £5,000 up front.

That really set me back. £5,000 and I had not a penny left – the solicitors had by now totally cleaned me out. Still, my credit was good – and the house had to be sold. I explained. My experiences with solicitors so far had not been good – I had just been throwing good money after bad, and £5,000 was quite a lot of money to throw…

Then I had a *brilliant* idea. We had agreed that finding a lost policy with no name or number *was* a problem, but… for £2,000, would he be prepared to instigate an initial enquiry into the £20,000 Scottish Widows *bonus*? The policy *had* a number, name and date of issue; it would take *one* phone call.

I should have received a £20,000 bonus in November – the details had been extensively televised. The media had confirmed this fact, but for some reason, Mr Brooks had insisted I would receive a couple of hundred. And, lo and behold – a couple of hundred was all I had received. I would merely like an explanation from Scottish Widows as to why I had not received it.

I should have received it in November and had, in desperation, cashed the policy in the following year, unable to wait any longer for funds. Presumably, if they had paid out the full bonus in November, they would have requested I pay it back when I cashed the policy in shortly afterwards?

Yes. That was it. A brilliant idea! "Mr Lloyd, would you, for an initial fee of £2,000, ask Scottish Widows what happened to the £20,000 bonus? If you can trace that it went to Mr Brooks, it would facilitate an investigation into the other £60,000 – £350,000 policy…"

It was agreed.

The file, having been retrieved from Mr Tye-Reeve, was posted directly to Mr Lloyd, together with a cheque for £2,000.

I was therefore surprised to find the postman on my doorstep the following week, with *my file.*

Mystified, I took it in. I read the accompanying letter. And re-read it. When I had climbed down from the chandelier, I read it again and then answered it, I felt, *very* politely.

I was sorry only 5% of my letter had any relevant value; it had seemed fairly straightforward at the time. For a £5,000 down payment, Mr Lloyd had assured me that the missing policy, for which I had no details, *could* be traced. Certainly, I had been dubious about parting with £5,000 after my previous experiences with solicitors, but I thought we had agreed that for £2,000, Mr Lloyd would be prepared to contact Scottish Widows and enquire what had happened to the £20,000 bonus due to be paid out in November… for which, as Mr

Brooks had uncannily and accurately predicted I would (and did) received £200.

I was not and never had been a maths teacher. I agreed I should take my son's advice: forget my losses and move forward with my life – or *get a life* – but, unfortunately, the lost policy represented my life's savings and without it, frankly, I was *unable* to get a life.

Without my ability in interior design, which had meant a lucrative profit on the sale of my house, I would now be in a B&B, my furniture having been cast out onto the pavement. However, Mr Lloyd was no longer interested in continuing with the case, which I must accept, and would he kindly therefore return my £2,000 after extracting his expenses incurred in glancing through Mr Andrews' file?

Mr Lloyd replied.

I wrote back; I quite accepted his comments. Kindly return my £2,000 – less his expenses, of course.

Three similar letters followed from Mr Lloyd. Then, finally, a letter with a bill. Each letter had cost £250. The cost so far was £1,468.75.

Clearly, Mr Lloyd would continue to write similar letters until the £2,000 had been expended. There seemed little point in continuing; evidently Mr Lloyd needed the money more than I did.

I never did receive the balance. In fact, I never heard from Mr Lloyd again.

However, courtesy demanded that I contact the Law Society and explain why the enquiry had ended. By now, I had used up the time allotted by Miss Warner, who only worked Tuesdays and Thursdays. I received a cheque for £50 to apologise for the delay caused by my inability to contact anyone there, and an assurance that a full-time member of staff was now available.

I had, again, reached a dead end; I had no option but to give up.

Of course, one appreciates – everyone *knows* – the law, traditionally, is an ass; but I hadn't appreciated that it extended to the Legal Ombudsman.

Eleven

Still, one thing – the house had proved successful. As I had hoped, the dockland area where I now lived was fast becoming a 'desirable area'. The docks were a thriving marina for jet-set sailors, and property was at a premium. An authentic Georgian property, it had now been extensively redecorated with cut-glass Victorian chandeliers and heavy duty Wilton carpet throughout. The garden had been transformed and was now a landscaped court garden. I advertised it at nearly three times the amount I paid for it and, as with all the properties I had lived in and decorated, it was advertised on Friday and sold on Saturday, provided I was prepared to vacate within a fortnight.

The problem was, two separate buyers had viewed the property together; a middle-aged couple who looked round and asked pertinent questions, and a single fellow who strode straight through, looking neither left nor right in the process.

I immediately rang Pearsons, the agents, and said the couple was interested, but do *not* send anyone else like the single fellow. "I can tell you," I said, "he would only be interested in a cheap, knock-down price, and I have spent considerable time and trouble on the house; it is pristine throughout, everything is top level luxury, and I want the price for it."

"Oh," said the girl. "I am surprised. I think the lone fellow has put in an offer."

"I wouldn't be interested," I told her. "He is looking for a 'Rackman' type of house, and this *isn't* it."

She rang me back. "Mrs Donnelly," she said. "This fellow is *very* keen. He *did* put in an offer and when I said no deal, he said he was prepared to pay the full asking price."

I told her *no*. I was *not* being difficult. It was imperative the buyer was *solvent* and could get a mortgage – *and* as fast as possible.

Pearsons sent out their Chief Negotiator, Mike Golding. "He doesn't have the money," I protested, "and the one thing I *cannot* afford is to be messed about."

Mike Golding was adamant. "First thing we do," he said, "is check the finance, and he *does* have the money. Now, you can't afford to choose your buyer – you can't refuse to let him buy your house because you don't trust him. In fact," he said, as I began to wilt, "if you don't accept his very generous offer, we would consider that very unreasonable and would have to take the house off our books."

Well, I certainly couldn't afford to re-advertise and time was of the essence. "He absolutely *has* the money?" I asked. "And it will be a cash sale, providing I can move out within a fortnight?"

"Absolutely," he replied. "I've been in this business for forty years and it is a straightforward sale. He is keen to move in – you can even leave your furniture."

What choice did I have? Here I was – again on the breadline – and if it worked, it would be a Godsend – the answer to a prayer.

I took a flight out to Gibraltar. Put a £3,000 deposit on a one-bed flat by the beach. He could keep the rest of the furniture. Then I had to return and tidy up my affairs.

I had taken one of my last treasures into Hammonds, a local jeweller – a 1704 carriage clock, by a well-known French clockmaker. I had taken it in 1999, when I bought myself a coral ring from the proceeds of the last house, and he had begged to borrow the clock. A retired watchmaker had to put in half a dozen clocks he had repaired for a show at Olympia. They had to be absolutely top quality – he very much doubted mine would qualify – but if I brought it in, he would at least show it to him.

"But it doesn't need repairing," I told him. "Certainly, it doesn't keep perfect time, but it *is* three hundred years old!"

I was told it would be returned to me in absolute first class condition, but the man was not to be hurried; he was a perfectionist.

I said that was fine. But the show was to take place 'next spring'. This was in 2000; it was now July 2001.

He was busy.

I went back again. The show had been spring *last* year, so either he had sorted out the timing, or he hadn't. Either way, I wanted the clock back.

The watchmaker had repaired the clock – it was so precious, he'd had to make all the parts himself.

Now I was seriously alarmed; the clock had been fully operational, it merely gained a few minutes a week.

Every fortnight I went in to Hammonds in Shirley High Street. Every time there was a different excuse. He'd gone on holiday… he was waiting for parts… he was *making* the parts…

Finally, it was being tested; he had to wait eight days to see if it gained, then it would be ready.

By now, I had sold the house and he'd had the clock *two years*.

Not a problem – it would be shipped out to me in Gibraltar by special messenger, but it was too valuable to be moved at the moment.

Eventually, I pointed out, the removal men had packed up my furniture, and were prepared to accept the little clock. But it still wasn't ready. The fact was, I didn't have the clock, Hammonds didn't have it, and I wasn't at all sure about this 'retired watchmaker'. I therefore had no alternative but to report it stolen and claim on the insurance for its value.

A police officer from Shirley police station visited Hammonds twice. The first time, the clock was 'in transit'; the second time, the police reported, Hammonds *had* the clock now, packaged and ready to go.

By now, I had packed up what I wanted from the house. There was exactly enough money to buy the little one-bed flat in Gibraltar, but just to be sure, I had also rented a flat for a short period. I had found the whole experience very traumatic – it was, I knew, time to make a fresh start. I would treat myself to a short cruise; living in Southampton, I'd spent my life watching the luxury liners leaving and returning, and dreamed my dreams…

Everything had finally been settled; I would go on my cruise and then move into my flat in Gibraltar. A dream come true! I couldn't wait for tropical nights – I'd get out all my old evening dresses, and there I'd be – ready for the formal evenings… everything was rosy!

I took my previous teaching assistant with me, sent off all the vans overland, and jetted to Gibraltar. I had a week to move the furniture, and I knew I would need help with that. We organised electricity and water. Then we sat down and waited for the furniture to arrive. And waited…

And waited.

In desperation, I rang them. My furniture (and clothes) were '…somewhere in Spain, we seem to have lost contact…'

My assistant and I carried on waiting until, finally, she was due to go home. I would have to move the furniture in as best I could when it eventually arrived. My fabulous cruise left Southampton on 10th October, and I literally had what I stood up in. Should I go, and be shamed, in slacks and sweater – or forego the cruise?

What the hell! I *needed* that cruise. I travelled back with my assistant and drove on to the Dock Hotel. That evening, I rushed out to Debenhams, frantically looking for evening dresses – *anything*.

There was nothing. All the 'evening' would be coming in next week for the Christmas festivities – but that was no use to me. Passing a model, I had a brainwave. She was swathed in deep crimson velvet, with lace overlay. I persuaded the bemused assistant to strip the model. Of course, the velvet is modelled as a dress, Madam, but no, we don't actually have any more – it's just for show. If it would go round the model, I was certain it would go round *me*. Off it came; the Manager was most helpful – no; he didn't in the least mind being left with a naked model in the busy run-up to Christmas…

I sat and tacked all evening. I now had an evening dress. Two, in fact; I'd picked up a black lace kaftan in Gibraltar, from a barrow for £15. I was all set. Next morning, still sewing, I was on board for my very first cruise; one top, one pair of slacks, one pair of shoes.

Off we set. As I'd seen all the film stars do, I waved enthusiastically as the mooring ropes were loosed. *This was living*! Actually, not *quite* as I had expected; I'd seen pictures of the film stars leaning gracefully over the side, the obligatory chiffon scarves wafting gently in the breeze. However, this was Southampton in October. I braved the gales that we suddenly picked up in the Solent and fought my way to the sharp end (I'd seen Kate Winslet do it), but I had to put an anorak on – it looked like rain – and I was immediately splattered against the foredeck like a gnat on a windscreen and pinned there. With my hood flattened against my face, I stood there for a while – I don't give up easily, and in any case, I was winded and needed to get my breath back.

But I had a *wonderful* cruise. Pampered and petted, I was on an eight-seater table, my seven companions being most impressed by my evening dress. When an ex-Chippendale asked me to dance, I almost (but not quite) passed out. Dutifully, I turned him down (as one does), but when he demurred, what could I do? There were half a dozen fellows who simply danced with any spare lady – and all magnificent dancers... *magnificent*! However, I had to warn him; my clothes, I explained, were 'somewhere in Spain' and my beautiful evening gown was only *tacked* together. But this was the *formal* evening and I was formal. "But don't tread on my hem," I warned. "Do that, and I will be very *informal* in two seconds flat!"

But he didn't, and neither did anyone else. They danced with me as if I were Dresden china, but they *danced*. A wonderful, *wonderful* cruise – and I have kept in touch with all of them.

And then finally, back to Southampton, and a flight to Gibraltar – and my new life. I'd left all my problems behind.

There was a message on my answerphone. Could I ring Pearsons? I did.

"Er, we appear to have a problem," Mike Golding told me. "Mr Singh now tells me: a) he doesn't have the cash, and b) he can't get a mortgage."

Chaos. I didn't have the money for my rented flat, and no money for the one I was buying. There followed a fortnight of absolute terror. I rang round all the agents. No, they were sorry; no, *they* could have got the full asking price *easily*, but it would be unethical as I was committed to Pearsons, etc. etc.

Finally, Pearsons informed me that Mr Singh *did* want the house, but for £18,000 less, (seeing as how I was over a barrel). I had no alternative at this stage. During the delay, my flat in Gibraltar had gone up by £20,000 – I simply didn't have enough to buy even a one-bed flat. Thank heavens I'd rented one. Nothing I could do about it.

I accepted the new offer and then spent a whole day ringing round for a removal and storage firm at very short notice – like twenty-four hours! Eventually I found one. He would do it as a personal favour, having moved me five times already. His men zipped round to the house at first light and moved practically all of the furniture out.

He phoned me. "There's still a lot of china left," he said. "But it's one o'clock and Mr Singh has turned up to move in, and at the moment is having a punch-up with my men."

Clearly, Mr Singh did have the money and was obviously crooked. (I'd had some experience with crooks by now.) He'd thought he could get away with paying less for the house *and* keeping all the furniture. His aim was obviously to let it, probably to students. He hadn't been the least bit interested in the luxury fittings, just how many students he could squash in – and using all my furniture.

As it was, he merely got what he paid for. Without the furniture, even his lower price was reasonable for an empty house. Still, at least I'd kept my furniture.

Having settled in, I wrote to Shirley police to see if I could get my carriage clock back. The way I eventually recovered it was by writing to my insurance company and claiming for theft. They accepted the claim without any problem, but it was their letter that finally worked the magic.

Hammonds said they would deliver it to my son in London. It was, they said, *far too valuable* to be sent to Gibraltar. Eventually it arrived. Broken. Obviously, the watchmaker, who was a *perfectionist* – well, he'd taken over two years on the clock – had broken it and didn't like to say so! At least I had it back; grateful for small mercies now.

And so… to Gibraltar.

At last, the mist began to clear and I soon got used to my new way of life – waking each morning to a sparkling, sunny day, overlooking the Atlas Mountains in the distance, and the Harbour below; strolling down to Casemates Square for coffee, which is put on the table before I can sit down; spending the afternoon lazing on a deserted, sandy beach, swimming in the crystal clear waters, then home to watch 71-channel TV, or out on the balcony to watch the African sunset. Who could complain?

Still, it did rankle. The Law Society *and* the police had said, *yes*, there *were* firms that could trace a lost policy. But *where* were they? As a last resort I had written to Mr Whitehead, but received no reply. So I wrote to Tony Blair – it was, after all, only an address I required.

I received a reply from Tony Blair. *He* couldn't tell me, but he knew a man who could…

A letter came from the Lord Chancellor, suggesting I contact my MP, Mr Whitehead. We had now gone full circle.

It was quite clear now that I was *never* going to get the stolen money back. I'd also cashed in the first policy, trying to get the second one back. £300,000 down the drain – not to mention the hundred and one nervous breakdowns.

I would have to accept defeat.

Even so, John Paul's scholarship had been vetoed, costing me £17,000 a year for his seven years at Charterhouse, and Desmond still owed me £450 a month since 1976. The Queen was the Principal Governor of Charterhouse, and, if nothing else, Desmond Donnelly was responsible for the whole miserable set of events.

Last shot before I gave up: John Paul had by now put on several quality plays, been hailed as Young Playwright of the Year, and just needed a little financial help which, in normal circumstances, most fathers would have given. I therefore wrote to the Queen. I appreciated that John Paul's scholarship was probably water under the bridge by now, but it should be possible to persuade Desmond to pay *something*, even at this late stage, since he had been ordered to do so by the High Courts of London *and* Hong Kong. He had been in Contempt of Court for the past thirty years but was still apparently able to practise, regardless.

I didn't get a letter back from Baroness Hollis of Heighman, but I did get one from the Ministry for Children and Family, and also from the Department for Constitutional Affairs.

And no, they couldn't help because I was now a resident of Gibraltar.

I didn't know that? I had thought I was still a resident of the UK.

But presumably I couldn't be both. Certainly, I had intended buying a property in Gibraltar, but in fact I was only renting, pending a dramatic improvement to my spinal injury after my final, *enforced* year of commuting and teaching in London.

I had looked upon retiring to Gibraltar in much the same way as retiring to the Isle of Wight. In fact, Gibraltar is much more British than Britain, except, of course, when it becomes convenient to say '… you live in Gibraltar, therefore your problems are no concern of the UK…'

However, John Paul was at that time offered the opportunity of writing another play for the Royal Court Theatre in London and – the pinnacle of achievements – a play for the National Theatre. Both were accepted and scheduled to run in 2006.

At which point, he met the girl of his dreams and had a ring on her finger within six weeks.

Success indeed!

Perhaps we don't need *any* of the money we are owed after all. And, well… there is nowhere nicer than Gibraltar to be stranded in – and I *am* certainly *stranded.*

That was my last chance, and my last house. It did brilliantly, and everything worked out as planned, except that I was right – Mr Singh *didn't* have the money, or at least very cleverly *said* he didn't.

Finally, I thought I would check the last policy that Albert Brooks had forced me to take out. Great. Now worth £19,000 – so I cashed it in. Of course, to date, I'd paid in £36,000 – another £17,000 Brooks had cost me. But with my pension, that will do me nicely – albeit on the breadline. But then, who needs more, when you can wake up in the morning and then walk out in glorious sunshine, look out over Marina Bay, and watch the sun set behind the Atlas Mountains in the evening?

So… what to do today? Lie out on golden sands at Catalan Beach and take tea afterwards in the Caleta Hotel?

See if Nanette and Michael are doing another trip to Morocco on their forty-foot ocean-going yacht?

Or a concert in St Michael's Cave?

Or just laze on my balcony with dry Martinis?

Or write my own cautionary tales? An autobiography?

What shall I call it… *The Black Hole?*

Hm, not bad; tomorrow, perhaps – Nanette has just rung; we're going sailing.

The future is rosy…

Epilogue

So, this is the Forest... again.

Once again I am back in my beloved New Forest. As I pass along the dappled rides, do I long for the sun-drenched beaches of Gibraltar? No. It is calm and peaceful here, with only the scut of deer or rabbit disturbing the air as they spring away, startled by my intrusion.

I had returned to Gibraltar for six months only – to recuperate – and went to visit Mr Phillips, my (tenth) solicitor, for the last time. My friend, Vivien, whose husband ran a renowned legal practice, had recommended a firm called Hassans.

Having been given a fortnight's notice to get out of my UK home and accept the full offer for the house, I put everything in store in Southampton and flew to Gibraltar, taking with me only the bare essentials.

Bishop's Move, a BFPO removal firm, had taken everything out. I'd found a flat overlooking the Botanical Gardens, and duly made my appointment to visit Hassans. I arrived in good time and was duly ushered in.

"Mrs Donnelly! Good to see you. Vivien sends her regards. She's in Hertfordshire now, of course. Husband retired and they are now enjoying country life. *Lovely* to see you, but... catastrophe! I have a yacht in the bay with massive drugs on board and I've been asked by the coastguards to attend the incident, as it were. Would you excuse me? I do have to dash."

"Of course." Well, obviously a massive drugs haul was more important than my tiny theft.

"May I make another appointment?"

"Of course, of course." He beamed toothily. "Please do... Miss Smith? Make an appointment for Mrs Donnelly would you? Must dash!" He swept out.

The following week, I turned up for my appointment ten minutes early – just in time to be met by a body hurtling through the swing doors and almost flattening me.

"Oh! Mrs Donnelly! *So* sorry to have missed you (almost). My wife has just rung. She suffers from depression, you know, and I am needed at home desperately."

Now, had she been knocked down by a bus, I could have believed in his haste to get home. But depression?

My friend was to tell me, later, "Oh yes, that is true. Quite genuine. She has been treated in a private hospital for depression. She is home now."

Fine. But she had a non-working son, daughters and a dear loving husband, and they were millionaires, and that being the case, I still felt that he could at least have spared me five minutes of the second appointment. As I explained, all I wanted was an answer – yes or no. Could he or couldn't he write two simple letters on my behalf – one to Lloyds Bank requesting statements, the other to the Financial Ombudsman requesting an investigation?

However, there was no alternative. I made another appointment.

And here I was again, at the third attempt. This time he didn't even bother turning up. The receptionist resignedly put up with me for three quarters of an hour, at which point I gave up and left. Before doing so, I left a message with her. I merely wanted two letters from him, one to Lloyds and the other to the Financial Ombudsman. If he said no, then I would consider the matter final and give up, the money was lost. But a solicitor's letter, I felt, might sway the balance.

"Oh, most assuredly," I was told. No problem, Another appointment was made.

He failed to turn up.

Finally, at the sixth attempt, I sat waiting, ten minutes early and poised for flight as soon as zero hour passed, when the door opened and a dapper, middle-aged fellow strode across the reception area to greet me.

"Mrs Donnelly? Delighted to meet you! Delighted! You need some help with a fraud case, I gather?" He ushered me into his adjoining office, introducing himself as Mr Phillips. One of Hassans' panel of solicitors, I thought.

"I gather," I began, "from my several abortive attempts to get an interview, that no one was prepared to deal with a case of fraud and were reluctant to even write a couple of letters on my behalf."

"Mrs Donnelly," he leaned forward importantly, "of all the solicitors in Gibraltar, I think I am probably the *only one* capable of dealing with a matter of fraud." Leaning back again, elbows on the arms of his leather executive armchair, he steepled his fingers. "I happen to have worked in London for twenty years, solely on insurance matters. And I know personally most of the staff at Scottish Widows that you mentioned."

Things were looking up. He gave the impression that he had been *selling* insurance.

"All you need are two letters to the Financial Ombudsman and Lloyds, and certainly a rational explanation from Scottish Widows. A straightforward phone call should do it."

I explained the need for a letter, especially to the Financial Ombudsman.

"Well, I think I can save you the trouble and expense of that," he said. "I think I can safely say that if *anyone* can get your money back, I can."

Clearly *he* was impressed with his own abilities, if no one else was!

"In that case," I said, "I'll leave you with a cheque for £1,000 to do so.

He was delighted. I was hopeful, and left. Later, I received a letter from Phillips, Solicitors – nothing to do with Hassans – they never appeared again. Apparently, I had somehow managed to switch lawyers with little or no effort.

Anyway, a further appointment was made. He had now solved the case. He had heard from his personal friends at Scottish Widows. *So* sorry to be the bearer of bad news, but it appeared I had cashed the policy in. There was therefore no bonus. End of the matter. Thanks for the £1,000. Goodbye Mrs Donnelly.

"*That* was made clear by Mr Andrews ten years ago," I told him. "The policy *was* cashed in, yes, a year *after* the takeover payment was due. The bonus should have been paid in November 1999; I cashed the policy in the following year."

His smile faltered. "Well, anyway, Mrs Donnelly," he blustered, "that appears to be the end of the matter."

Had he, as he'd said, known the staff at Scottish Widows personally, I would have hoped for an explanation for not only the non-payment of any bonus, but also the miraculous appearance of 'an extra £200' in the final cash-in, as prophesied by the psychic Mr

Brooks. But the main point was the stolen principal policy, not a small bonus.

All I wanted now was a straightforward letter to Lloyds demanding back statements, and a letter to the Financial Ombudsman on my behalf to beg (a second time) for an investigation.

"I believe I'm only allowed one crack of the whip, officially," I told him, "but since solicitor number three deliberately withheld the file the first time, I feel I should be given a second chance. Could you, would you write such a letter on my behalf?"

Of course he could, and of course, he would.

I made another appointment. This time I left him with a cheque for £2,000, an offer he couldn't refuse, I felt.

However, he said he would continue to write to Scottish Widows about the lost bonus. "I fear you did not give me all the information I needed, Mrs Donnelly. Since there was full media coverage at the time, *that* was what I needed."

"It would all have been recorded in the *Financial Times*, I'm sure," I said, "and it had full coverage on TV and radio."

"*That's* what I need," he beamed.

I rang the research department of the *FT.* Yes, John, their researcher was up to that.

John was delighted. "I'll look them out for you. Afraid it will have to go Special Delivery to Gibraltar."

Thirty copies of *FT* via Avion cost £500, but worth it.

A further appointment with Mr Phillips was made. Had he heard from the Financial Ombudsman? No. Anything from Lloyds? No.

"One thing at a time, Mrs Donnelly, one thing at a time," he beamed.

He now only needed to cut out all the relevant articles and put them in order, and he would solve the problem.

Meanwhile, my six month contract on the flat was coming to an end. I had arrived barely able to stand for more than a couple of days before being consigned to my bed with massive spasms from the damaged spinal fusion. Then I began swimming or walking daily, sunbathing on the sandy beaches, and now I was meeting up with friends, had joined the Cathedral choir and helped in an animal sanctuary. I hadn't realised until now – my back was cured and life here was fun

Anyway, I still hadn't heard from the Financial Ombudsman and I didn't really want to leave yet, so I signed a further six-month contract. This was fun!

Christmas came and went. From my balcony I surveyed the £40m firework display celebrating the New Year. It lit up the entire bay and from my 40ft balcony I had a fantastic view of the midnight sky, with the Atlas Mountains on the far horizon. For the first time in years, there were barbecues, outdoor theatres and parties. I unpacked the Waterford, the Crown Derby and the Spode and gave parties and *celebrated!*

Early in the New Year I asked for a further appointment with Mr Phillips. Mr Phillips was not available. He had gone on a two-month cruise. (I had just given him a cheque for £2,000… not surprising.) Who cared? Everything was in hand. I went sailing. The days grew hotter and life was a drowsy round of lotus eating. My back was completely cured and life was fun! I could get used to this!

One day there was a phone call from John Paul. Could he come out for a visit?

"Of course. Delighted! Bring Becky."

"Er… no," he stuttered, "not this time. This is *important*, Mum. Prepare yourself for a *shock*."

(My dear, I am BOMB-proof by now!) Patter of tiny feet? I wondered… there had been great excitement over the wedding, the previous year.

"I hope you think it's *good* news," he continued, "but I'd better come out and tell you *myself* – it's going to be *quite a shock*. Well, it was to *me*, so I'd better come out and tell you *myself*."

He sounded quite grim. (Not the patter of tiny feet, then.)

He arrived two days later.

I greeted him at the airport. "So what's the news, then?"

"Can't tell you here," he muttered. He was in a nervous, excitable state, most unlike John Paul.

We arrived at my flat.

"So?" I asked.

"Not here. Not here. I'll tell you tomorrow when I've had a chance to recover."

The following day we beached, swam and sunbathed. Finally, in the evening, I took him out to the Marina Restaurant. We had a table overlooking the bay, with a soft, African sunset, calm blue sea and ice cool drinks...

"Now!" I insisted.

He took a hefty swig from his glass. "Well... it's like this. Er... are you *sure* you're ready for this, Mum?" he asked anxiously. "I don't want you to collapse on me, or anything..."

"Just *tell* me!"

"Okay. Well, it's like this... I had a phone call..." he inhaled deeply, "from *my brother*!"

Just as well I was sitting down. Just as well *he'd* been sitting down at the time, apparently.

"I just had a phone call out of the blue," he said, "and a voice asked 'is your name John Donnelly?' Yes. 'Is your name John Paul Desmond Donnelly?' Yes. 'Oh well, it seems I am your brother. Your mother, apparently, wrote a story called *The Black Hole* and put it on the internet.'

"I'm afraid another shock for you, Mum," he said then. "You see, Desmond died last year and his family were trawling the internet, looking for Donnellys to invite to the funeral. His obituary was on the internet at that time. Anyway, they found the story by Wendy Donnelly."

I was about to learn a great deal more about Desmond Donnelly, QC. Apparently, he had not *decided* to work in Singapore and Hong Kong for his health – he had been *sent* there. The eldest son and heir to vast estates in Ireland, he had been disinherited by his father, together with his young family and then *sent* to Singapore, *never to darken the family portals again.*

It seemed I was not the only one to find Desmond a total and complete disappointment. Upon discovering *The Black Hole* containing my tales of Desmond, his first wife had confirmed the general suspicions by exclaiming, "*That's* the bastard!"

He had, apparently, walked out on his young family – the youngest was five year old Brendon – leaving them stranded in Singapore, penniless. The Donnelly estate had then provided them with a London home with the approval of his mother and two sisters.

"Did... er, did Desmond ever show any personal violence towards you?" John Paul asked, anxiously.

"No. He wouldn't have dared." I never have been able to understand how some women could accept violence with apparent equanimity. Discussing the subject once with friends, I remembered he had said, "I dare not argue with Binky. I'm afraid my coffee might have a funny taste next morning!"

He had apparently beaten up his first wife and remonstrations (legal?) had followed.

"He told me," I said, "that he had *three daughters* and his cruel wife had walked out on *him* and never allowed him to see them again." (Tears would roll down his cheeks as he related this sad tale, and worried and sympathetic women had crowded round him to offer sympathy and understanding.)

"Well," I said, my thoughts reeling, "I suppose that leaves you as the only legitimate heir? *You* were never disinherited."

"Brendon," he said happily, "*my brother*, rang me and we had a *long* conversation. Several, in fact. Then *Brendon* invited me over to *Ireland* to see the estate. It's being run by Desmond's eldest daughter – there's no one else – and her husband." (I thought they'd been disinherited?)

"It was her *birthday*," he continued, "so, having seen *The Black Hole* on the internet, they invited me over, and it turned into a party for *me*!!"

Much champagne and wine generally, I gathered. He had then been taken out on their America's Cup class yacht for a drunken sail, and generally feted. I didn't dare say, 'Yes, but what about your claim to the estate?' (I hoped he hadn't signed anything.) Clearly, the important thing was that he now had a *family* and was being asked over to Ireland regularly, where there were stables, racehorses, etc, etc, etc.

"Look," I said, "it's *your* family. I gave up on Desmond and I have *no* interest in any of his family. If you want to meet up with them, go, and enjoy them. You're welcome to them."

He still looked anxious. "You don't mind?"

"Not in the least."

He had always desperately wanted to be part of a *family* – now he was. At that time I had enough problems on my mind to cope with and I didn't want to have to take on John Paul's lost opportunities, or any more fights on his behalf.

So he kept in touch. Visited Ireland. One family member was living in LA; John Paul had invited them all to London. All, it seemed, was well with John Paul.

If that was his *bad* news, I'd heard worse.

Only one thing bothered me. Liz's husband, an Army QC, had visited Hong Kong – and Desmond – on many occasions. Desmond had never had a day's illness in his life. He had simply chosen, as before, not to pay *any* maintenance for *any* family. Apparently, he had boasted that, as Hong Kong's leading Counsel, he had undertaken the takeover of Hong Kong by China, initially single handed. Being Desmond, he had made a fortune out of playing the triads one against the other, to win incredible concessions to the highest bidder, etc. and had made millions! If he made Xmillions, he would then have set about spending Xmillions *plus one* as he had clearly tried to spend his father's inheritance.

I couldn't help wondering… whatever happened to the money?

Eventually, I contacted Mr Phillips again. "Have you heard from the Financial Ombudsman yet?"

"No."

"Have you heard from Lloyds Bank?"

"No."

I wanted to make another appointment.

"No, no. That won't be necessary. I can deal with this. Anyone who pays me £3,000 in advance gets my *full* attention." He would get in touch as soon as there was any news.

I had suddenly realised that the flat's rent had risen by £100 each time I renewed the contract. I was fast coming to the end of my resources.

I made another appointment.

"Ah, Mrs Donnelly! I've been looking at your file. I think I've solved the problem. I've *found* your lost policy."

I nearly fainted with joy.

"Yes. I've looked through the list of policies Scottish Widows sent me. But I'm sorry to say you cashed it in for £1,000. Look, see for yourself… I have it here."

I couldn't believe what I was hearing. A policy that I'd paid into for twelve years out of twenty – cashed in for £1,000? The man was talking nonsense, of course. I told him that I remembered that particular policy. "If you check," I said, "I think you will find it was a policy I had taken out two or three years earlier and, being in a desperate situation, I cashed it in for what it was worth, £1,000."

He looked at it again. "Oh, yes," he said, disappointed. "It would appear so."

"I think I have to make it clear," I said, "that my time here is limited. I came for six months and have now been here three years and achieved nothing. I am now in a position where, financially, I must return to the UK."

(Not soon enough, his face said.)

"Have you heard from the Financial Ombudsman or Lloyds Bank?"

"No."

"Well, will you please check with them both today? I will wait a fortnight. If there is no news I will have to make arrangements to move back to the UK."

I made an appointment two weeks later.

"Mrs Donnelly," he said, "I've solved your problem... er, the two envelopes containing the Scottish Widows policy and the stolen policy?"

"What about them?"

The numbers on the envelopes *are* the number of the policy! You have the number of the stolen policy. All you have to do is check it out when you get back to the UK!"

"You mean," I said slowly, "that I have been walking round with details of the stolen policy in my pocket all this time?"

"Yes," he beamed.

"And all *nine* solicitors failed to realise that?"

"They probably don't understand insurance policies as I do," he said modestly.

I returned home thoughtfully. If Lloyds could confirm that the number on the envelope they had given me was in fact the number of the stolen policy, then the matter was indeed solved.

I checked the Scottish Widows policy number with the number on the other envelope. Completely different. One of us was an idiot (probably me), but no, the numbers on both envelopes were for bank use only. They were for administration purposes and had nothing whatever to do with the policies.

No word from Financial Ombudsman.

No word from Lloyds.

Time to go. I made a last appointment with Mr Phillips.

"May I see the letter to the Financial Ombudsman?" I asked.

He showed it to me, dated 8th August 2007. There had been no reply. And none from Lloyds.

"There *must* be a reply soon," I said. "I will keep in touch and see if I can find out from there what the problem is."

I contacted Bishop's Move. Yes, they could move me out in three weeks. Their man came to view the flat. They still had the inventory of when I'd come out (£2,500). There were still a few bits left to collect in their depository, I explained. I had ditched most of my heavy winter clothing and would be travelling back considerably lighter, but £3,100 in all was what he said. The deal was struck. I imagined that petrol, as well as everything else, had increased in the interim. Certainly my rent had risen a frightening £300 during three years.

Delivery date was set for 30th October 2007 and frantic preparations followed.

John Paul rang. He had finally managed to obtain a mortgage for Becky and himself. A flat of their own! I had been about to congratulate them on *not* achieving this, since the news from America was bad, and getting worse. Rows of FOR SALE boards dominated the news programmes. A recession was imminent.

I kept quiet. But the UK *always* followed America's example. It did not bode well.

Suddenly our own Northern Rock crashed. Definitely time to go home but, fortunately, I thought, it could not possibly affect *me*!

Dozens of boxes arrived, all to be filled. Then, out of the blue, my back collapsed. There was no alternative, it would mean three weeks strict bed rest or I wouldn't be able to travel. I rang the hospital. Since it had gone into spasm, I could hardly breathe, let alone move.

I was impressed. A young doctor arrived within half an hour. He apologised; he would have to charge me £5. Imagine getting a home call-out in the UK for that!

He gave me a prescription. "Be very careful," he said. "Don't take more than two at a time, and no more than six in any one day. They will get you on your feet, but they are strong. Whatever you do, don't take an overdose. They can cause liver damage. If there is still a problem after the recommended dose, call me."

He was right. They were far stronger than those prescribed in the UK and I was back on my feet the next day.

One of my cats, a stray, had found herself a millionairess in a house further up the mountain, with a huge garden. She was happily playing one off against the other – a small child in the next block had also been trying to tempt her away from me, her mother told me, with *prawns*.

"I hope you don't mind," her mother said, "but she's such a pretty cat. My daughter has quite fallen for her."

I explained the situation; I would be leaving shortly.

"I'll tell my daughter," she said with delight. "We can have her?"

Matilda appeared next day. Her somewhat tatty collar was now replaced by a rhinestone-studded silver one with the name and address of the millionairess inscribed upon it, proudly declaring ownership. I explained to the daughter that she would have to share Matilda's affections (there were about five others that she also scrounged from).

Leo was different. A beautiful white Persian with golden eyes, he had been brought into the cat sanctuary eaten alive by fleas and ringworm. When taken to the vet he was pronounced 'moribund.' A year later, with twice weekly 'poison baths' and regular shaving of his beautiful fur, he was now completely cured, but somewhat shaken if not stirred. He looked at me expectantly.

"Sorry," I said, "We're going back to the UK. It's the vet again for you." Fortunately, both cats had received every injection available, including rabies, so it merely involved at least six visits to the vet, six more to the airport, a ticket costing exactly three times more than mine, and he could travel.

Me? I rang the airport and booked a ticket electronically for one third of the price. We were both ready to travel to the UK.

There was a phone call from Bishop's Move. It was Claire. "Mrs Donnelly, sorry to have to call you. Slight oversight on our part, I'm afraid. My manager has pointed out that when he visited your flat (three times), he slightly under-estimated the total of goods to go to the UK..."

Too right. I had all my valuables – silver, ivory, jade and jewellery – that I hadn't dared to leave in store in Southampton. Having spent a lifetime re-accumulating all the heirlooms lost from my family's home, nothing was less than an authentic antique.

"House full of bloody *clocks*!" Commander Woods had said in disgust, "and not *one* to tell the right time."

"Let us hope," I had said acidly, "that you will be in as good condition after three hundred years as that fourteenth century carriage clock. It is merely running five minutes slow."

"… so," Claire continued, "there will be a further £1,000 to pay."

Now, having moved house (of necessity, after my disastrous liaison with Desmond), steadily moving lower down the tracks, at least five times, with Roberts – the same removal firm each time – I had a fairly shrewd idea that an 'estimate' was not a wild guess as to what the carrier *might* charge, but heretofore and ever after a final and definite *quote*. On top of which, my savings were now down to £3,500 and nothing was left in my current account.

"Well," I told her, "I've paid the original estimate of £3,100. I'll see what I can do, but at the moment I have no option but to accept your original estimate. On the other hand, all my goods will be in store with you at Wokingham and, certainly, if I find the query to be justified, it will be paid. You hold the value of the goods. I will take advice once I am back in the UK as to any extra payment."

There were three more phone calls, each one becoming more desperate. "Mrs Donnelly, we must have that extra £1,000."

I checked all my statements. If it had been there I would certainly have paid it – anything to just GET ME HOME! All I had now was a £16,000 facility on my credit cards and a small savings account.

Came yet *another* phone call – this time triumphant. "Mrs Donnelly, your credit card has bounced!"

"Now that *is* nonsense," I said sharply. I'd had enough of this. "To my knowledge, there is £6,000 credit on that card. There must be some mistake."

"No mistake," she crowed. "It bounced. Oh, and do you realise that October 30th is the *only* date available this year to move you? As I told you, we are undertaking a *mammoth* MOD movement after that, which will take us right up to the new year."

"I'll get on to the bank right away," I told her. I rang the bank.

"Yes, I'm sorry," said the girl disinterestedly. "You may have heard of the crash of Northern Rock? I'm afraid all our credit facilities have been cancelled."

I was shocked. "But I've heard nothing from you."

"Well, no," she admitted, "but there's been so many queries we really haven't been able to cope."

Recovering, I rang Claire. "My apologies," I said. "I'll have to give you another card – Barclays this time – I assume that will be safe enough."

Three days later Claire was on the phone again. "Your credit card has bounced *again*, Mrs Donnelly."

I was shattered. Banks didn't crash, did they? Barclays had been inundating me with new and better offers of unending credit facilities – would I like a holiday? A cruise? "You haven't used it, so we've topped it up; *now* will you use it?"

So I had. Just once. For Bishop's Move. My timing, as always, was impeccable. I rang Barclays.

"So sorry, Mrs Donnelly. You've probably heard about the havoc caused by the crash of Northern Rock. We have had to cancel the credit. So sorry." The phone was put down with some finality.

I sat down. Rethink. I now had less than two weeks to get out of Gibraltar. I went through my bank statements. There was exactly enough to pay Bishop's Move if I wrote and cashed in all my savings immediately. I wrote and posted the letter there and then. It would take 7/10 days to get transferred to my current account.

I took a deep breath and swallowed what was left of my pride. "I'm afraid," I told Claire, "I had not appreciated the effect of Northern Rock crashing, All my credit facilities have gone. I do have the money in a savings account but it will take seven to ten days to be transferred. But it will be paid before the thirtieth."

"*Three* days before, in fact," said Claire, nastily I thought, "or we don't pack up the goods. *And* there's the extra £1,000 to be paid."

"With respect," I said, "that was *your* error. I have now checked the incoming inventory. £2,500. And there is considerably less going back. However, it will be dealt with, as I said, on my return to the UK. Otherwise, I will refer it to the MOD here and let them decide."

There was no answer so I presumed it had been accepted.

Better check everything. Leo was ready to travel after about twenty trips to vet and airport in readiness. All in order.

Check my flight. Ah, a problem: "... due to the recent terrorist threat only ONE piece of hand luggage will be accepted."

Okay. Repack. All necessities could go in the three boxes labelled URGENT. At least I would have a change of underwear and immediate necessities within three weeks.

Without thinking, I began packing up clothes in bits and pieces, quite aimlessly. My back was numb, fortunately. I would have to get the cat to airport, and see the removals people off, and check this and that... could I do it? I would need those pills.

There would be no one to meet me at the other end. It would be Just Me, with a cat box and the clothes I stood up in... needed money for a hotel... find a flat... and a cattery...

The pills had begun to settle now. No pain at all. I surveyed the mess around me. No way was I going to finish all that packing. I was just not going to make it and there was little alternative, but at least I could put things in order...

I fetched the only bottle of wine from the kitchen and the rest of the boxes of pills the doctor had given me – to my surprise *four* boxes 'for emergency use only.' What was this if not an emergency?

Clearly, I was never going to make it to the UK and if I did, I hadn't even the resources to buy a cup of coffee when I arrived there... I would be homeless and penniless. Whereas if I left now, John Paul would come in for all the antiques and heirlooms I had spent a lifetime collecting to replace my parents' lost inheritance in the black hole.

It was quite easy to take the pills. Two had abated the spasms... slowly, I downed the first eight with some wine, then a further eight, and so on until the box was empty.

The second box took a little longer.

Then the third.

The fourth took some time, even with the wine, but eventually I realised the box was half-empty. Still, in all there must have been well over a hundred. Enough, anyway.

Suddenly, it didn't seem very important any more. The chaos of packing, Claire's constant hectoring for extra payment... AN EXTRA £1,000, MRS DONNELLY... AN EXTRA... an extra...

It all faded and I became aware of an overwhelming lassitude. I gazed at the four boxes with surprise. There were just a few pills left, scattered near the empty wine bottle. I hadn't taken them *all*, but enough was enough...

I wandered into the bedroom. All was well now. The cats would be taken care of by someone else. I certainly couldn't help any more.

I had never known a bed could be so *comfortable*.

I slept.

I became aware of floating on soft grey clouds, and a feeling of blissful satisfaction. I had clearly *arrived*. Shouldn't there be music? Harps? There was certainly a *noise*...

I now had a feeling of dissatisfaction. *Grey* clouds? GREY? Had I not lived an entirely exemplary life? Had I not contributed to all and sundry welfare projects? Had I not, in fact, been little short of perfection in earthly life?

What, then, was I doing with grey clouds? Moreover, now that I came to think of it, not only was that sound *not* music, but it was also an abominable noise. A mobile ringing.

A MOBILE? UP HERE?

Cautiously, I prised open one eyelid. A picture of the Chateau de Chillon greeted me. I had painted it during my first trip abroad. I was back in my own bedroom.

I glanced at the clock. 3pm. I had started packing that morning at 7am and keeled over at midday. Not to worry. I felt very relaxed. I was pleased to note that I had prepared myself properly – hands on breast – just like the old medieval crusaders. In fact, fine for a siesta...

Suddenly, a violent eruption occurred mid-bed, and I lurched to the bathroom, where I deposited almost four boxes of strong painkillers neatly down the loo.

I leaned against the wall, breathless, waiting for that BLOODY phone to stop ringing. Too faint to argue, I picked it up.

"Wendy? Maureen. Don't forget we are picking you up at ten o'clock tomorrow for Granada. I've collected the car and I'll be there at ten o'clock sharp."

"Granada?" I murmured. My head cleared a little. "But that wasn't till Saturday..."

"It's Friday now, you idiot. Ten o'clock *tomorrow*, okay?"

I had slept the clock round,

Ten o'clock sharp and we were on the road. A pleasant stop for lunch at a medieval convent, now an exclusive restaurant known only to the initiated. Maureen, a travel courier, knew all the secret hide-outs of the elite. Watching the deer as we drove through the grounds and back on course, I began to regain my senses.

The Alhambra was magnificent, the weather gorgeous, the views unparalleled. We sat on a seat to rest, halfway. Madge, who liked to know things, had bought a tourist guide at every single stop on the way, so far.

"*We'll* go on to the gardens," she told me. "*You've* been before." She dropped the guidebook on the seat beside me. They had not failed to notice my lack of concentration.

"No, no," I protested, struggling to catch up. "I'm fine."

"No," Madge said firmly. "You stay there with my guidebook..."

We all turned back to look at the seat. The book had gone. It was too far to go back to get another one; we'd come halfway. Hell.

I had been before and desperately tried to remember all I knew about the Alhambra... the line of the canal of fountains... how the canal narrows, giving the impression of being much longer than it actually is... the fountains getting smaller, giving an impression of depth...

My brain slowly began to function again.

"Sorry about the guide book," I said. Finally, over a coffee on the terrace overlooking the stupendous views, I gave my explanation.

"I really am sorry I've been so dozy today, but I wasn't expecting to come. To be honest, I'd forgotten all about it."

"We wondered what had happened to you on Thursday," Maureen said. "We were supposed to meet up in the evening and when I rang you next morning you sounded really weird."

I told them what had happened.

"We wondered," Maureen said. "We saw the mess the flat was in, with everything tipped out. We just couldn't think how you were going to get everything packed up in three days."

"The boxes only arrived last week," I said, "and it took me the rest of the day to assemble them. And then bombshell after bombshell. All credit cancelled, an extra £1,000 to pay at the last minute, and then only hand luggage on the plane."

Maureen, the experienced traveller, took over. "Absolutely do not pay the extra £1,000," she insisted. "If they assessed it at £3,100, then £3,100 is all you pay."

I explained that Bishop's Move had, it seemed, finally accepted it would be dealt with in the UK.

"I didn't realise that credit facilities had been cancelled," she said. "And if you get stuck, we'll both come and help you to pack up."

"Actually," I said, "it's not all that bad. I've got everything out of the cupboards – that's why it looks a mess – but I've arranged for specialist packing facilities for all the nice stuff I brought out with me. The rest is in store in Southampton. I've left Mr Phillips in charge of all the legal stuff and I've packed all the files and papers and labelled them with a thick black marker, URGENT LEGAL PAPERS. All I have to do is give them my new address and they will see that those three boxes are hand delivered, personally."

I heaved a sigh. "It's just getting back to Southampton now, that's the problem, with a dodgy back, a cat, no car and no CASH!"

"Not a problem," said the invincible Maureen. "I'm finishing as a courier here at the weekend. I *may* come back; I've been offered a job in an estate agent's office. But I'm going home for Christmas. I'll pick up my car in Surrey, meet you at Gatwick on the 2nd November and take you down to Southampton. We'll stay in a hotel until your flat is ready and see a bit of the New Forest. Nice!"

All my problems were now solved.

"Phew," said Madge. "I thought you might have done something silly."

"Madge rang me," said Maureen. "She was worried. So I rang you. I thought you'd been drinking – you sounded different."

"I had," I said. "It took most of the bottle of wine just to get all the pills down."

There was a silence. Madge and Maureen looked at each other, and then at me.

"I wouldn't have gone on ringing, but Madge kept on. Finally, I kept on and on until you did answer. Madge threatened to come and bash the door down if you didn't!"

With everything now settled, we drove home. The following day Bishop's Move arrived at 8am to begin packing. They packed non-stop until 5pm. Finally, I threw the last dress in and checked the sitting room.

"You are *sure* you've packed those three urgent boxes ready to be offloaded en route as Charlie promised?" I asked, looking round the room.

"Already packed. Oh, er, one of the boxes was too heavy. Had to redistribute some of those heavy files."

"WHAT?" I screamed. "Never mind, never mind," I then said hastily. It will be there, waiting, inside three weeks.

And as yet I'd not heard from Mr Phillips that the Financial Ombudsman was ready to open the case. Don't panic! No rush...

But it was odd that I hadn't heard from the Ombudsman.

At last the two lorries drove off. The taxi came for the cat to be left at the vet's for a final check, to be collected the next morning and dropped off at the airport.

Finally, with my one piece of hand luggage, I climbed the steps to board the midday flight back to the UK.

At the end of the second week I rang Claire of Bishop's Move. When was my furniture likely to arrive?

"Soon," she said, happily.

I hadn't sufficient funds to stay any longer in the hotel. The flat was ready and waiting, and had been since the beginning of the month. But I needed my furniture to move in.

The flat was convenient and economical but it was a retirement flat. John Paul had thought, rightly, I might need a little peace and quiet, BUT I would need a medical card and other personal details before I could move in. THAT, together with my driving licence, phone/address book, etc. was of course still in Gibraltar in one of the three boxes clearly marked URGENT, LEGAL DOCUMENTS.

I would get a replacement. There was a doctors' surgery nearby.

"No problem," they said. "We just need your PERMANENT ADDRESS."

I went back to the flat.

"We'll need details of your doctor, medical card, etc. before you can move in."

I began to see how some ended up living in cardboard boxes under a bridge. There was also the fact that it was unfurnished and I had no furniture.

The flat manager had a solution."I'll move you into the guest flat," she said, "just while you wait for your things to arrive."

December arrived. I rang Claire.

"Where the hell is my furniture?"

"Oh, I'm so sorry," she said, "it's the Credit Crunch. Nothing has moved out of here since you left. It's affected everyone."

Christmas came and went.

I went out and bought a small toaster. HOT TOAST! Wonderful, even with cold baked beans – well, you can't have everything. But I couldn't help thinking of my beautiful Cannon cooker in store in Southampton, and three microwaves, one of which was still in Gibraltar.

The flat manager pointed out that I could stay in the guest flat no longer. It had now been out of use to weekend visitors for six weeks. Finally, by employing various devious methods, we managed to move me in.

I bought an orthopaedic bed (essential), a chair and table and a TV. Bliss! I collected little Leo and paid his horrendous cattery bill for two months and we settled in.

It was freezing. Daren't turn the heating up. Fortunately, with the Credit Crunch, the sales had begun and I picked up some warm slacks for £4.99, a warm top £4.99, and some hot water bottles.

I couldn't ring Claire. My phone was still in one of the URGENT boxes in Gibraltar, so I bought a mobile and rang her.

"Any sign of delivery?"

Absolutely not. Not a single lorry had left Gibraltar since October. It was the Credit Crunch.

I rang Phillips. "Any news from Lloyds or the Financial Ombudsman?"

No on both counts.

By February 2008 I was desperate. I had left Gibraltar in October 2007 and paid for immediate delivery. Since then, I'd paid storage charges to prevent it being disposed of and there was *still* no sign of it.

I rang Commander Chapman at Forces HQ.

ALL MOVEMENT IN AND OUT OF GIBRALTAR HAD BEEN AS NORMAL SINCE OCTOBER 2007.

He would send another Commander out to Bishop's Move to investigate.

The Commander reported back, "Goods now en route."

Three days later, Lorry One arrived. Lorry One contained all the heavy furniture including bed, dining table and chairs, and three boxes. The furniture, of course, I had already replaced. Still, I could no longer afford to pay storage charges, so I took most of it in.

My tiny flat was now reduced to a furniture store. I could barely ease round it. Leo, of course, was having a ball. He hated being combed anyway and except for feeding time, I never saw him.

But where was Lorry Two? I had paid £300 just to have the three boxes delivered. The *wrong* boxes. One had burst open and the two mink coats inside had come into contact with old batteries. The contents were damp. Both coats were ruined, of course, and *no papers*. No clothes, either. At least I could – and would – claim compensation.

Eventually, I received a letter from Claire. Pity about the coats, but the boxes weren't covered by insurance anyway.

That was most odd. The flat manager had been furious when they smashed a lamp on the way in, and rang the firm, demanding £16 for replacement. It was paid by return. To date, I had paid £5,000 for safe delivery. But my goods, apparently, were not insured.

Now they told me it would cost another £1,000 if I wanted my goods delivered from Wokingham to my flat. I explained that I had already paid £3,100 for door to door delivery.

All the staff at Bishop's Move in Gibraltar had been sacked and replaced, they said. "What you paid them is no concern of ours." Did I or did I not want it delivered?

I paid another £1,000 – it was either that, or continue to pay for storage. Eventually I found copies of *The Black Hole* but no supporting evidence, ie the legal papers that the Financial Ombudsman would need.

And still no sign of Lorry Two. I was still without clothes, telephone, driving licence, medical card, address/phone book, etc. Since I left the hotel I had not eaten one hot meal and was still without a radio, microwave, vacuum cleaner, etc.

'Look on the bright side,' I told myself. 'Your energy bill will be ZERO. All I had after five months was an electric kettle and toaster and one electric light.

Again I rang the new staff in Gibraltar. Again they said it was no concern of theirs.

I needed those papers. I had left copies with Mr Phillips in Gibraltar.

He wrote back immediately. Yes, certainly he would forward them on. "Shall we say £1,000?"

Shall we not.

Unable to afford Mr Phillips' fee of £1,000 to forward the file, I decided to ring the Financial Ombudsman myself. I explained that my solicitor in Gibraltar had dealt with the matter and I quite appreciated there was a waiting list, but I had been waiting now for months.

How far down the list was I now?

"Donnelly? You did say Donnelly?"

No, I was not on the list at all. Did I wish to make a complaint?

I lost it completely. How incompetent!

I took a deep breath. "Mr Phillips has been in touch with you," I stated, slowly and clearly, "and I have been waiting well over a year for a reply. I checked the last letter *myself*. I *saw* it, it was dated 8th August 2007. I have been waiting for a reply EVER SINCE!"

"Mrs Donnelly," said the receptionist, gently and patiently, "Mr Phillips may well have *written* the letter, and you may well have *seen* it, but that does not mean that he *posted* it and we most certainly have never *received* it. However, I have now noted that you have a complaint and have registered it as such, dated 8th February 2008. There is of course a waiting list, but at least your complaint has now been filed and dated."

I was speechless. Gutted. I could only hang up.

But I had checked the letter myself... I'd *seen* it! So he *deliberately* hadn't posted it. He had accepted the first £1,000 and then a further £2,000 with no intention whatsoever of contacting either the Financial Ombudsman or Lloyds Bank.

A fool and his money are soon parted. Still, I was now on the waiting list for an investigation.

But there was just one small matter... they would require some evidence and I had no file. I was clearly in the same position I'd been in with Tye-Reeve – while he kept the file, there could be no investigation.

By June I had paid £2,000 storage charges to Bishop's Move. Without credit facilities, I could afford to do so no longer. I was also becoming aware of a totally unacceptable set of facts.

Lorry One had finally arrived after a five month succession of deliberate lies by Claire of Bishop's Move. The entire staff, including Claire, in Gibraltar had been sacked and replaced. The new staff had, presumably accepted, after Commander Chapman's intervention, that transport *had* been paid for. So why send one lorry, and not two?

Lorry Two had contained a collection of unique and antique valuables – small, easily disposable objects. Plus, of course, the legal papers that the Financial Ombudsman now required. I *must* get those papers back, whatever it cost.

I rang Roberts Removals. They had moved me at least half a dozen times, going down the scale from det.des.res. to semi… and finally, hovel, but they had always been quick, courteous and efficient.

Mr Roberts answered. "When did the lorry leave Gibraltar?"

"30th October, 2007."

"Mrs Donnelly, that was months ago."

"I know, it gives a whole new meaning to *immediate delivery*," I said, bitterly. I told him of my various difficulties due to the 'credit crunch.' "And I need you to collect the rest of the stuff I stored in Southampton. But I don't have the details of the storage company – they are all in the three boxes labelled URGENT. I haven't even been able to call them – my address and phone book are in Gibraltar as well. If you take any large items from Lorry Two, I simply can't get any more in. But at least I would have them all under one roof. I know I must have accumulated the most *enormous* bill, but I think I have just enough to clear it. Then, once I have all the goods together with someone I can trust, I can concentrate on the Financial Ombudsman investigation…"

"Oh, *no*, Mrs Donnelly," he groaned. "Where are we now? March 2008. And you left Gibraltar last October. No way would they keep your furniture for that long without payment, or even a phone call from them…"

"But *you* recommended them," I said, "don't you remember?"

"I gave you about a dozen names as I recall," he said, "as I was unable to accommodate you at such short notice. There's no easy way to tell you this, Mrs Donnelly, but it will all have gone, I'm afraid."

"Gone? But it can't have, surely. I knew it would have accumulated a massive sum, but I had prepared for that."

Too late. It had all GONE!

Everything. John Paul's soft toys, Victorian rocking horse, Steinway Baby Grand – fetched and lovingly restored by Winston's of Winchester. I had taught both his children and he had returned the favour in style, since I had got them both into Westminster School.

Lorry One had brought the dining table, but the eight heavily carved rosewood chairs I'd had to leave behind. The two carvers had been on sale in Harrods Oriental Department for over £1,000 each (now they were not allowed to cut down the trees in the rainforest to make them any more). I had brought them all the way from China. Then I met up with Bishop's Move… and they had GONE!

GONE too were all John Paul's Charterhouse School photographs – pride of place in each one of them as Top Scholar; cricket eleven and football teams with John Paul growing ever larger, but always Captain. Tennis trophies and cups as Hampshire's Junior Hopeful, and then School Captain. At least four hundred books, all purchased from the Charterhouse Bookshop – complete sets of Shakespeare, Dickens, etc. Family photo albums – dozens of them, going back to 1880. Then University, his degree and more trophies, more photos. His gap year and his first play. Top award for best writer, best director AND best actor – a first in the history of the Edinburgh Festival. Rave reviews in the *Guardian*, his first play at the Court Royal…

"Look after them for me, Mum," he'd said.

I thought I had. But GONE!

Hockey sticks, football gear, PGA golf clubs – his treasured Hole-in-One certificate from Charterhouse Golf Club… GONE!

A complete set of mahogany dining room furniture – admittedly not rainforest rosewood, but close enough… GONE!

Everything… GONE!

Still, I could do nothing about it. It wasn't even insured as I had only expected to be there for six months.

Now, though, the main thing was to get back the legal papers for the Financial Ombudsman.

"I don't want your money, Mrs Donnelly," said Mr Roberts. "Take my advice and ring BAR, *now*."

British Association of Removals answered. They were astounded. Was I *quite* sure? I *had* paid delivery charges? When? OCTOBER 30TH 2007? For *immediate* delivery? *Guaranteed* within *three* weeks? Containing *essential* legal papers clearly marked URGENT?

I assured them my solicitor had checked and they had cashed the cheque for £3,100 for immediate delivery.

"Leave it with us," they said. "We will see that it is delivered *immediately*."

Then came a letter from Bishop's Move. "We will certainly deliver Lorry Two immediately upon receipt of further payment of £2,000." To date, that lorry had cost me £6,000 and STILL HAD NOT DELIVERED!

With no credit facilities there was nothing I could do, as they very well knew. Not even BAR could persuade them. I sat there, devastated, with one thought in my head – my beautiful clock. The first thing I had ever bought with my first hard-earned pocket money, scrubbing hospital floors during teaching college vacations.

It had cost me half my earnings – a whole £10! A fortune then. For many years it had sat in broken splendour on my mantlepiece until I finally plucked up courage and took it to a London jeweller to be mended.

"Louis fourteenth," he breathed, picking it up tenderly and turning it over. "And made by the best clockmaker in Paris. Wonderful!"

"It's broken," I had told him, apologetically.

"It's an eight day clock... fantastic! May I just give it to our clockmaker? If anyone can repair it, he can."

"How much would it cost?" I asked anxiously.

"Nothing." The Tessiers' man smiled. "You can't put a price on a thing like this, but if you are prepared to pay for the cost of materials, I think he would jump at the chance. It's impossible to *buy* the spares," he explained. "He'll have to make them all by hand."

Déjà vu, but we agreed.

It had taken the clockmaker six months. Tessiers proudly presented it to me, in full working order. The price? A mere £200. A fortune in those days and, for me, an impossible sum. I scrubbed floors every holiday after that, and finally collected it. Then I would stand still, wherever I was, just to hear those beautiful, melodic chimes.

And now... GONE!

All the (easily disposable) contents of Lorry Two – the ivory and jade, the Capo di Monte, Crown Derby, Waterford Crystal, etc., the medieval tapestries I'd lavished time on to produce authentic cushions for the six Elizabethan hall chairs... all of them, GONE!

I suddenly realised – with that awful blankness of total loss – *exactly* how my parents had felt, driving out to their house, to be faced with…

… A BIG BLACK HOLE. Total devastation.

We had come full circle.

It had taken me forty years in my determination to replace all those lost memories and heirlooms and finally, *finally*, I'd achieved it… and I went to Gibraltar to recuperate. And, just like my parents, IN ONE INSTANT…

… IT WAS GONE!

The only difference being, I had paid Bishop's Move six grand for the privilege. At least the Luftwaffe had done it for my parents FOR FREE!

© Wendy Donnelly 2009